THE MODERN HISTORY
OF JORDAN

THE MODERN HISTORY OF JORDAN

KAMAL SALIBI

WITHDRAWN

I.B. Tauris & Co Ltd
Publishers
London · New York

Published in 1993 by
I.B.Tauris & Co Ltd
45 Bloomsbury Square
London WC1A 2HY

175 Fifth Avenue
New York
NY 10010

In the United States of America
and Canada distributed by
St Martin's Press
175 Fifth Avenue
New York
NY 10010

A CIP record for this book is available from the British Library

A full CIP record is available from the Library of Congress

ISBN 1-85043-610-X

Printed and bound in Great Britain by
WBC Ltd, Bridgend, Mid Glamorgan

Contents

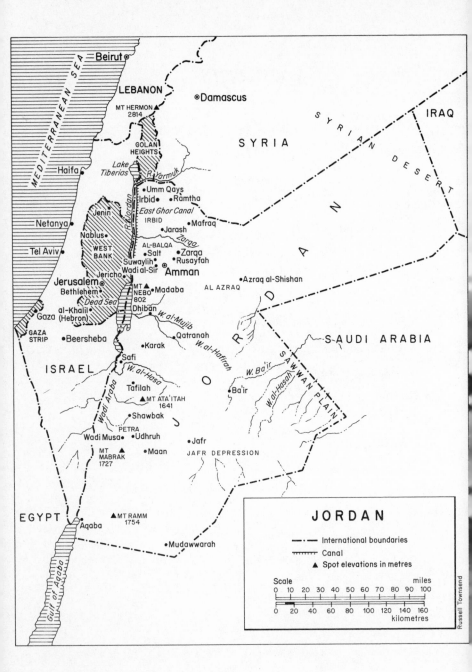

JORDAN

— · — International boundaries
〜〜〜 Canal
▲ Spot elevations in metres

Scale
miles
0 10 20 30 40 50 60 70 80 90 100
0 20 40 60 80 100 120 140 160
kilometres

Russell Townsend

Preface

This book attempts to reduce the history of modern Jordan into a readable narrative, tracing the stages of the country's political and demographic development under the Hashemite monarchy, and explaining the internal, regional and international circumstances and constraints within which the Jordanian state has functioned since it was first established. The study, for the most part, involves no new research, but is mostly an interpretation of what to scholars would be common knowledge: information derived from monographs, biographies, memoirs and other historical and documentary materials which already exist in print.

Because the book is addressed as much to the general reader as to the specialist, it dispenses with all but the most necessary endnotes for special explanation or reference, and only special Arabic terms and expressions are rendered in accurate transliteration. Others which have passed into English usage are given their accepted English dictionary form (for example, Koran instead of *Qur'an* and Shiah or Shiite instead of *Shi'ah* or *Shi'i*). Personal and place names are spelt in the manner most familiar to readers of English, or most easily pronounceable in English.

The first four chapters of the book are intended to provide the necessary background information: the history of the land of Jordan before it came to be organized as a state under Emir Abdullah; the history of the Hashemite dynasty in the Hijaz, and the early career of Emir Abdullah before he became the founder of the Emirate of Transjordan in the wake of the First World War. The remainder of the book, comprising seven chapters, relates the history of Jordan from the time the country took its present form, with special concentration on the involvement of the Jordanian state and its Hashemite rulers with the Palestinian question, and the development of this involvement to date. In treating the Jordanian-Palestinian controversy, I have endeavoured to explain the essence and details of the issue as seen from both sides to the best of my ability.

In writing this book, I received invaluable help from many directions. HRH Crown Prince Hassan of Jordan kindly placed the resources of his personal library at my disposal for my work. For his gracious help and encouragement, I am especially grateful.

Among the people who accorded me valuable interviews at different stages of my work were Akram Zuayter, Walid Salah, Rajai Dajani, Jamil Barakat and Mrs Malek al-Husseini. The bibliographer of the Centre for Arab and Middle Eastern Studies at the American University of Beirut, Yusuf Khuri, provided me with the Arabic documentation I needed and assisted me in establishing the chronology of events.

I also received help and encouragement from a number of friends and colleagues who read the book as first drafted, in part or in full, suggesting corrections and changes in content or expression, most of which I accepted. I mention, especially, Ihsan Abbas, Abdul-Rahim Abu-Husayn, Adnan Bakhit, Mustafa Hiyari, Taher Kanaan, Abbas Kelidar, Usama Khalidi, Jim Muir, Randa Muqhar and Wahib Shair. I also profited from critical comments by Zeid Rifai, Hazem Nuseibeh and Raouf Abujaber. Carl Brown and Albert Hourani read the completed work in the final draft, suggesting important revisions. While I acknowledge the debt I owe to all the individuals mentioned, apologizing beforehand for any unintended omissions, I naturally hold myself to be solely responsible for the interpretation of the history of Jordan which this book presents.

Kamal Salibi

1

The Land and its Story

The present book, as indicated in the preface, will relate the history of the Hashemite Kingdon of Jordan from 1920 to the present. At the outset, however, something must be said about the geographical and historical character of the land on which this story unfolds. This land which geographers call Transjordania, or more simply Transjordan, occupies an area of just over 90,000 square kilometres, to which the Palestinian West Bank (total area under 5,500 square kilometres) was officially united from 1951 to 1988. The population of the Transjordanian territory has varied in size from one historical period to another. From one of its lower ebbs of less than 400,000 in the 1920s, it is estimated today at approximately four million, nearly a quarter of them living in the capital, Amman, and a clear majority among them of Palestinian origin.

West to east, the country consists of three natural regions which converge in the south on the port of Aqaba – Jordan's only outlet to the sea. Originally, the Aqaba coastal strip was limited to about eight kilometres. It was later extended to about twenty-six by special agreement between Jordan and Saudi Arabia which re-adjusted the frontiers between the two countries in 1965.

The first natural region of Jordan comprises the eastern parts of the great rift valley of the Ghor (meaning, in Arabic, 'the sunken land') and Wadi Araba. The Ghor, in the north, follows the course of the Jordan river from Lake Tiberias as it descends from about 190 metres below sea level to pour into the Dead Sea at 435 metres below sea level – the lowest point on earth. From the southern end of the Dead Sea, Wadi Araba rises gradually to a point 300 metres above sea level, then falls as gradually to reach the Red Sea at the Gulf of Aqaba. This Wadi Araba, as its name indicates, is mostly gravel or sandy desert (the term *'araba* seems to derive from a Canaanite and Aramaic term denoting a steppe or a desert). The Ghor, on the other hand, with its rich alluvial soil, is irrigated by the Jordan river and its tributaries, which makes it highly arable. What adds to its fertility is the hot-house effect caused by its enclosure between the Palestinian and Transjordanian highlands rising, on average, between 800 and 900 metres above sea level on either side. The intense heat of the Ghor, however, except for the winter months, has historically kept its resident population limited for the most part to the local peasantry working the land. The parts of the Ghor and Wadi Araba belonging today to Jordan are those east of the Jordan river and the inland and maritime drains of the Wadi Araba water divide.

Next come the highlands bordering the Ghor and Wadi Araba from the east. When geographers speak of Transjordan, it is principally this region that they have in mind. Of the three regions of the country, this one has been, historically, the most densely populated. The highlands begin in the north, from the tributary of the Jordan called the Yarmuk, which connects with the main course of the river directly south of Lake Tiberias, and they taper to an end in the south at the approaches to Aqaba. North to south, the highlands are divided by valleys and gorges into different parts, which are naturally grouped in three distinct areas. Between the Yarmuk and the Zarqa – the next tributary of the Jordan river – lie the highlands which the classical Arab geographers used to call the Sawad *(sawad al-Urdun),* meaning 'the fertile land'. This region comprises the high plain of Irbid and the hill country of Ajlun. The highlands of al-Balqa, which follow, span the area between the Zarqa and the Wadi al-Mujib canyon, which drains into the Dead Sea. The water divide of al-Balqa divides it naturally into two parts: an eastern part, dominated by Amman, and a western part opening on to the Ghor by way of the fertile Wadi Shu'ayb, and dominated by the town of Salt. Finally, there is the range of higher hills called in Arabic Bilad al-Sharat, rising from Wadi al-Mujib to reach summits of 1,200 metres above sea level in the north, and over 1,500 metres in the south. The principal town here is Karak, overlooking the southern end of the Dead Sea.[1]

The Transjordanian highlands enjoy on the whole a dry and temperate climate, and, lying in the rain shadow of the Palestinian highlands to the west, they are mostly steppes. Before the water table began to be systematically exploited in recent decades, the local agriculture was traditionally limited to dry-farming, except for the fruit orchards and vegetable plots irrigated here and there by wells or springs, or by the perennial or seasonal streams in the valleys draining directly or indirectly towards the rift valley to the west. Down the ages, the more arable parts of the Transjordanian highlands have been known mainly as producers of grain. Some of the higher elevations, however, have also been famed for their vineyards.

Beyond the Transjordanian highlands lies the third natural region: the gravel plateau of the Syro-Arabian desert, patched with areas of basalt and tilting gradually eastwards towards the frontier with Iraq. This desert today forms more than three-quarters of the total area of Jordan. Historically, the inhabitants of this desert which, geographically, continues northwards into Syria, eastwards into Iraq, and southwards into Saudi Arabia, have been bedouin pastoralists. When there were strong governments in the area, the movement of bedouins from the desert into the more attractive grazing lands of the Transjordanian highlands was carefully controlled. During the long periods when strong government was absent, however, the bedouin tribes pressed into these highlands, raiding the agricultural areas to prey on their harvests, and establishing permanent tribal settlements not only between the local towns and villages, but also in the Ghor and the Palestinian highlands further to the west. In the western part of the desert, the broad valley of Wadi Sirhan, descending from the central highlands of northern Arabia, ends with the self-contained depression of al-Azraq, approximately 60 kilometres east-south-east of Amman. Al-Azraq, with its perennial pools, is the only major oasis of this desert region.

The administrative divisions (*muhafazat,* singular *muhafaza*) of the Jordanian kingdom follow the natural divisions of the Transjordanian highlands, and include the adjacent parts of the rift valley to the west and the desert to the east. All in all, there are five *muhafazat*. That of Irbid, in the north, centres around the Sawad highlands. That of the capital, Amman, comprises the parts of the Balqa highlands east of the water divide, along with the adjacent desert. That of Salt, on the other hand, comprises the parts of the same highlands west of the water divide along with the adjacent parts of the Ghor. The muhafaza of Karak, starting from the shore of the Dead Sea and the northward drain of Wadi Araba, centres around the northern stretch of Bilad al-Sharat. In the extreme south, the muhafaza of Maan, starting from the southward drain of Wadi Araba, comprises the southern and more arid stretch of Bilad al-Sharat and the Aqaba coastal strip, along with Maan and the adjoining desert.

To place this in a broader geographical perspective, the Palestinian and Transjordanian hill country, along with the rift valley in between, forms the southernmost part of broken highlands bordering the North Arabian and Syrian deserts from the approaches of Aqaba in the south to those of Anatolia (today Turkey) in the north. From south to north, these highlands consist of two parallel ranges of hills and mountains, divided by a continuing stretch of valley. On the western side bordering the Mediterranean coast, the Palestinian highlands are followed in the direction of the north by the Galilean hills, the Lebanon mountains, and the Alawite mountains. On the eastern side bordering the desert, the Transjordanian highlands are followed in the same direction by the mountains of the Anti-Lebanon and the inland hill country of northern Syria.

Southwards, however, the highlands of Palestine and Transjordan continue in different directions. The first merge with the highlands of Sinai, west of the Gulf of Aqaba, and in the direction of Egypt. The second continue into Western Arabia, on the eastern side of the Gulf of Aqaba and the Red Sea, as the mountains of the Hijaz. This makes Palestine the natural point of connection between Syria and Egypt. On the other hand, it makes Transjordan the natural point of connection between Syria and Arabia.

To Arab travellers coming from Arabia, the territory of present-day Jordan was *masharif al-Sham* – literally, 'the approaches of Syria'. To those travelling back to the peninsula, it was *masharif al-Hijaz* – 'the approaches of the Hijaz'. Across this territory, a number of caravan trails, starting from diverse parts of peninsular Arabia, followed the natural configurations of the land in different areas to reach their Syrian destinations. One of them was the Wadi Sirhan trail, which entered Syria by way of the oasis of al-Azraq. There was also the trail further to the west which followed the folds of the mountains of the Hijaz, to reach Syria by way of

Maan. Yet another trail followed the coast of the Hijaz, to pass through Aqaba before reaching Maan. From this point, these last two trails merged into one – the so-called King's Highway (the *Via Nova Trajana* of the Romans) – following the length of the Transjordanian hill country to reach the Syrian regions further north. The town of Amman, at the headwaters of the Zarqa tributary of the Jordan river, was a natural meeting point for all the Syro-Arabian caravan trails, which accounts for the prominence it enjoyed in antiquity. The modern revival of Amman began in 1908, when it became one of the principal stations of the new Hijaz railway constructed by the Ottomans to connect the Syrian city of Damascus with the Hijazi holy city of Medina.

Down the ages, the importance of the present land of Jordan derived to a great extent from its status as a major highway. Since antiquity, traders had followed this highway as they carried the products of the lands of the Indian Ocean basin to Syria, to be distributed from there to other parts of the Mediterranean world. In Islamic times, this same highway gained special importance as the *Darb al-Hajj* or *Tariq al-Hajj* – the 'pilgrimage road' annually taken by Muslims converging on Damascus from different directions on their way to the holy land of the Hijaz.

Historically, however, today's Jordan was not only the highway between Arabia and Syria. It was also the area where all the natural highways of what is today called the Middle East met and crossed. Despite its great depth, the rift valley separating Transjordan from Palestine is far from being impassable. It can easily be crossed at various points, north and south of the Dead Sea, to connect the Syro-Arabian routes passing through Transjordan with the Syrian coastal route skirting the highlands of Palestine and Sinai on its way to Egypt. From Damascus, which is the natural meeting point of the various inland routes coming from the direction of Iraq and Iran in the east, and Anatolia in the north, the easier natural passages to the Mediterranean coast – and hence to the main highway to Egypt – pass through Transjordan. Thus, down the centuries, the present Jordanian territory has been one of prime strategic importance.

* * * * * * * * *

Very little is known for certain of the history of this territory before the third century BC. Speculations on the subject are mainly based on local archaeological findings and passages from ancient Egyptian and Mesopotamian records interpreted in accordance with the standing tenets of biblical scholarship. These speculations, and the tenets on which they are based, are not adequately substantiated as yet, and for this reason they will not be surveyed in the present chapter.

One of the very few informative local records regarding the ancient history of the area is the stele called the Moabite stone, dating from the ninth century BC. The long inscription on this stele speaks of the military, town-building and road-construction achievements of Mesha, the Moabite king of Qarha (*qrhh*) – today, possibly the village of Jahra in the Karak region of Bilad al-Sharat. Unfortunately, no one knows exactly where the Mesha stele was originally found. It was first brought to the attention of travelling orientalists by local bedouins in 1868, then broken into pieces and sold to them, piece by piece. The reconstructed stele – with some parts still missing – is housed today in the Louvre Museum in Paris.

The Mesha whose achievements are recorded on this stele was none other than the Mesha described in the Bible (2 Kings 3:4) as the 'shepherd' (*noged*) king of Moab. His Transjordanian kingdom apparently straddled the canyon of Wadi al-Mujib to include the adjacent parts of Bilad al-Sharat to the south, and al-Balqa to the north. The inscription on his stele indicates that his cattle (*baqaran*), goats (*ma'az*) and sheep (*sa'an*) were able to graze the pasture lands all the way north to *haranan*[2] – obviously the plain of Hawran, directly north of the Yarmuk river, and today part of Syria.

Judging by this Mesha inscription, the language of the king of Qarha and his subjects – which scholars call Moabite – was a form of Canaanite not much different from biblical Hebrew and Phoenician. The evidence of place names indicates that Canaanite, in one dialect or another, was the dominant language of most of the western parts of Syria and Arabia in early historical times. After the sixth century BC, the Canaanite language in these areas began to give way to Aramaic; and in the early centuries of the Christian era, Arabic began to make its first incursions in the Aramaic-speaking lands, until its general dominance was established with the coming of Islam. All three of these languages – Canaanite, Aramaic and Arabic – belong to the so-called Semitic family, which includes other languages, living and dead, such as Ancient South Arabian and Ethiopic. The term 'Semitic', to describe these related languages, derives from the name of Shem, son of Noah, who is depicted in the Bible as the common ancestor of the Hebrews, Arameans and Arabs. It was first introduced into scholarly usage by the Orientalist, A.L. Schlözer, in 1781.

According to speculations by linguists, Canaanite, Aramaic and Arabic were originally dialectical variants of a parent mother tongue – sometimes called proto-Semitic – whose closest living relative may be classical Arabic. This is thought to be so because classical Arabic retains archaic linguistic features which were dropped or became vestigial in Canaanite, Aramaic and other related languages. The original homeland of proto-Semitic speakers was apparently the Syro-Arabian desert. As the pastoral tribes of this desert arrived to settle in the peripheral lands, always by gradual infiltration, but sometimes in massive waves, the tribal settlers at each stage were mainly speakers of a particular group of related proto-Semitic dialects which were subsequently homogenized into a unified language. This established the dominance first of Canaanite, then of Aramaic, and finally of Arabic in the settled areas. The picture as described here simplifies what must have been a far more complicated process, but it may be considered roughly correct.

Between the different linguistic stages in the history of the area, there were periods of transition from one dominant language to the next. This is illustrated by inscriptions dating from such periods. For example, the Moabite of the Mesha stele is basically Canaanite, with some features of Aramaic, and possibly also of Arabic. The next transitional stage, between Aramaic and Arabic, is documented by a considerable body of inscriptions – among them the Safaitic, Palmyrene, Lihyanite, Thamudic and Nabatean – which have been found in different parts of Syria and Arabia. The languages of these inscriptions may be called Arameo-Arabic. In some cases, the text is clearly Aramaic, but cites personal names and names of gods which are clearly Arabic. This indicates that the authors of such inscriptions wrote Aramaic, but most probably spoke some form of Arabic or Arameo-Arabic. Among the historical people who appear to have done this were the

Transjordanian Nabateans of Petra, whose inscriptions are written entirely in Aramaic.

* * * * * * * * * *

It was during the Aramaic linguistic stage in the history of the area that the Nabatean kingdom of Petra was established in the southern parts of Bilad al-Sharat. Apart from the occasional mention of the name of a king, the Nabatean inscriptions say nothing about the actual history of this kingdom, which is known mainly from the extensive references to it in contemporary Classical and Jewish writings. This was because the Greeks and the Romans on the one hand, and the Jews of Palestine on the other, had good reason to take an interest in Nabatean affairs.

The Nabateans of Petra, whatever their antiquity, first emerged to historical notice in the Hellenistic period, starting from the time when Alexander the Great (d. 323 BC) was undertaking the conquest of the Persian empire in the lands of the Near East. Once this conquest was completed, and Alexander was dead, his generals divided the conquered lands between them into three empires, of which two have special relevance to the present story. One was the Seleucid empire of Syria, with its capital in Antioch; the other was the Ptolemaic empire of Egypt, with its capital in Alexandria. Between these two rival Greek empires of the Near East, there was a continuous tug-of-war. The Nabateans, whose territory fell in between, exploited the power balance between the Seleucids and the Ptolemies to emerge as an independent Transjordanian kingdom by about 169 BC. The same power balance between the Seleucids and the Ptolemies opened the way, in about 167 BC, for a Jewish revolt in Palestine led by the priestly house of the Hasmoneans, or Maccabees, who finally succeeded in about 142 BC in establishing their quasi-independent rule as high priests, then as priest-kings. The Greek rulers of Syria and Egypt took an interest in the affairs of the Nabateans of Petra because they coveted their control over the lucrative trans-Arabian trade. To the Jews of the Hasmonean state in Palestine, the Nabateans were sometimes friends and allies, and sometimes rivals and enemies. In either case, however, they were their immediate neighbours.

The same continued to be the situation after the Roman conquest of Syria in 63 BC, and the completion of the Roman takeover of Egypt by 30 BC. Like the Seleucids and Ptolemies before them, the Romans were interested in controlling the prosperous Nabatean kingdom. Meanwhile, the Hasmonean territory in Palestine passed into the hands of a Jew of Arameo-Arab origin called Herod the Great (37–4 BC).[3] His rule, and that of his successors after him, extended across the Jordan river to include the Transjordanian highlands of al-Balqa and the adjacent parts of the Sawad to the north and Bilad al-Sharat to the south – the area then known as Perea (from the Greek *peraios*, meaning 'on the other side'). This made the Herodians closer neighbours to the Nabateans of Petra than the Hasmoneans before them had normally been.

The earliest Classical references to the Nabateans, relating to the late fourth century BC, speak of them in terms indicating that they were still bedouins at the time. They did not build houses and disdained agriculture, but were skilful in desert warfare, and derived considerable wealth from dabbling in the trans-Arabian caravan trade. Most probably, they were originally a tribal folk from the neighbouring desert who took advantage of the recession of the Persian imperial control over the lands of the Near East, starting from the late fifth century BC, to infiltrate and settle in the highlands south-east of the Dead Sea.

These highlands, presumably along with the Hijaz mountains to the south, formed the area which the Greeks called *Arabia Petrea*, or 'Rocky Arabia'. The name of Petra itself is Greek for 'rock'. Judging from their own inscriptions, the Nabateans themselves called their capital Reqem, meaning 'of varied colours' – apparently in reference to the varied colours and shades of the sandstone cliffs which formed the narrow confines of the city. When the Nabateans finally became a sedentary people, with a flourishing economy based on agriculture, industry and the traditional pastoralism, as well as on the continuing control of the trans-Arabian trade, they constructed the principal public buildings of their capital by actually cutting into the sandstone of these cliffs, as can be seen to this day.

The territorial extent of the Nabatean kingdom varied with circumstances. In the south, it reached the port of Aqaba – then called Aela – and even extended further south along the eastern coast of the Red Sea into the Hijaz, where the Nabateans maintained another seaport called Leuke Kome (Greek for 'white

village'). The exact site of this second seaport remains uncertain.
From Aela and Leuke Kome, however, the Nabateans could offer
stiff competition to the Ptolemies of Egypt in the Red Sea trade.
In the north, the Nabatean dominion had, by about 85 BC,
already reached Bosra, today in Syria, and even Damascus. Here
the Nabatean rulers were still appointing governors as late as the
middle decades of the first century AD, judging by the direct
evidence of St Paul who lived in the city at the time (2 Corinthians
11:32).

By this time, however, the Nabatean kingdom had lost its
independence and become a Roman client state. Under its last
king, its capital was removed from Petra to Bosra. Subsequently,
in AD 106, the emperor Trajan abolished the kingdom and
reorganized its territories into the Roman Province of Arabia,
with Bosra as its capital. The establishment of this *Provincia
Arabia* marked the beginning of a new era for local dating which
continued to be used until the end of the Roman period, and – at
least to some extent – even in the first two centuries of Islam. This
is attested by a dated Greek inscription of this late period found
on a Transjordanian church mosaic discovered in 1986.

* * * * * * * * * *

During the period of the Seleucid and Ptolemaic empire, urban
life in Transjordan – including the Nabatean kingdom – became
thoroughly Hellenized, and Greek replaced Aramaic in official as
well as in sophisticated social use. This was largely the outcome of
the increasing settlement of the principal cities of the area by
Greeks. The marked Hellenization of Transjordan as of other
parts of Syria at that time is reflected, among other things, by the
local architecture of the age, which fuses architectural styles which
are basically Greek with indigenous decorative motifs. The Hellenistic character of urban Syria continued during the Roman
period.

When the Romans arrived on the scene, one of their first acts
was to give the Greek cities of southern Syria and Transjordan
what may be described as a chartered freedom, whereby each city
could enjoy a considerable degree of autonomy while remaining
subject to the Roman governor of Syria. These free cities together
formed a league called the Decapolis, meaning 'ten cities'. The

round number indicated by the name does not necessarily mean that the cities involved were strictly ten. Among the Transjordanian cities of the Decapolis were Gadara (Umm Qays) and Gerasa (Jarash) in the Sawad, and Philadelphia (Amman) in al-Balqa. The ancient Semitic name of Amman was first changed to Philadelphia (Greek for 'brotherly love') by Ptolemy II (285–c. 247 BC) who occupied and rebuilt this city in the course of a Transjordanian military campaign against the Seleucids. Ptolemy II was the first Greek ruler of Egypt to follow the Egyptian royal custom of marrying his own sister. He was given the nickname of 'Philadelphos' with reference to his incestuous marriage and the rebuilt city was called Philadelphia after him.

Socially, Hellenistic and early Roman Syria – including Transjordan – was a land of sharp contrasts. On the one hand, there were the highly developed cities – such as those of the Decapolis – where the upper classes among the native population regularly associated with the Greek colonists, shared their tastes, and spoke and wrote the Greek language often in preference to Aramaic. On the other hand, there were the native Aramaic-speaking villages where life followed older, traditional patterns. Among the towns and villages lived the bedouin Arabs, whose proper home was in the desert. Those, one would assume, spoke Arabic among themselves and communicated with their sedentary neighbours either in Arabic or in Aramaic, depending on which of these two related languages was the dominant one in any given area. Arab tribesmen and Aramaic-speaking villagers who did business with the Greek colonists in the cities must also have possessed a smattering of Greek.

To what extent the sedentary parts of Syria were already infiltrated by Arabs in Hellenistic and early Roman times is anyone's guess. By the second century AD, however, the Romans, from their base in Egypt, had gained full mastery over the Red Sea, and their maritime trade with the countries of the Indian Ocean basin dealt a serious blow to the trans-Arabian caravan trade. Peninsular Arabia was consequently thrown into serious economic recession, which was reflected in social and political upheavals. This triggered successive waves of migration from the impoverished and troubled Arabian lands – the sedentary as well as the tribal – in the direction of Roman Syria, where the prospects of life seemed more promising.

The story of these migrations from Arabia to Syria – *tasha'um al-'Arab*, as this historical phenomenon is called in Arabic – is so fused with legend that it is difficult to tell exactly when and how the migrations actually occurred. In any case, by the fourth century AD, the Arab population of Syria was already considerably swelled by the newcomers from Arabia, many of whom were tribal bedouins. The Roman state had to fortify the cities and towns on the edges of the desert, and keep them well garrisoned, to stop bedouin encroachments, or at least set a limit to them. This, however, did not prevent the Arab immigrants from infiltrating the sedentary areas and settling in the existing towns and villages, or even establishing new ones for themselves.

Meanwhile, in AD 324, the emperor Constantine the Great moved the capital of the Roman empire from Rome to Byzantium, an old Greek town on the Bosphorus which he renamed Constantinople. At the same time, Constantine recognized Christianity as one of the accepted religions of the empire. This was the beginning of the so-called Byzantine period in Roman history. Later, under Theodosius the Great (379–395), Christianity was made the official religion of the Roman state, and the followers of other religions – pagans and Jews – were subjected to persecution. After 395, the Roman empire was divided into western and eastern parts, and Rome was re-established as the capital of the western part. When Rome fell to the Ostrogoths in 476, the Roman empire in the west disappeared, and only the eastern and essentially Greek Byzantine empire remained in existence.

* * * * * * * * * *

The Byzantine period in the history of the present land of Jordan was one of the most prosperous. Except for the open desert, the whole countryside was dotted with flourishing cities and towns, indicating a high density of population. The religious policies of Constantine, then of Theodosius the Great and his successors, encouraged the building of Christian churches everywhere. The remnants of these churches, with their elaborate mosaic floors, continue to be discovered on sites throughout Transjordan, even in areas which today are completely desert. Obviously, the tapped water resources of the land in that period, as in earlier periods, were more ample than in later times. Their subsequent decline can certainly be attributed to increased natural desiccation, but perhaps it was also due to growing neglect.

The desert, in any case, remained close by, ready to impinge on the settled areas at the first opportunity. In this desert, a succession of Arab tribal kingdoms rose and fell during this period: some as client states to the Byzantine state, others as clients to the chief adversaries of the Byzantines, namely the Sassanid rulers of Persia (AD 229–651). The Arab desert kingdoms in question had no fixed territories or boundaries; their rulers simply exercised a measure of informal jurisdiction over the tribes that accepted their leadership, wherever they happened to be located. Thus, the territories of these kingdoms – if one may speak of them formally as territories – dovetailed in many parts. During the reign of Constantine the Great, the founder of one such desert kingdom – a man called Mar' al-Qays, probably a Roman client – apparently claimed some form of jurisdiction over a territory extending from the vicinity of Bosra, south of Damascus, to the desert approaches of the Yemen. This claim is made on his tombstone which was discovered in the northern part of the present Jordanian territory (assuming that the readings so far made of the Arabic inscription on this tombstone are correct).

By the time of Justinian the Great (527–565), the Arabian tribes which had arrived to settle in Transjordan and other parts of Syria were already beyond count. Among them were those in Transjordan and the regions south and south-east of Damascus who recognized the leadership of the house of Jifna – the chiefs of the Christian Arab tribe of Ghassan, originally from the Yemen. Justinian recognized the royal title claimed by the Ghassanid chief of his time, who was his faithful client; and the Ghassanid tribal kingdom remained on the Syrian scene until the time of the Arab conquests. The last Ghassanid king, failing to come to terms with the Muslim conquerors, retired to Constantinople.

* * * * * * * * * *

The security and prosperity enjoyed by Transjordan during the Byzantine period did not long survive Justinian. It came to a catastrophic end after 610, when the emperor Heraclius (d. 641) came to the throne in Constantinople, determined to renew the Byzantine offensive against Persia. In the same year, the Prophet

Muhammad (c. 575–632) began to preach Islam in Mecca. In the course of the great Byzantine–Persian war that followed (613–628), the Persians overran Syria all the way to Egypt, but were ultimately defeated and forced to retreat. Thereupon, Byzantine rule in Syria was tenuously re-established.

Meanwhile, in 622, Muhammad left Mecca in the Hijaz for Medina, where he established a state (the *umma*) based on Islam as the one true religion valid for all mankind and for all time. This event is called in Arabic the *hijra*, and its date was later chosen to mark the first day of the Muslim calendar, and the beginning of the Muslim era. The success of Muhammad's *umma* was indeed phenomenal. Arab tribal delegations from every part of peninsular Arabia, and also from Syria and Iraq, arrived in Medina to declare acceptance of Islam and proclaim religious and political allegiance to the Prophet on behalf of their people. Among these delegations, it seems, were Arab tribes settled in and around the Transjordanian hill country of Bilad al-Sharat. Here the Byzantines, after their victory over the Persians, had taken measures to refortify the town of Mu'ta, where the local Byzantine garrison had traditionally kept strict watch over the tribal movements in the adjacent desert.

Originally, the control of the desert vicinity of Mu'ta by the town garrison was a routine matter, because the local Arab tribes had no point of political reference other than the Byzantine. Now, however, their allegiance went to the Islamic *umma* at Medina. In 629, these Muslim Arab tribes waged two successive attacks on the town. On the second occasion, they received reinforcements from Medina under the command of leading members of the Prophet's family and close entourage. Both these attacks were repelled, and the Prophet was reportedly planning a third offensive against Mu'ta, on a larger scale, when he died.

When this offensive was finally taken in 634, two years after the Prophet's death, it went far beyond the conquest of this marginal garrison town, to become a much wider military operation involving the Muslim Arab conquest of Syria in general. The Transjordanian highlands were rapidly overrun and the decisive battle was fought in 636 on the banks of the Yarmuk stream – today the border between Jordan and Syria. During the three years that followed, the whole of Syria fell to the Muslim Arabs, and the last remaining Byzantine troops were forced to retire across the

Taurus mountains into Anatolia in 641. Meanwhile, the conquest of Egypt had been virtually accomplished, while Muslim Arab armies in the east, having captured the whole of Iraq from the Sassanids by 638, were proceeding with the conquest of Persia. By 651, the Muslim Arabs were already masters of a far-flung empire extending from the borders of India and Central Asia in the east, to the Sahara desert in the west; and further expansion was continuing in both directions.

At the head of this new empire of Islam stood the caliphs (Arabic *khulafa'*, singular *khalifa*), the successors of the Prophet in the political leadership of the umma. First came the orthodox caliphs (*al-khulafa' al-rashidun*): Abu Bakr (632–634), Omar (634–644), Othman (644–656), and finally the Prophet's cousin and son-in-law, Ali (656–661). The first three maintained the old Islamic capital in Medina; the last, Ali, established his capital in Kufa, in Iraq. His succession as fourth caliph was disputed in a number of quarters: most of all by Muawiya, the governor of Syria, who belonged to the Meccan family of the Umayyads, and whose capital was Damascus.

The conflict between Ali and Muawiya was put to arbitration in 659, but remained undecided until the caliph was murdered by one of his former followers in 661. Thereupon Muawiya established a dynastic Umayyad caliphate in Damascus. In 750, the last caliph of this Umayyad dynasty was defeated and overthrown by a revolt which started in Persia, claiming the caliphate of Islam for the descendants of the Prophet's uncle, Abbas. What followed was the dynastic caliphate of the Abbasids who transferred the capital again to Iraq – first to Kufa, then to a new city, Baghdad, which was built on a magnificent scale on the borders of the Tigris river, a short distance to the north of the old Sassanid capital at Ctesiphon.

* * * * * * * * * *

After its conquest by the Arabs, Syria was divided, south to north, into four (and later five) administrative regions called *ajnad* (singular *jund*). The present land of Jordan, from the very beginning, was divided between two of these *ajnad*. The highlands of the Sawad, and those of al-Balqa west of the water divide (the region of Salt), belonged together to the Jund of Jordan (*Jund al-Urdun*). This jund extended westwards, across the adjacent Ghor and the Galilean hill country, to reach the Mediterranean coast between the mouth of the Litani river, north of the seaport of Tyre, and the promontory of Mount Carmel, overlooking the seaport of Haifa. The administrative centre of the Jund of Jordan was the town of Tiberias. The parts of al-Balqa east of the water divide (the region of Amman), along with Bilad al-Sharat all the way south to Aqaba, originally formed part of the Jund of Damascus (*Jund Dimashq*). Starting from the late ninth century, however, Bilad al-Sharat, while remaining in theory part of the Jund of Damascus, was attached for practical purposes to the Jund of Palestine (*Jund Falastin*), whose administrative centre was the town of Ramla.[4]

The Islamic conquests did not result in the eradication of Christianity among the Arabs and Arameo-Arabs of Syria. In fact, there are historians who reckon that the Christian population – not only in Syria, but also in Egypt – was not reduced to the level of a minority until after the end of the period of the crusades (1097–1291). Even then, the Christian population of Syria remained a large minority, which only became smaller with time, and by gradual stages. This reduction in the proportion of Christians to Muslims in the country was largely relative to the steady growth in the Muslim population as a result of increased Arab and non-Arab Muslim immigration. To the extent that it was absolute rather than relative, it was apparently due more to sporadic waves of large-scale Christian emigration from one part of Syria to another, and ultimately to other lands, than to the limited individual conversions of Syrian Christians to Islam. In the early decades of the twentieth century, the Christians of the Transjordanian highlands still formed about 15 per cent of the total population, and included townspeople and villagers as well as bedouin or semi-bedouin clans. Today, they stand at an estimate of only 5 per cent, largely because of increased emigration.

Until at least the ninth century AD, a number of Christian towns in Transjordan remained more or less autonomous, each under its own *archon* – the Greek title by which the chief magistrate in each of these towns was known. The local Christians, it appears, also maintained direct relations with the Byzantine church in Constantinople. This is attested by the Greek-inscribed and dated mosaics of two adjoining churches recently discovered on the desert site of Umm al-Rasas, south-south-west of Amman, where a town called Mefa once flourished. The mosaic in the first church was made about the middle of the sixth century, during the reign of the Byzantine emperor, Justinian the Great; the one in the second church was made during the reign of the Abbasid caliph Harun al-Rashid (AD 786–809). The coloured inlays in both mosaics have been carefully removed from the parts depicting animate objects (people or animals) and replaced by blank tesserae. This means that they were removed from the two mosaics some time after the second of the two churches was built. The most reasonable explanation would be that they were removed in the first half of the ninth century, between 817 and 842, under instructions from Constantinople. In the history of the Byzantine empire, this was the second active period of the so-called iconoclast controversy, when the official Byzantine church strictly forbade the use of religious images and issued orders that pictures of animate subjects in all churches were to be destroyed or defaced. Clearly, the Christians of Mefa, in Transjordan, were among those who received and meticulously followed these instructions, although they lived under Islamic rule, which made them immune to punishment by Byzantium if they resisted its ecclesiastical orders.

Until probably the end of the ninth century, Transjordan continued to enjoy a measure of prosperity under the Umayyads and the Abbasids. Starting from the time of the Muslim Arab conquests, the maritime trade in the Red Sea and the Mediterranean came to a standstill, and the overland routes between the different Islamic countries acquired predominant importance – not only for trade, but also for troop movements and ordinary travel. From whatever direction they came, these routes, as already indicated, had their central juncture in the present land of Jordan. It was along one of these routes that the armies of Islam advanced from the Hijaz, through Transjordan, to conquer Syria. The place chosen for the attempted political arbitration of the issue of the caliphate between Ali and Muawiya was Udhruh, on the main highway from Maan to Bilad al-Sharat. During the years when the Abbasids were plotting the overthrow of the Umayyads, the place they chose for their headquarters was Humayma, north of Aqaba and close by the same Maan–Udhruh highway. Here, at a safe distance from Damascus, the Abbasids could host politically influential travellers on their way back or forth between the eastern lands of Islam and Egypt, to canvass support for their revolutionary schemes. From the same Humayma, they might also have been able, now and then, to intercept the *barid* – the official post-horse relay of the Islamic empire – between Damascus and Egypt. Today, Udhruh is a small village, and Humayma little more than a tiny bedouin encampment. In Umayyad and early Abbasid times, they must have been towns of some importance.

Some reminders of the prosperity enjoyed by Transjordan during the first century of Islam survive to this day. They are the ruins of Umayyad palaces that have been found in different places between the Jordan valley and the open desert. Judging by the location, some of these palaces must have been used for regional administration. Others could well have been hunting lodges or pleasure haunts.

By the late ninth century, however, the maritime trade of the Red Sea and the Mediterranean was already beginning to revive, to an increasing extent at the expense of the overland trade passing through Transjordan. This brought particular prosperity and importance to Egypt, which had ports on both the Red Sea and the Mediterranean. Here, the Abbasid caliphs of Baghdad condoned the establishment of two quasi-independent dynastic states in succession: that of the Tulunids (868–905), followed by that of the Ikhshidids (935–969). Each of these two dynasties, in turn, was founded by a Turkish officer of the Abbasid army owing allegiance to the caliph of Baghdad; and both of them were permitted to bring the southern parts of Syria – including the present land of Jordan – under their control. It was actually the Tulunids who first removed Bilad al-Sharat from the control of Damascus to make it, for all practical purposes, part of the Jund of Palestine.

The rule of the Ikhshidids bears on the history of Jordan in another, more indirect manner. In addition to Syria, these Ikhshidids also had control over the Hijaz. There, in 964, they appointed the first emir of Mecca – a *sharif*, or recognized descendant of the Prophet – placing the guardianship of the Holy Places in his trust. King Hussein of the Hijaz, the father of the founder of the Hashemite Kingdom of Jordan, was the last sharif to be appointed to this historical Islamic institution, originally founded by the Ikhshidids of Egypt.

* * * * * * * * * *

As the maritime trade between the Indian Ocean and Mediterranean Sea continued to grow at the expense of the overland trade, the Transjordanian territory lost its central position in the world of Islam, and the country became rapidly impoverished. Most of its once flourishing towns dwindled into villages, or vanished from existence to become desert sites. The *Darb al-Hajj* (pilgrimage road) remained the only source of annual income to supplement the languishing agricultural and pastoral economy. From the nearby desert, wave after wave of bedouin tribes penetrated the highlands to terrorize the local peasants, and ultimately to settle among them. With the arrival of every new wave of bedouin tribes, the older ones, having already lost their original desert vigour, made common cause with the local peasants to resist the invaders. As this happened again and again, the local peasants became bedouinized in their folkways, and the Christians among them, in particular, found it expedient to enter into tribal or quasi-tribal alliances with the settlers from the desert.

This bedouinization of Transjordan probably began towards the end of the ninth century and the beginning of the tenth with the movement of the Qaramita – a heretical Islamic sect, opposed to all standing government control. The movement originated among the peasant tribes and bedouins of southern Iraq and came to have its main base in the eastern parts of Arabia, where its followers established a militant rebel state which was not finally subdued until 1071. The emergence of the Qaramita movement unleashed a tribal anarchy which spread in different directions to touch the furthest reaches of Arabia and Syria. Among the Arab tribes who took advantage of this anarchy were the Tayy of the Hail region of North Arabia, who pressed in the direction of Transjordan, crossed into Palestine, and established a tribal state for themselves in Ramla, the administrative centre of what was originally *Jund Falastin*. There the Tayy chiefs of the house of Jarrah maintained their tribal hegemony until the later decades of the eleventh century.

After 977, the Jarrah chiefs of Ramla became tributary to the

Fatimid caliphs. The Fatimids were the religious heads of the Ismaili Shiite Muslims, and they based their Islamic political legitimacy on claimed descent from the Prophet. Called after Fatima, the daughter of the Prophet who became the ancestress of all his descendants, they originally established their caliphate in Tunisia in 909. From there, they challenged the legitimacy of Abbasid rule over the lands of Islam, and proceeded to seize Egypt from the Ikhshidids in 969, establishing a new capital for themselves in Cairo by 973. From Egypt, the Fatimids expanded their empire northwards to include most of Syria, starting with Palestine and Transjordan. Their regular rule in Syria continued until 1070.

Meanwhile, in Baghdad, the weakened Abbasid caliphs handed over their temporal authority in 1058 to the Seljuk sultans, who became their associates in sovereign Islamic power. The Seljuks were the paramount chiefs of the Central Asian Turkish tribes which had recently overrun Persia, and their capital, from 1044 until the death of the last sultan of the main Seljuk line in 1157, was established in the Persian city of Isfahan. In 1070, Turkish freebooters were allowed by the Seljuks to sweep into Syria from northern Iraq. This put an end to Fatimid sovereignty over Syria, paving the way for its formal conquest by the Seljuks, which was finally completed in 1086. As the Seljuks proceeded to threaten Egypt, the Fatimids reacted by re-occupying the coastal parts of Palestine in 1089.

The first Seljuk viceroy of Syria was Tutush, the brother of the Seljuk sultan reigning in Isfahan, and his capital was in Aleppo. After his death, his Syrian realm was divided between his two sons: Ridwan in Aleppo, and Duqaq in Damascus. Transjordan was part of the Damascene kingdom of Duqaq. The actual ruler of the Damascene kingdom, however, was not Duqaq himself, but his *atabeg*, or guardian-regent,[5] called Tughtekin. The descendants of this Tughtekin, called the Burid atabegs – apparently after the name of Tughtekin's father, which was also the name of the atabeg's eldest son – continued to rule Damascus and its dependent territories until 1154.

It was while Ridwan and Duqaq were still quarrelling over the rule of Syria that the armies of the first crusade crossed the Taurus mountains to capture Antioch in 1098, then continued southwards to capture Jerusalem in 1099. During the early decades of the next century, the crusaders – or Franks (*Faranj*), as they were locally known – expanded their conquests to include the whole of Palestine, along with the Syrian coastal territory all the way to Anatolia. Their Palestinian territory was organized as the Latin Kingdom of Jerusalem. At its greatest extent, this Frankish kingdom included the coastal parts of present-day Lebanon as far north as Beirut, and also the Transjordanian hill country of Bilad al-Sharat. It was organized in sixteen feudal fiefs, one of them being Bilad al-Sharat, which was officially called the Seig-neury of Oultre Jourdain (Old French for Transjordan), or the Seigneury of Crac (Karak) and Montreal (Shawbak) – the latter being a fortified position south of Karak, in the same hill country.

The Transjordanian highlands north of Bilad al-Sharat – the Balqa and the Sawad – remained part of the Burid atabegate of Damascus. In 1154, a new dynasty of atabegs called the Zengids, who were already established in Aleppo, seized Damascus from the Burids and made it their capital, and the same parts of Transjordan became part of the Zengid realm. Meanwhile, in 1171, a Kurdish officer called Salah al-Din Yusuf ibn Ayyub (better known as Saladin), who had been sent by the Zengids of Damascus to Egypt, overthrew the last of the Fatimid caliphs of Cairo and began to rule in his place, nominally on behalf of his Zengid overlord. From Egypt, Saladin extended his rule over the Hijaz and the Yemen, where he appointed a member of his Ayyubid family as viceroy in 1173. The following year, when his Zengid overlord died, Saladin left Egypt to seize Damascus, then Aleppo, after which he came to be recognized as the sultan – or paramount Islamic sovereign – of his day. One of the fortresses he built in the Transjordanian part of his realm stands to this day as the citadel of Rabad, near the town of Ajlun. Saladin, and his successors after him, also rebuilt the older crusader fortresses – notably those of Karak and Shawbak – in Bilad al-Sharat, to use them as military outposts against the Franks.

In 1187, Saladin crossed the Transjordanian highlands of the Sawad, around Ajlun, to inflict a decisive defeat on the Franks at the battle of Hattin, near Lake Tiberias. During the months that followed, all but a few outposts of the Latin Kingdom of Jerusalem fell into his hands. This spelt the end of Frankish rule in Bilad al-Sharat. Shortly after, the coastal strip between Jaffa and Beirut was reconquered for the Franks by the third crusade, but the inland parts of Palestine, including Jerusalem, were kept by Saladin. The capital of the restored Latin kingdom still carrying the name of Jerusalem was actually the seaport of Acre.

After the death of Saladin in 1193, his empire was divided between his sons and other members of the Ayyubid family. The most prominent among them was his brother, al-Adel Sayf al-Din Abu Bakr (known to the Franks as Saphadin), who established himself in Cairo as the recognized Ayyubid sultan. His descendants in Cairo continued to hold this title of supreme Islamic sovereignty until 1250. Where the history of the Hashemite Kingdom of Jordan is concerned, the reign of al-Adel has a special, though indirect, significance. It was he, in 1200, who appointed a new emir for Mecca – the sharif Qitada ibn Idris of Yanbu – to replace the last of the older sharifian dynasty in the holy city. After that date the emirate of Mecca remained the preserve of Qitada's descendants, the last emir of Mecca being Hussein, the father of the founder of the present Jordanian kingdom.

While al-Adel and his descendants were established in Cairo as sultans, other members of the Ayyubid family – some descendants of Saladin, some of al-Adel or other brothers of Saladin – became the rulers of principalities of different sizes in different parts of Syria, including Transjordan. These local Ayyubid rulers were not called sultans, but *muluk* – the plural of *malik*, which was the title used at the time to distinguish provincial kings from their sovereign overlords. When the last Ayyubid sultan died in Egypt in 1250, his title was assumed by the Ayyubid malik of Damascus. In 1258, however, the Mongols conquered Iraq and sacked Baghdad. The following year, they conquered Syria, where they put an end to the existing Ayyubid principalities.

In Cairo, the last Ayyubid sultan was replaced in power by one of the leading officers of the so-called Mamluks – the Turkish military slaves who formed the crack regiment of the dead sultan's army. The Mamluks refused to accept the Ayyubid ruler of Damascus as the new sultan, and the conflict between the two sides continued until Damascus fell to the Mongols. Then, in 1260, the Mamluks entered Syria, defeated the Mongols at the battle of Ayn Jalut, near Lake Tiberias, and proceeded to establish their rule in all parts of the country formerly belonging to the Ayyubids. Next, they went to war against the Franks, to put a complete end to crusader rule in coastal Syria by 1291. Like the Ayyubids before them, the Mamluk rulers of Egypt and Syria assumed the title of sultan.

* * * * * * * * * *

During the crusader period, the present land of Jordan provided outposts for the military campaigns waged by the Muslim rulers of Damascus against the Frankish kings of Jerusalem. Otherwise, the territory remained of marginal importance. By this time, the trade between the Indian Ocean basin and the Mediterranean had come to be wholly restricted to the maritime route of the Red Sea; and this continued to be the case during the Mamluk period that followed. The trade from Persia and the Asian lands beyond arrived in Syria by overland routes which terminated in Aleppo and Damascus, without reaching Transjordan. Thus, under the Mamluks, the commercial prosperity of Syria was limited to the great inland cities and the seaports – mainly Beirut and Tripoli. These seaports received the overland trade from the inland cities, and also the maritime trade which coasted its way from Egypt to Byzantium and Italy by way of the Syrian littoral. Transjordan had no part in this commerce.

After their conquest of Syria, the Mamluks divided its territory into six provinces called *mamalik* (singular *mamlaka*, in the sense of 'vice-regency'). The largest of them, the mamlaka of Damascus, was too large to be administered as one unit, so it was subdivided into four main regions called *safaqat* (singular *safaqa*). One of those, the 'southern safaqa' (*al-safaqa al-qibliyya*), had its administrative centre in what is today the Syrian town of Deraa, just across the present Jordanian frontier, and it included the northern highlands of Transjordan and the adjacent parts of the Ghor. South of Wadi al-Mujib, the hill country of Bilad al-Sharat formed a separate mamlaka – that of Karak – which ranked last in importance among the Syrian provinces of the Mamluk empire. It was chiefly used as a place of political exile for discredited Mamluk sultans and officers, many of whom spent long years as prisoners in the great Karak fortress originally built by the crusaders. Sometimes, the territory of the mamlaka of Karak was extended northwards to include the highlands of al-Balqa in whole or in part.

In the course of the fifteenth century, as the Mamluks' control over Syria began to weaken, the district of Jabal Ajlun, in the Sawad highlands, became the centre of a tribal emirate, or principality, headed by a family known as the Ghzawis. Reportedly of local peasant stock, the Ghzawis claimed for themselves a bedouin origin, and actually developed their power by forming alliances with neighbouring bedouin tribes. Towards the end of the century, their originally Transjordanian territory extended westwards to include the rural parts of Palestine around Jerusalem and Hebron.

* * * * * * * * * *

When the Ottomans wrested Syria from the Mamluks in 1516, the district of Ajlun was established as a sanjak (adminstrative district) of the eyalet (or province, later called vilayet) of Damascus, with the local Ghzawi chiefs as its sanjakbeyis. This remained the case until about the middle of the seventeenth century. Meanwhile, successive Ghzawi emirs of Ajlun were appointed – with some interruptions – to the important and lucrative post of *amir al-Hajj*, to provide military escort for the pilgrims proceeding from Damascus to Mecca.

During the first two centuries of the Ottoman period, new bedouin tribes from the Syrian and Arabian deserts entered Transjordan. One such tribe were the reportedly North Arabian Adwan, who arrived in the first half of the seventeenth century to lay claim to the parts of al-Balqa west of the water divide. Starting from about the middle of that century, the Ottomans undertook a succession of measures to tighten their grip over Syria. In the process, the hegemony of the Ghzawis over the sanjak of Ajlun was gradually brought to an end.

By the turn of that century, however, the ability of the Ottoman state to control its vast territories was visibly declining; and this decline was noticeable throughout Syria, and particularly in Transjordan. Meanwhile, the northward thrust of the Anaza bedouins from central Arabia, which came to be associated in the second half of the eighteenth century with the rise of the Wahhabi movement in Najd, pushed more of the North Arabian desert tribes in the direction of Transjordan. Among the Anaza bedouin were the Banu Sakhr, whose tribal claims in the parts of al-Balqa east of the water divide were already established by about 1730. By the end of the eighteenth century, the Huwaytat bedouins were already laying claim to the steppes between Aqaba and the southern reaches of Bilad al-Sharat.

The bedouin anarchy which came to prevail in Transjordan by this time was temporarily checked betweeen 1832 and 1841 when Ottoman Syria was occupied by the forces of Muhammad Ali Pasha of Egypt, under the command of his formidable son Ibrahim (for the circumstances which brought about this short-lived Egyptian occupation of Syria, see Chapter 2). Once this occupation was brought to an end by the intervention of the European powers on the side of the Ottoman sultan against his rebel vassal from Egypt, the Transjordanian territory reverted to anarchy on an even greater scale. It was in these troubled circumstances that the Christians of Tafila, in the southern parts of Bilad al-Sharat, abandoned their town and dispersed in different directions. Later, in 1880, a number of Christian families left Karak to establish themselves on the abandoned site of Madaba, east of Amman, under the care of the Roman Catholic missionaries who were stationed there. Ottoman attempts to restore a semblance of law and order in Transjordan, particularly after the administrative re-organization of the vilayet of Damascus in 1864, provoked a succession of tribal rebellions in the different parts. Considerable efforts had to be exerted to pacify the country before the Hijaz railway between Damascus and Medina could be completed by 1908.

The principal support on which the Ottomans could safely rely in the area, as they sought to pacify it, were the Circassian farming communities settled in and around Amman. A stalwart Muslim people from the Caucasus region, the Circassians were subjected to persecution when the Russians took over their land in the latter decades of the nineteenth century. They began to arrive in Transjordan as refugees in 1878,[6] and continued to do so until 1909, with the encouragement of the Ottoman government. Before long, they were provided with arms to defend themselves against their bedouin neighbours and became loyal subjects of the sultan.

In 1914, the First World War broke out. Two years later, Sharif Hussein proclaimed the Great Arab Revolt against the Ottomans in Mecca, after which he was acclaimed as King of the Arab

Countries. As the forces of Hussein, led by his son Feisal, fought their way through Transjordan to reach Damascus, whatever stability the Ottomans had recently restored to the country broke down, and the land again reverted to rampant disorder. In Damascus, the Arab government subsequently established by Feisal was too preoccupied with the consolidation of its central authority to pay adequate attention to the administrative collapse in the outlying areas.

When Sharif Abdullah, the son of King Hussein and older brother of Feisal, arrived in Transjordan to reclaim its territory for the cause of the Great Arab Revolt, no one could have envied him his lot. What the British ceded to him out of their newly acquired Palestinian mandate were areas which were deemed virtually ungovernable, in addition to being extremely poor and undeveloped. He himself accepted this territory only as a first instalment of a greater Syrian territorial claim.

At this point, it would be necessary to determine exactly what conditions were like in Transjordan when Abdullah arrived in the country. For this purpose, the local developments of the last decades of the Ottoman period, and those of the two years immediately following the First World War, must be considered in more detail.

NOTES

1. The Roman names Galaaditis (Gilead) and Moabitis (Moab), applied respectively to the Sawad and the northern section of Bilad al-Sharat, appear to be borrowings from the Palestinian Jewish literature of the Hellenistic and early Roman periods (the books of Maccabees and the historical works of Flavius Josephus). The same applies to Esbonitis, the Roman name for the part of al-Balqa east of the water divide. Ammanitis (Amman), as the Roman name for al-Balqa as a whole, first appears in a Ptolemaic document of the Hellenistic period. The southern section of Bilad al-Sharat, during the same period, was called Gabalitis. European geographers generally follow this Classical terminology.
2. The vocalization of the four words cited here from Mesha's inscription, including the place names rendered as *qrhh* and *hrnn*, is arbitrary. The alphabetical script in which the inscription is written is purely consonantal, and lacks vowels.
3. See Stewart Perowne, *The Life and Times of Herod the Great* (London, 1956).
4. This precise delimitation of the *ajnad* in question derives from the

detailed work recently done on the subject by Mustafa Hiyari, of the University of Jordan in Amman.

5. It was customary for Seljuk rulers to entrust the care of each of their sons to one of their leading officers, who came to be called in Turkish *atabeg* (from *ata*, meaning 'father', and *beg*, meaning 'prince'). Once an officer received this title, he held it for life, and even passed it on to his descendants – hence the rulers and dynasties which held this title at the time.

6. Norman N. Lewis, *Nomads and Settlers in Syria and Jordan, 1800–1980* (Cambridge, 1987), p. 107.

2

'The Stone which the Builders Refused'

Until the middle decades of the nineteenth century, Ottoman administration in the Arab world had seldom followed uniform patterns. In the Syrian provinces, as in Iraq and the parts of Arabia where Ottoman sovereignty was recognized, special circumstances prevailed which made it difficult to maintain regular control from Istanbul for extended periods. Every now and then, military expeditions had to be sent here or there to crush a local rebellion, impose discipline on a seditious tribe, or put a brusque end to the career of some troublesome political adventurer. At different times, makeshift arrangements had to be improvised to keep the more intractable parts somehow answerable to Istanbul. By the eighteenth century, administrative irregularity, in the Arab provinces as elsewhere, had grown so rampant that it became the rule rather than the exception. In some areas – among them Transjordan – actual Ottoman control was so slight that it was virtually non-existent.

It was only in the middle decades of the nineteenth century that the Ottoman government in Istanbul finally set itself to regularize the administration of the empire. This was precipitated in the case of the Arab world by the rebellion of Muhammad Ali Pasha in Egypt. When he first came to power in Cairo in 1805, Muhammad Ali, in theory, was no more than a regular vali (governor) appointed from Istanbul to govern Egypt as an Ottoman vilayet (province). He soon developed enough power to become a match and potential rival to the Ottoman sultan, but he was careful to remain co-operative. When the Wahhabis of Arabia, from their small beginnings as a puritan religious movement in Najd in the middle years of the eighteenth century, rose to challenge Ottoman rule and began to threaten Iraq, Syria and Hijaz, the sultan found

himself powerless to stop them. Consequently, he asked Muhammad Ali to undertake the conquest of the peninsula on his behalf,
to root out Wahhabi power in its home grounds in a campaign
which lasted from 1811 to 1818. A few years later, in the 1820s,
the same sultan called upon Muhammad Ali's help once more,
this time to help put down the revolt of the Greeks in Morea.
Here again, the intervention of the Egyptian Pasha was on the
point of achieving complete success when the European powers,
in 1827, intervened in full force on the Greek side and compelled
him to abandon the project. Morea was subsequently lost to the
Ottomans, and an independent Greek kingdom was established
on its territory.

The quarrels which developed between Muhammad Ali and the
sultan after the failure of the Egyptian intervention in the Greek
war finally led to the Egyptian occupation of Syria in 1832. When
this happened, the same European powers who had helped the
Greeks gain their independence from Ottoman rule turned to
support the Ottoman sultan against his rebel Egyptian vassal.
Consequently, the Egyptian occupation of Syria was forcibly
brought to an end in 1841, and Ottoman authority over the region
was restored.

The Ottomans returned to Syria in that year fully determined
to regularize its affairs. Shortly before, in 1839, an imperial
rescript called the Hatti-Sherif of Gulhane had launched a programme of general reforms called the *Tanzimat*. Among them
were new vilayet laws issued in 1864, and again in 1888, to re-
organize the provincial administration, among other places in
Syria. The Tanzimat culminated in 1876 with the promulgation of
a constitution for the empire and the election of the first Ottoman
parliament. Two years later, the sultan Abdul-Hamid II
(1876–1909) suspended the constitution, dismissed the parliament,
and began ruling the empire as a despot. In most other respects,
however, the principles on which the Tanzimat of the preceding
decades were based remained virtually unaltered. Among them
was the principle which called for increased centralization in the
management of the empire.

Despite the efforts exerted by Abdul-Hamid II to keep the
empire together, some important territories were lost during his
reign. Among them was Egypt, which was occupied by Britain
in 1882. Technically, the descendants of Muhammad Ali who

succeeded him in Cairo as pashas, subsequently adopting the honorific title of khedive, continued to rule as vassals of the Ottoman sultan until 1914. Effectively, however, Egypt after 1882 was a British protectorate.

During the thirty years of the so-called Hamidian despotism, the political ideals of the Tanzimat remained alive in Istanbul among a group of intellectuals and European-educated officials and army officers who came to be known as the Young Turks. The idea of nationalism had already begun to permeate the Ottoman world at the time, and the Young Turks were Turkish nationalists. They maintained that the Ottoman empire, while remaining the empire of Islam, was essentially a Turkish concern. In keeping with the spirit of the Tanzimat, the Young Turks were firm believers in the principle of political centralization. In addition, they believed that the empire must be Turkified. These two principles – centralization and Turkification – became the underlying ideals of a group of officials and army officers who secretly organized themselves as the Committee of Union and Progress (CUP).

In 1908, an army revolution led by the CUP in Istanbul brought the period of Hamidian despotism to an end, and the Ottoman constitution of 1876 was restored. Within five years, however, the Young Turk regime in Istanbul was transformed by stages into a military dictatorship for which the democractic institutions reintroduced in 1908 – among them the Ottoman parliament – served as a mere cover. A succession of military catastrophes which were blamed on civilian politicians, among them the defeat in the war of 1911–12 which ended with the loss of Libya to Italy, hastened the process by which the military finally seized power in Istanbul.

The army officers who became the actual rulers of the Ottoman state by 1913 were all German-trained, which made them naturally pro-German. As newcomers to power, they lacked the resilience of their political predecessors, and were generally inclined to take hard-and-fast positions on debatable issues. When the First World War (or the Great War, as it was called at the time) broke out in 1914 between the Central Powers (Germany and Austria–Hungary) and the Allies (Britain, France and Russia), the Young Turk regime threw the Ottoman empire into the war on the side of the Central Powers. When these lost the war in 1918, the Ottoman empire was doomed.

Meanwhile, starting from 1908, the policies of increased centralization and Turkification relentlessly pursued by the Young Turk regime were beginning to provoke negative reactions in the Arab countries. In many Arab circles, particularly among the educated and politically ambitious classes in the cities, there were people who were beginning to sense that they were being rapidly transformed from Ottoman citizens into Turkish sujects. Among the general run of Muslim Arabs, however, the Ottoman empire continued to be revered as the empire of Islam, ruled by the sultan-caliph in Istanbul not only as a temporal sovereign, but also as a defender of the Islamic faith.

Naturally, Christian Arabs had never subscribed to this popular Muslim view of the empire, and the idea of a secular Arab nationalism had been developing among them for some time, particularly in Beirut. After the coming of the Young Turks to power, increasing numbers of Muslims were attracted to the Arab nationalist idea. Some of these went no further than demanding a measure of autonomy for the Arab countries within the existing Ottoman political context, on the basis of what they termed *lamarkaziyya* or decentralization. But others aspired to nothing less than complete Arab independence. Among the latter group were the members of the secret Arab nationalist society called *al-Fatat* (short for *al-Jam'iyya al-'Arabiyya al-Fatat*, or 'the Young Arab Society'), based in Damascus. A sister organization was the secret society called *al-'Ahd* ('the Covenant'), which was founded by Arab nationalist officers of the Ottoman army, most of whom were from Iraq. In 1913, an Arab congress was convened in Paris in which the different views regarding the future of the Arab nation were openly voiced before the world for the first time.

From the very beginning, the British, from their base in Egypt, maintained contacts with the secret Arab nationalist organizations, most directly with *al-Fatat*. The leaders of this society were made to believe that Britain would support the establishment of an independent pan-Arab state when the right moment came, provided that the Arab nationalists were prepared to co-operate politically with Britain. After the outbreak of the Great War in 1914, these contacts with the Arab nationalists in Syria were intensified by the special Arab Bureau which the British had established in Cairo. From this same Arab Bureau, the British also approached Sharif Hussein, the emir of Mecca, encouraging him to proclaim a general Arab revolt against the Ottomans, particularly after the Ottoman empire entered the war on the side of Germany. This Arab revolt was finally proclaimed in June 1916. The Sharif, as its leader, was now recognized by the British government as King of the Hijaz (for more details, see Chapter 3).

Within a year, the forces of the Arab revolt were beginning to fight their way into Syria under the leadership of Sharif Feisal, the third of King Hussein's four sons. They were subsequently joined in Transjordan by the British forces which had completed their own advance from Egypt through Palestine. On 1 October 1918, Sharif Feisal, supported by the British, entered Damascus and established an Arab government on behalf of his father in that ancient seat of Arab empire. Shortly after, the last Ottoman troops left Syria, and the Ottoman government signed the so-called Mudros armistice which brought the hostilities between the Ottoman empire and the Allies to an end.

At that particular point, the Arab nationalists who rallied around Sharif Feisal in Damascus were convinced that their aspirations, at long last, were about to be achieved. In the course of the war, however, their British supporters had made commitments to other parties. By the so-called Sykes–Picot agreement of 1916, Britain had recognized the political interests of France in Syria and northern Iraq. In 1917, the British foreign secretary Arthur James Balfour, in a letter to Lionel Rothschild, one of the most famous Jews in England, had committed Britain to support the Zionist aspiration to establish a Jewish 'national home' in Palestine (the so-called Balfour Declaration).

Shortly after Feisal entered Damascus, French forces landed in Beirut to abort the claim of his newly formed Arab government over that city and the adjacent Lebanese territory. At the peace talks which followed the end of the war, France insisted that her own claims to Syria be recognized. In 1919, the treaty of Versailles, between the Allies and Germany, provided for the establishment of an international body called the League of Nations; and it was agreed that the German colonies, and also the Arab lands which were formerly part of the Ottoman empire, must be taken over by the League of Nations, to be assigned as mandates to one or another of the Allied powers. The Arab territories in question, in Syria and Iraq, were to be classified as class A mandates, because they were considered developed enough already to be prepared for independence. This was to distinguish them from the German colonies in Africa and other parts of the world, which were to be mandates of class B.

To pre-empt the French designs on its territory, the Arab government in Damascus convened a General Syrian Congress in March 1920, to proclaim Syria an independent Arab kingdom with Feisal at its head. In the following month, however, the Supreme Allied Council meeting at San Remo, on the Italian riviera, formally assigned all parts of Syria north of the Yarmuk river to the mandate of France, along with the Lebanese territory which the French already occupied. Britain, already in occupation of Palestine and Iraq, was to have her mandate over both these lands and the territory in between, including the highlands of Transjordan. While Britain made no attempt to challenge the sovereignty of King Feisal over the Transjordanian territory now assigned as part of her Palestinian mandate, the French were determined to act differently in the parts of Syria allotted to them. In July 1920, the newly appointed French high commissioner in Beirut, General Henri Gouraud, sent the troops under his command to defeat a small group of hastily gathered Arab fighters at the Maysalun pass in the mountains of the Anti-Lebanon, and then proceeded to occupy Damascus. Forced to abandon his kingdom, Feisal left Damascus for Deraa, at the Transjordanian border, from where he proceeded to Haifa in Palestine. From there, he continued his journey to Britain, where his wartime allies had other plans for his future.

It is against this general background of regional and world developments, starting from the mid-nineteenth century, that the particular situation of Transjordan during this period can be brought into focus.

* * * * * * * * * *

In the last decades of Ottoman rule, Transjordan was administered, north to south, in three divisions: the sanjak of Ajlun, the kaza of al-Balqa, and the *mutasarrifiyya* of Karak. The last centred around Bilad al-Sharat, stopping just short of Aqaba. This strategic port was kept by Muhammad Ali after the end of the

Egyptian occupation of Syria in 1841 as part of the Egyptian territory of Sinai, which bordered the Gulf of Aqaba from the west. In 1892, however, the port was ceded back to the Ottomans to become part of the *muhafaza* of Medina, in the vilayet of the Hijaz. North of Aqaba, the town of Maan, in the desert, straddled the border between the mutasarrifiyya of Karak and the Hijazi territory of Medina.

In the Ottoman administrative system of the late nineteenth century, a kaza was a subdivision of a sanjak, and a sanjak was a subdivision of a vilayet (formerly called an *eyalet*), which was the largest unit in the Ottoman provincial administration. In 1861, the European powers compelled the Ottomans to provide a special status for the Christian-dominated territory of Mount Lebanon, which was originally divided between the vilayets of Sidon and Tripoli. Accordingly, this Lebanese territory was removed from the regular vilayet system of Syria and turned into a privileged administrative unit called a mutasarrifiyya, guaranteed by the European powers and governed by a *mutasarrif* appointed directly from Istanbul. Because the Ottomans were actually averse to this arrangement, they proceeded to call some other sanjaks 'mutasarrifiyyas', to detract from the special administrative significance of the term as applied originally in the case of Mount Lebanon. Among these was the Transjordanian mutasarrifiyya of Karak, which was essentially no more than an ordinary sanjak, as will be seen.

In northern Transjordan, the sanjak of Ajlun already existed as part of the eyalet of Damascus in the sixteenth and seventeenth centuries. It was reconstituted as a regular sanjak of the same province – now called a vilayet – in 1851, ten years after the Egyptian forces of Muhammad Ali retired from Syria. It was only in 1894, however, that an Ottoman military expedition was finally sent to subdue Bilad al-Sharat, where the local population had been in a state of rebellion for more than four decades. Once the region was pacified, it was organized as a mutasarrifiyya of the vilayet of Damascus. In Karak, which was made the administrative centre of this mutasarrifiyya, an Ottoman garrison was stationed to help the Ottoman mutasarrif maintain law and order. Similar garrisons were maintained in other parts of the region. At the same time, the former rebels in the area were granted a general amnesty, and the sheikhs who headed the clans of Karak and its immediate vicinity were assigned monthly stipends to secure their political co-operation.

Meanwhile, following the first re-organization of the Syrian vilayets in 1864, attempts were made to introduce land and tax reforms in the different provinces, among them the vilayet of Damascus. This provoked negative reactions in many parts. In the Transjordanian Balqa region, the governor of the sanjak of Nablus tried to impose taxes on the local Adwan bedouins in the early 1880s, from his base in Palestine. The Adwan were determined to resist this, whereupon their leading sheikh was seized and put in prison. After his release in 1882, the Balqa region became a regular kaza of the sanjak of Nablus, and remained so after this sanjak in 1888 became a mutasarrifiyya attached to the newly established vilayet of Beirut. Later, in 1905, the kaza of Balqa was separated from the mutasarrifiyya of Nablus and made part of the mutasarrifiyya of Karak, in the vilayet of Damascus.

When the Young Turk revolution in Istanbul restored constitutional life to the empire, only one Transjordanian deputy from the town of Karak was returned to the Ottoman parliament, first in 1908, then again in 1914. This parliament, however, was not the only representative institution re-introduced at the time in accordance with the restored constitution. There were also the general councils of the vilayets, among them Damascus; plus the administrative councils of the sanjaks or mutasarrifiyyas, and those of the kazas. The different Transjordanian regions were naturally represented in all these provincial, regional and district councils.

As the Ottoman administration in the Transjordanian territory was thus regularized, some agricultural prosperity returned, and new villages re-emerged here and there on sites that had earlier been abandoned. One was the Christian village of Madaba, in the Balqa region (see Chapter 1), which grew into a small town. In the more turbulent parts, however, the Ottoman efforts to impose law and order and introduce innovations clashed with local interests as well as with the traditional way of life, particularly when the Ottoman officials in charge happened to be brusque and insensitive to local customs. More important, the modernizing state policies pressed by both civilian and military Ottoman officials threatened the traditional power enjoyed by the established local sheikhs.

Normally, these sheikhs were not the chiefs of the bedouin tribes, so the state could buy their allegiance with cash payments or ceremonial honours, as was the time-honoured practice. Rather, they were the crafty town and village notables who headed the more important sedentary clans in the region. These notables came from families which were more sophisticated politically than their bedouin peers, and were experienced masters in political intrigue. In general, they maintained close connections with the bedouin tribes of the area, and their attitude towards the state, or *hukuma* (literally, 'government'), was opportunistic and cynical. While they vied with one another for Ottoman favour, they lost no opportunity to discredit Ottoman state policies which threatened their traditional power. This they did by fanning popular opposition to these policies, and by charging the officials who carried them out with mismanagement, neglect, corruption and deliberate cruelty, regardless of whether or not such charges were justified. In this manner, they could present themselves as the defenders of the people against governmental oppression, and so enhance their own local power.

In the town of Karak and its vicinity, the most prominent and traditionally powerful among the local notables were the sheikhs of the Majali clan, whose ancestors had first arrived in that area towards the middle of the seventeenth century as immigrants from the Palestinian town of al-Khalil (Hebron). When Karak became the administrative centre of the mutasarrifiyya bearing its name, the Majali sheikhs had most reason to fear the erosion of their local power. In league with other sheikhly families of the area, and also with the neighbouring bedouin chiefs, they sought to maintain their influence by instigating popular resistance against the local Ottoman administration whenever they found the opportunity to do so.

In the mutasarrifiyya of Karak, the clash of interest between the town and village sheikhs backed by their followers on the one hand, and the Ottoman administration on the other, was more serious than in most other Syrian parts. Before long, two revolts followed one another in the region, both of which were crushed with the utmost severity.

The first of these two revolts broke out in 1905 in the village of Shawbak (the medieval Frankish outpost of Montreal) south of the town of Karak. In that year, the officers of the local Ottoman garrison began to put the women of the village to forced labour, carrying water to the old crusader fortress, where the troops were stationed, from the springs in the valley below. This may well have been done deliberately to punish the village for repeated insubordination. In any case, it provided the direct excuse for an uprising not only among the people of the village itself, but also among the neighbouring bedouins who rallied to their support. A special expedition had to be sent from Karak to put down the Shawbak uprising by military force, and brutal punishments were meted out to its perpetrators.

The second revolt in the region broke out in Karak itself in 1910, and was far more serious. Also, the circumstances that brought it about were more complex. Here the problem began in 1908, when the monthly stipends paid to the local sheikhs since 1894 were stopped. Apparently, the new Young Turk regime which came to power in that year did not feel that the Karak notables were performing services to the state deserving of recompense. At the same time, elections to the administrative council of the mutasarrifiyya of Karak had returned a leading member of the Majali clan to this council, but the governor of the vilayet, in Damascus, refused to approve his appointment. Meanwhile, the Ottoman state had frightened the rural population not only in Transjordan, but throughout Syria, by introducing military conscription, and also by ordering the general disarmament of the civilian population – the sort of measure to which the tribal people of the country, peasants or bedouins, were particularly sensitive.

In Transjordan, matters became more critical by 1910. In that year, the Ottomans sent a large expedition to put down an uprising by the Druzes of Hawran, south of Damascus, and the perpetrators of this uprising were brought before military tribunals which dealt death sentences to some, and prison sentences to others. At the same time, the Druzes of the area were forcibly disarmed, and the men among them who were of the appropriate age were conscripted and sent for military service in the Balkans. Once the Hawran region was pacified, the Ottoman government in Damascus sent a census committee to Karak, to determine which of its men were of military age, so that they too could be conscripted. This naturally alarmed the local people as well as the local chiefs, who forthwith rallied around the Majalis to lead them in resistance.

Seizing the opportunity of the absence of a large part of the Karak garrison from the town on a special mission to the bedouin areas nearby, the tribesmen of Karak and its neighbourhood, led by the Majalis, attacked the government house in the town, killing the officials they found there, and setting fire to all the official records. When the troops in the town fortress attempted a sortie to stem the rebellion, they were forced to retreat back into the fortress, which was effectively besieged. From Karak and its immediate vicinity, the rebellion rapidly spread to other parts of the mutasarrifiyya, to reach Tafila and Maan. Wherever they could, the rebels seized stations of the recently completed Hijaz railway and destroyed bridges and telegraph lines.

The Karak uprising continued for eight days, until forces arrived from Damascus, covering most of the distance by rail, to put down the rebellion in the town by a random massacre. Of the leaders of the uprising who were arrested and brought to trial, five were executed in Damascus, and another five in Karak itself, to set an example to their fellow townsmen. The Majalis, who were regarded as the chief perpetrators of the uprising, were declared outlaws. Later, a settlement was imposed, whereby the people of Karak – including the Majalis – were to pay compensation in annual instalments for all state property destroyed in the course of the insurrection. The payment of the compensation was subsequently allowed to lapse. In 1912, a general amnesty declared throughout the Ottoman empire brought the whole matter to an end.

* * * * * * * * * *

The Ottoman control over Transjordan was already complete and firmly established by 1914, when the Great War broke out. Two years later, Sharif Hussein of Mecca proclaimed the Great Arab Revolt. Arab nationalists – some civilians, others officers defecting from the Ottoman army, in some cases after they had been taken prisoners of war by the British – arrived in the Hijaz from different Arab provinces to join the Arab forces of Sharif Feisal and acclaim his father as their leader and king.

In the course of his Transjordanian campaign in 1917–18, which was financed by Britain, Feisal was assisted and advised by British officers detailed from Cairo, among them the famous and controversial T. E. Lawrence, who immortalized the story of the Arab revolt in his book *The Seven Pillars of Wisdom*. Feisal also received invaluable local support from a number of desert tribes, the most important among them being the Ruwala and their Shaalan chiefs, from the North Arabian region of Jawf, and the Huwaytat of the steppe country north of Aqaba. Some of the Banu Sakhr bedouins of the Balqa region also joined the forces of the Arab revolt.

Other Transjordanian tribes, however, including most of the Banu Sakhr, tended to hedge; and the same was true of the sedentary clans in the different Transjordanian regions. Among these, the Christian clans generally favoured the Sharifian side, and leading Christian notables from towns such as Karak and Madaba were actually seized by the Ottoman military authorities and sent into exile in the vilayet of Adana, in southern Anatolia, because of their pro-Sharifian sympathies. The same was not generally true among the Transjordanian Muslims, who regarded the Ottoman state as standing ultimately for the political cause of Islam, and were suspicious of King Hussein of the Hijaz and his sons because of their political relations with Britain. To secure the continued loyalty of the Transjordanian Muslim clans, or at least prevent them from openly opting for the Sharifian side, the Ottoman authorities repeatedly invited their more prominent sheikhs to Damascus, where they were feasted and honoured. It was only when it became clear that the Ottomans could no longer hold out in Transjordan that some of these sheikhs began to declare their support for Feisal and the Arab cause.

* * * * * * * * * *

Once the war in Syria was over, and Feisal established his Arab government in Damascus, the Transjordanian territory fell under the jurisdiction of this government. From the Balqa southwards, it was placed under a military administration answering to one commander-in-chief – a former Iraqi officer of the Ottoman army called Jaafar al-Askari. Other officers and officials from different Arab countries – Iraq, Syria, Palestine, Lebanon, and even North Africa – were placed in military charge of the different parts. In each place, the local notables were summoned to take solemn oaths of allegiance to the Sharifian government, and to the red, black, white and green banner of the Arab revolt.

Towards the end of 1919, Feisal's government in Damascus divided its Syrian territory into eight administrative units, called *liwas* (*liwa'*, formerly the Arabic term for an Ottoman sanjak). Of these eight liwas, the one of the Balqa consisted entirely of Transjordanian territory. Its administrative centre was the town of Salt, and it also included Madaba and Amman. The remaining Transjordanian regions were included in two other liwas. In the north, the territory of the former sanjak of Ajlun became part of the liwa of Hawran, whose administrative centre was the now Syrian town of Deraa. In the south, the former mutasarrifiyya of Karak simply became the liwa of Karak, except that its territory was extended into the northern Hijaz, to include the vicinity of Tabuk. Of these three liwas, none was headed by a native Transjordanian; but an effort was made to placate the local population in each liwa by appointing members of the more prominent local families to a number of official positions. Also, a special tribal council headed by a member of the Sharifian family was instituted in the area to arbitrate on tribal disputes according to the accepted conventions. Otherwise, the Transjordanian territory remained a neglected part of Sharifian Syria, receiving little attention from the central government in Damascus which was preoccupied at the time with more pressing matters.

When Feisal was forced by the French to abandon Damascus in 1920, he could easily have remained in Transjordan had he chosen to do so, considering that France had no claim to that territory. Feisal's British allies, for their part, could hardly have stopped him from keeping at least this small remnant of his lost Syrian realm. As the generally accepted hero of the Arab national cause, however, Feisal evisaged his future differently, and so did his British friends. Earlier in that year, he had been proclaimed King of Syria by the General Syrian Congress convening in Damascus. At that same congress, delegates from Iraq had announced the independence of their own country as a kingdom under Feisal's older brother, Abdullah (see Chapter 4). In the following year, however, when Britain, as the mandatory power, finally agreed to the establishment of an Iraqi kingdom, it was Feisal, not Abdullah, who was formally installed as king in Baghdad.

* * * * * * * * * *

Once Feisal was out of Syria, many of his political entourage – Syrian, Iraqi and Lebanese – fled Damascus to seek refuge in Transjordan. In the northern regions, they could enjoy the protection of former political associates who still held the administrative posts in towns such as Irbid and Salt, to which they had been appointed in Feisal's time. Outside the larger towns, however, the sudden collapse of the central authority in Damascus was reflected in a general breakdown of law and order. In the rural areas, the sheikhs of the more powerful sedentary clans felt free to behave as they pleased, each of them set on becoming a government unto himself. Among the bedouins of the desert regions, the sheikhs of the more powerful tribes did the same.

During the last decades of the Ottoman period, the Transjordanian bedouins, no less than the town and village folk, had been brought around to obey the state and even to pay taxes. Feisal, in his time, was unable to maintain the same degree of control over these bedouins, although a number of their more powerful chiefs – among them his wartime allies of the Huwaytat – willingly accorded him their personal allegiance. Now, however, with Feisal out of the way, the bedouins throughout Transjordan completely reverted to their original ways, refusing to recognize any local authority, and imposing their own control on the sedentary areas wherever they could. In some places, they came up against the organized resistance of sedentary clans who were able to defend their villages and repel the bedouin raiders. In other areas, different bedouin tribes fought one another to determine which of them would have the local monopoly over village raiding.

Meanwhile, the British mandatory authority in Jerusalem undertook the administration of Transjordan as part of the Palestinian mandate, but only in a somewhat offhand manner. The principal concern of the mandatory government in Jerusalem was with the Palestinian part of the territory, where the project to establish a national home for the Jews was being militantly resisted by the local Arab population (see Chapter 6). In some British political circles, Transjordan was viewed as no more than a part of the Palestinian mandate to which Arabs unwilling to live with the Jews could ultimately go to settle. Moreover, the question of the exact frontier between the British- and French-mandated territories was as yet unsettled. Under Feisal, the liwa of Hawran had included the Transjordanian region of Irbid and Ajlun.

Hawran subsequently became part of the French-mandated Syrian territory. Until 1921, however, it still included the town and vicinity of Ramtha, south of the Yarmuk river, which was geographically part of the Irbid area. This frontier question was certainly one factor which made the British reluctant to make too much of an issue of their mandatory administration of Transjordan. What added considerably to their reluctance was the continued presence of many of Feisal's men in Transjordan, which was a source of grave concern for the French in Damascus. The French continually blamed the British for any trouble they received from that direction.

Rather than treat Transjordan as one administrative unit composed of different parts, the British mandatory authorities recognized no fewer than three separate governments in the area, each of which went its own way. And to each of the three governments there was a special British adviser assigned from Jerusalem. The northern region became the territory of what was called the Government of Ajlun, although the administrative centre of this government was not Ajlun, but the town of Irbid. The central region, comprising the Balqa territory, was organized as the Government of Salt, with an administration actually established in Salt. In the south, the territory of Karak was stripped of the Maan and Tabuk regions, which were re-appropriated by the Hijaz; and the rest of the territory was placed under an administration which chose to call itself, in all seriousness, the Arab Government of Moab (*al-Hukuma al-'Arabiyya al-Mu'abiyya*). Shortly after this government was set up in the town of Karak, a young British officer, Major Alec Kirkbride, was sent from Jerusalem to become its adviser.

Of these three regional governments which emerged from the Transjordanian ruins of Feisal's Syrian kingdom, the only one which was moderately successful was the government of Salt. Here, the administration remained in the hands of the mostly non-local administrative and security officials appointed in Feisal's time, who were relatively efficient. Here, also, the sedentary population, which included the Christians of Salt and Madaba and the Circassians of Amman, was generally docile, so that taxes could be collected from the townspeople and the villagers without much difficulty. This provided the Salt government with financial resources which were more or less adequate to pay the salaries of the officials. It was only the bedouin tribes of the region, such as the Banu Sakhr and the Adwan, who were given to causing trouble, by refusing to pay taxes and making a point of remaining outside the pale of the established jurisdiction.

In the north, the government of Ajlun, operating from Irbid, was totally unable to maintain the integrity of its territory, let alone exercise any degree of central control over it. In Irbid itself, as in Salt, the administration set up in the days of King Feisal continued to function. Also, the flag of Feisal's Syrian kingdom – the four-coloured banner of the Arab revolt, with a white star featuring on the triangular red strip – was maintained. The government here, in fact, regarded itself as representing the last remaining outpost of Arab independence in Syria; and for this reason, the men at its helm wished to make of it as much of a success as possible.

Irbid was only a small town at the time, but it had a special character. It was the principal market of the rich grainlands which Arab geographers used to call the Sawad of Jordan (see Chapter 1), and its people had traditionally dealt with grain merchants in Damascus and other Syrian cities. Unlike the inhabitants of the more typically Transjordanian towns, the families of Irbid were not tribally organized into clans headed by sheikhs. Some of these families were actually of Damascene origin, or came from the larger provincial towns of adjacent areas, such as Safad in northern Palestine. The town of Salt, as the principal market of the Balqa region, was not unlike Irbid in these respects, and was actually larger and more evolved, having better schools and other social facilities, among them a British missionary hospital. Here, the population included families originally from Palestinian towns such as Nablus or Nazareth. While the population of Salt included a large proportion of Christians who had traditionally shied away from politics, that of Irbid, being more solidly Muslim, acted more as one body politically, which made a considerable difference.

This special social character of Irbid set the town apart not only from the rest of Transjordan, but also from its immediate surroundings. While remaining basically provincial, the people of Irbid were affected more than other Transjordanians by political influences from the outside, especially from Damascus. Also, they were politically ambitious. The nationalist spirit which had lately come to pervade urban society throughout Syria was rife among them, and they considered themselves among its torchbearers.

With all this ostensibly to its credit, however, Irbid was out of tune with the rural surroundings which its government sought to control. In this area, which could boast the largest sedentary population in Transjordan, townspeople and villagers, organized in compact clans, could hold their own against bedouin raiders without much difficulty. On the other hand, they fought bitter feuds among themselves, and also with clans of the adjacent Balqa region. The sheikhs of the local clans, being extremely ambitious, were for the most part unwilling to obey the established government authority. From Damascus, the French mandatory administration could easily exploit their ambitions and the rivalries among them to consolidate its position in the Hawran region of Syria, which bordered the territory of Irbid from the north. Little wonder that a number of the rebel Transjordan sheikhs of the area were actually in the pay of the French at the time.

In Irbid, as in Salt, the administration inherited from the Feisal regime came to be assisted by a council of sheikhs representing the different local clans, called the Administrative and Legislative Council. However, despite the best efforts exerted by the government and council to administer the Irbid territory as a unit, the sheikhs of the more powerful clans in the area – notably the Shuraydas of the Kura district, the Furayhat of Ajlun, the Kayids of Jarash and the Azzams of al-Wustiyya – rebelled against the established order, one after another, each of them setting up a separate government of his own. The immediate cause of the rebellion, in nearly every case, was the determination of the Irbid government to collect taxes from everybody on a regular basis. The first and most serious of the resulting rebellions was the one led by Sheikh Kulayb al-Shurayda in the Kura district, which received virtually open support from the French in Damascus. The British authorities in Palestine, for their part, appear to have condoned the Kura rebellion, as they condoned others that followed, perhaps because they did not have much patience for the intense nationalism exhibited by the Irbid administration. In one instance, when the rebellion of the Kayid clan resulted in the establishment of a separate government in the town of Jarash, it received what amounted to official British recognition when a British officer was detailed to become its resident adviser.

If the performance of the government of Ajlun, based in Irbid, was ultimately unsuccessful, that of the Arab government of Moab, in the Karak region, which was advised by Major Kirkbride, was little better than a farce. From the first book of Kirkbride's political memoirs, *A Crackle of Thorns*, and also from other sources, it is possible to reconstruct a picture of the anarchic manner in which this government was run. After the destruction of Feisal's Arab regime in Damascus, the man who had been serving as its mutasarrif in Karak was replaced in office by a local sheikh called Rufayfan al-Majali – one of the recognized heads of the Majali clan. Major Kirkbride arrived in the town shortly afterwards, with no clear instructions from Jerusalem as to what precisely he was expected to do. A High Council had recently been elected to assist the new mutasarrif in the local administration. It was composed of eight sheikhs representing the more prominent clans of the area, one among them being a Greek Orthodox priest representing the Halasa, the largest of the local Christian clans.

When Kirkbride arrived to meet this High Council in formal session for the first time, he found its members looking at their solemn and dignified best, but it was clear that there was a conflict between them which they were taking in good humour. It soon transpired that they were unable to agree as to which of them should head the council, because each, with the possible exception of the Christian priest, felt equally qualified for the position. Moreover, none of the major clans of the region was prepared to concede the headship of the council to the representative of any of the other clans. An exchange of furtive looks between the men present indicated to the young British officer that it was he who was expected to preside over them. When he remonstrated, he was told quite plainly that he alone would be acceptable: first, because he was an outsider, which made him politically noncontroversial; and second, because he was the representative of Britain, and was thus the only person present who could secure for the Moabite government financial and other assistance from the British administration in Palestine.

Having prevailed on Kirkbride to accept its presidency, the High Council of the Arab government of Moab proceeded to inaugurate its tenure of power by dismissing all non-locals who had formerly been appointed to the liwa of Karak from Damascus, so that men from the Karak region could be appointed in their place. The political sensitivities between the major clans naturally took precedence over the question of competence in the new appointments. Next, a sub-committee of the council was set up to draft a code of acceptable civil and criminal procedure. This piece of legislation, after much give and take, was ultimately formulated in sixteen articles, which had to be further discussed and scrutinized before they were finally approved by the council in full session shortly before the end of that year.

The Moabite government of Karak appears to have expected the British administration in Jerusalem to provide it with all the money it needed. The sheikhs who sat in the High Council were in no position to force their tribal constituents to pay direct taxes, considering that they themselves remained disinclined to set an example for them. Other matters were also problematic. For example, the local post had no stamps of its own, and no means to print them; so Kirkbride had to beg for consignments of Palestinian stamps from Jerusalem, which were then super-imprinted with the seal of the Arab government of Moab. The fiscal stamps, which were issued locally, bore the imprint of the High Council and had their value written in by hand.

To maintain security, Kirkbride was assigned about thirty-five Arab policemen who were detailed to him from Palestine. For six months, these policemen received no pay because the cash sent from Jerusalem by way of Amman took that long to arrive. The reason for this was that the road between Amman and Karak was so infested by desert raiders and highwaymen that it was unsafe even for escorted officials to travel if they carried any money. The Moabite police force, in any case, was inadequate to impose law and order on a region which had been turbulent at the best of times; and it could do hardly anything against the bedouins of the broader vicinity. Among these bedouins, each tribe could now attack the other without fear of government intervention. A state verging on utter lawlessness thus came to prevail throughout the entire countryside, and there were occasions when Kirkbride, caught in a foray, had to defend himself with his personal arms. Before long, a feud broke out inside Karak between the rival 'eastern' and 'western' alliances of the clans of the town and its vicinity: the *sharagah* and the *gharabah*. The fighting that followed reduced the authority of the Moabite government, even in its administrative centre, to little more than a name.

* * * * * * * * * *

This was the situtaion that had come to prevail in Transjordan when Sharif Abdullah, the second son of King Hussein of the Hijaz, arrived from Medina by train in the border town of Maan on 11 November 1920. Until that time, Abdullah had been serving his father as foreign minister in the Hijaz. Now, he was coming to Transjordan with a special purpose. In the first formal announcement he made upon his arrival in Maan, he declared his determination to redeem the Arab Kingdom of Syria which his younger brother Feisal had lost four months earlier.

Of this lost Syrian kingdom, Abdullah managed to reclaim only the Transjordanian remnants: a territory, mostly desert, which had come to be regarded as being virtually ungovernable, and which no-one seemed particularly interested in keeping or acquiring. Out of this neglected territory, however, Abdullah was able to create a remarkably well-administered state: the Emirate of Transjordan, which later became the Hashemite Kingdom of Jordan.

Here we must interrupt the story of the land of Jordan and turn to the story of Abdullah. For the man who became the founder of the modern Jordanian state did not emerge from a historical vacuum, and his political credentials were substantial. Behind him was dynastic political experience going back many centuries.

3

The Dynastic Background

Carrying the name of the branch of the Qureish tribe to which the Prophet Muhammad belonged, the Hashemites, historically, have existed in two main lines: the Abbasids, descending from Muhammad's uncle Abbas; and the Alids, descending from the Prophet's daughter Fatima and his first cousin Ali, who was Fatima's husband. Since the extinction of the recognized Abbasid line towards the middle of the sixteenth century, the only Hashemites have been the Alids: the *Ahl al-Bayt*, or 'Dynasty of the House', as they have been called, the reference being to the house of the Prophet.[1] Consequently, only the Alids continue to be referred to as Hashemites in modern usage.

Fatima and Ali had two sons, Hassan and Hussein: the only grandsons of the Prophet, and hence the ancestors of all his descendants. Our concern here is with the Hassanid branch, to which the Hashemites of Jordan belong. But first, some general remarks applying to both branches would be in order. Ali, the father of Hassan and Hussein, was the fourth and last of the orthodox caliphs of Islam. After his death, Muslim rule became dynastic: first under the Umayyads, who established their capital in Damascus (661–750); and then under the Abbasids, who established their capital in Baghdad (750–1258). The Umayyads belonged to the Qureish tribe, but were not Hashemites. Once they had established themselves in the caliphate, they made a point of keeping the Hashemites – and especially the Alids – away from public life, using force against them on a number of occasions. The Abbasids, who finally managed to wrest the caliphate from the Umayyads, were Hashemites, as already observed. Their anxiety, however, was to keep the caliphate as their own preserve, to the exclusion of their Alid cousins who had the better dynastic claim to the rule of Islam. Consequently, the Abbasid policy towards the Alids was no less repressive than that of the Umayyads.

Muslims who accepted the legitimacy of Umayyad and Abbasid rule as a fact of history ultimately came to be called Sunnis (from the Arabic *sunna*, meaning 'tradition'). Others who maintained that only descendants of the Prophet could be rightful caliphs were called the Shiah (Arabic *shi'a*, meaning 'party, faction'). And before long, different sects developed among the Shiah. Among them was the sect of the Zeidis, who believed that any member of the Ahl al-Bayt was acceptable as caliph, provided he managed to secure the office, which they preferred to call the imamate rather than the caliphate. A Zeidi imamate was actually established in due course in the Yemen (see below). Another Shiah sect were the Ismailis, who believed that the true imam could only be the descendant of Hussein's great-great-grandson Ismail in the line of primogeniture. These two particular Shiah sects are singled out for mention here, because subsequent reference will be made to them in this chapter.

Sunni Muslims, however, no less than the Shiah, accorded the Hashemites of the Ahl al-Bayt special reverence. And it is important to consider briefly why this was so. By the time of the Umayyads and the early Abbasids, Islam was already established as a world empire, and the worldly demands of imperial sway were already taking a heavy toll on the purity of the Muslim faith and its egalitarian social principles. This, compounded by various other factors, created a widening rift between the ruling caliphs and their Muslim subjects, resulting in an endemic state of religious and political unrest. Though kept out of actual power by the reigning caliphs, the Alid Hashemites continued to occupy a position of great moral authority in the Muslim world by virtue of their descent from the Prophet, and most Muslims – Sunni or Shiah – naturally turned to them for leadership when fundamental political or social issues were at stake, or when there were serious grievances to be redressed. Consequently, Sunni as well as Shiah Muslims rallied around the Ahl al-Bayt in opposition to the established order whenever the occasion demanded.

Because the Alid Hashemites were direct descendants of the Prophet, they were naturally regarded as the best representatives of the interests of Islam and of the Muslims as one body. It was taken for granted that their commitment to the faith of the Prophet, who was their ancestor, ultimately transcended all other interests. Throughout the history of Islam, movements of Muslim protest have exhibited a marked tendency to seek leadership among members of the Hashemites of the Ahl al-Bayt, regardless of whether these movements were Sunni or Shiah in character. Even when Hashemite leadership for such movements was not actually sought, the Alid Hashemites have historically considered themselves the legitimate candidates for it. From an early time, their readiness to espouse public causes became a dynastic tradition.

Originally, all Hashemites descended from the Prophet or his uncle Abbas carried the title of *sharif*, meaning 'nobleman'. By later convention, this became the title accorded in a special way to descendants of the Prophet in the Hassanid line. Their Husseinid cousins, in time, came to be increasingly distinguished from them by the title of *sayyid*, meaning 'lord, master', although the two titles were often used interchangeably. In early Abbasid times, one line of Hassanid sharifs established themselves as an independent ruling dynasty in Morocco, while another seized power in the Yemen as the first dynasty of Zeidi imams. Our special concern, however, is limited to one particular group of Hassanid sharifs: those who stayed in the Hijaz, in the regions of Mecca and Medina. Originally, these Hijazi sharifs made a point of staying out of public life. It was only in the second half of the tenth century AD that circumstances brought them out of their political retirement.

In the annals of Islam, this was the period when the heretical sect of the Qaramita was at the height of its power (see Chapter 1). From their political base in eastern Arabia, the Qaramita directed tribal raids against Iraq, Syria, and every corner of Arabia, intercepting the overland passage of pilgrims to Mecca from every direction. The only pilgrims who remained able to reach the holy city were those arriving by sea from Egypt. In 930, Qaramita raiders attacked and plundered Mecca itself, carrying away the sacred Black Stone of the Kaaba as a trophy.

From the general Muslim point of view, the scandal was intolerable. To the Abbasids in Baghdad, it was a source of grave embarrassment. One of the first duties of a caliph was to make it possible for all Muslims to practise their religion as prescribed;

most important of all, to see to it that the pilgrim roads to Mecca were safe and the Muslim shrines of the holy city properly maintained. Unable to handle the emergency in person, the reigning Abbasid caliph in Baghdad left the matter to the care of his vassal, Kafur – the black eunuch who ruled Egypt between 946 and 968 as regent under the later Ikhshidids (see Chapter 1). In 950, Kafur persuaded the Qaramita to return the Black Stone to Mecca, and also to stop their raids in the direction of the Hijaz and Syria, so that pilgrims travelling by land could again reach Mecca without trouble. In return, the Qaramita were promised an annual tribute.

As a further measure to secure the Meccan pilgrimage, Kafur chose one of the Hijazi sharifs – a man called Jaafar al-Musawi – and installed him as emir of Mecca in about 964. In present Arabic usage, the title of emir denotes a reigning prince, or a non-reigning member of a royal family. In its original use, however, the term meant 'commander, commanding officer', from the Arabic verb *amara*, meaning 'order, command'. Thus the emirate of Mecca, as originally instituted by Kafur, was envisaged primarily as a military office. The duty of the emir of Mecca was to guard and defend the sanctuaries of the holy city and to take the necessary local measures to facilitate the annual pilgrimage.

As emir of Mecca, Jaafar al-Musawi was by no means the recognized ruler of all the Hijaz. It appears, however, that he did proceed to act in this capacity under the supervision of his Egyptian suzerain. When the death of Kafur was followed by the Fatimid conquest of Egypt in 969, and by the establishment of the new Fatimid capital in Cairo in 973, it was the Fatimid caliphs who began to appoint the sharifs of Mecca from among the descendants of Jaafar al-Musawi.

These Fatimid caliphs, who were at the same time the imams of the Ismaili Shiah, based the legitimacy of their Islamic rule on a claim of descent from Prophet – one which neither the Sunnis nor the non-Ismaili Shiah were willing to recognize. The Musawi emirs of Mecca, being Sunnis and also accepted descendants of the Prophet, could not easily have admitted the legitimacy of the Fatimid caliphs who appointed them, and it can hardly be doubted that, in their hearts, they mocked the Fatimid pretensions. One of these emirs, called Abul-Futuh, did more than this, however. In 1012, he availed himself of special political circumstances to get himself installed as caliph in the Palestinian town of Ramla, by right of his recognized descent from the Prophet. Within the same year, however, Abul-Futuh was persuaded to give up the caliphal title and return to Mecca.

To the Fatimids, the desire to control the Hijaz did not derive solely from religious motives. In fact, their Ismaili Shiah followers did not set much store by ordinary Islamic practices, such as pilgrimage. According to the esoteric religious theory they followed, the recognition of the living presence of the imam in the world absolved the faithful from the need to perform conventional religious duties and rites. As Ismaili imams, the Fatimid caliphs, therefore, had no special reason to be concerned with the Hijaz, except that they needed to control the pilgrimage to Mecca to justify their title to the caliphate in the eyes of non-Ismaili Muslims. What was vitally important to the Fatimids, however, was the control of the Red Sea. By their time, the revival of maritime commerce had already made Egypt the leading *entrepôt* for the Asian spice trade which came by way of these waters to the Mediterranean world.

To control the Red Sea trade, the Fatimids had first to extend their dominion over the Yemen. Here, in 1037, they managed to install a vassal Ismaili dynasty called the Sulayhids, whose rule in some parts of the country continued until 1138. The first ruler of this dynasty conquered the whole of the Yemen in 1062, then immediately proceeded northwards to occupy the Hijaz on behalf of his Fatimid overlords. The emirs of Mecca, for a time, became his own appointees from among the local sharifs.

When Sunni power in the Islamic world began to revive after 1058, the Meccan emirs apparently maintained an equivocal position between the Fatimid caliphs in Cairo and the Seljuk sultans of Isfahan (see Chapter 1). In 1171, however, Saladin overthrew the last of the Fatimid caliphs in Cairo, seized power in Egypt, and subsequently became the founder of the so-called Ayyubid sultanate. Of Saladin and his Ayyubid successors, enough has already been said in the opening chapter of this book. Here, however, it is important to emphasize that Saladin, like the Fatimids before him, was interested in controlling the Red Sea trade on which the flourishing economy of Egypt depended. For this reason, in 1173 he sent one of his brothers to conquer the

Yemen, where a special branch of the Ayyubid dynasty continued to hold power until 1228.

From the Yemen, as from Egypt, the Ayyubids were determined to tighten their grip on the Hijaz, where the Red Sea trade had an important stop at Yanbu, the seaport of Medina. Also, the Ayyubid sultans of Cairo aspired to establish their Islamic sovereignty over Mecca, to enhance their claim to supreme Islamic dominion. After the death of Saladin, however, these sultans became so involved in dynastic quarrels between uncles and nephews, brothers and cousins, that they could do little to strengthen their hold over the Hijaz. The region, for a while, was left more or less free of external interference.

* * * * * * * * * *

In about 1200, a local sharif called Qitada ibn Idris seized power in Mecca and was recognized as emir of the holy city by the Ayyubid sultan reigning in Cairo. Qitada became the first of a new dynasty of sharifs who continued to hold the Meccan emirate until the office was abolished in 1925. Sharif Qitada came originally from the seaport of Yanbu, in the Medina region, where his family had held a considerable estate since Umayyad times. Without seeking the permission of the Ayyubids, he went on to subdue most of the Hijaz. In his native Yanbu, he maintained a garrisoned fortress by the sea, which made it possible for him to exact a good share of the profits of the Red Sea trade as it stopped at this port before proceeding to Egypt.

The Ayyubids apparently thought it prudent to leave Sharif Qitada at peace while he lived. Shortly after his death, however, a new dynasty called the Rasulids established its rule over the Yemen (1228–1454) and proceeded to dispute the Ayyubid claim to the Hijaz. As the descendants of Sharif Qitada, starting in 1241, began to quarrel over the emirate of Mecca, the Rasulids exploited their quarrels to end the Ayyubid suzerainty over the Hijaz and bring the area under their own control.

In 1250, however, when the last Ayyubid sultan died, his leading Mamluk officers usurped power in Cairo and began, one after another, to search for ways and means to gain recognition of themselves as sultans. After the Mongols sacked Baghdad in 1258 and the last Abbasid caliph in that city was killed, a new line of

Abbasid caliphs came to be installed in Cairo. Their only political function was to invest the Mamluk rulers in Egypt with the authority of sultans – a function which only reigning caliphs could perform. Meanwhile, as a further boost to their position as sultans, the Mamluks, from the very beginning, sought control over the Muslim holy places in the Hijaz.

Like their Fatimid and Ayyubid predecessors, the Mamluks were also determined to establish an unquestioned Egyptian ascendancy over the Red Sea, and this was what brought them into direct conflict with the Rasulids of the Yemen. In the course of this conflict, the Mamluks succeeded in taking over the Hijaz, which became a regular province of their empire after 1350. By the fifteenth century, a regular Mamluk cavalry force had come to be stationed in Mecca. At the same time, Egyptian warships were moored in the Meccan seaport of Jidda, which the Mamluks used as a base for their naval operations in the Red Sea and the Indian Ocean. With the Mamluks in control of the harbour of Jidda, this town rapidly replaced Yanbu as the leading maritime trading centre on the Hijazi coast.

The Mamluks managed to achieve their high degree of political and military control over the Hijaz by playing off different members of the established sharifian house against one another more effectively than the Rasulids had done before them. As the Hijaz became increasingly integrated into the Mamluk empire, these sharifs, as emirs of Mecca, became the chief local aides to the Mamluk government. They provided useful contacts with the Arabian tribes, and also assisted in other ways. Being natives of the country, familiar with its extremely rugged topography and highly experienced in local warfare, they could be called upon to take part in military campaigns whenever needed.

After 1454, the Yemen was under the rule of a new dynasty, the Tahirids, who, like their Rasulid predecessors, had their winter capital in Zabid, close by the Red Sea coast. From the seaport of Aden, they controlled the mouth of the Red Sea. Originally, the Tahirids had co-operated politically with the Mamluks, who therefore left them undisturbed. By the early years of the sixteenth century, however, the Portuguese, having rounded the African continent for the first time in 1497, were already establishing themselves as a formidable naval power in the Indian Ocean. From their own naval base in Jidda, the Mamluks sent their fleet out into the Indian Ocean in 1508 to engage the Portuguese in battle south of Bombay and put their ships to flight. In the following year, the Portuguese retaliated in force, compelling the Egyptian ships to escape back to Jidda.

Next, the Portuguese began to threaten the Tahirid port of Aden, which controlled access to the Egyptian waters, and the Mamluk government felt that the Tahirids were not strong enough to maintain the needed defence of these waters in the long run. To stop the Portuguese from entering the Red Sea, the Mamluks became convinced that they had no choice but to conquer the Yemen. The whole economic future of Egypt – and also the future of their regime in Cairo – seemed to them to depend on this matter. The emirate of Mecca at the time was held by Sharif Barakat (1499–1524) in association with his son Abu Numai (1512–41), both of them men of considerable political and military ability who stood ready to help. When the conquest of the Tahirid kingdom was finally undertaken, it was these two sharifs who advanced with their Hijazi forces to occupy Zabid on behalf of the Mamluk state in May 1516, forcing the Tahirids to retire to Aden.

The conquest of Zabid, however, was to be the last military triumph of the Mamluk empire. In August of that same year, the Ottoman army under sultan Selim I entered Syria from the north, routing the Mamluk forces near Aleppo, and proceeding to occupy Damascus. From there, Selim I advanced to Egypt and entered Cairo in January 1517. The last Mamluk sultan, Tuman Bay (1516–17), continued to resist outside Cairo until April, when he was finally defeated, captured and hanged. In the Red Sea, an Ottoman naval officer shortly afterwards attacked Jidda, seizing its Mamluk governor and putting him to death, reportedly by having him drowned. Promptly, Sharif Barakat and his son Abu Numai turned against the Mamluks and proceeded to arrest the two leading representatives of the Mamluk government in Mecca – the commander of the local cavalry force and the *muhtasib*, or fiscal superintendent. They also arranged to have the Mamluk governor in the Yemen killed, in preparation for the imminent Ottoman takeover of that country.

On 3 July 1517, Sharif Abu Numai arrived in Cairo to surrender his Mamluk prisoners to Selim I and pay him homage, recognizing his suzerainty over the Hijaz as the 'Servant and Protector of the

Holy Places' (*Khadim wa Hami al-Haramayn al-Sharifayn*). In return, the Ottoman conqueror confirmed Abu Numai and his father in the emirate of Mecca, with all the traditional privileges of the office. The two sharifs were also recognized as effective masters of the whole of the Hijaz and assigned the three important positions formerly held by Mamluk officers: the governorship of Jidda, and the military command and fiscal superintendence of Mecca. Throughout the five weeks of his stay in Cairo, Abu Numai was treated as a reigning prince, and a special guard of honour was provided for him as escort when he left the city to return home. Some explanation would be necessary to understand why Selim I chose to accord the emirs of Mecca such generous treatment. While the Mamluk rulers, since the 1260s, had made a point of establishing a line of Abbasid caliphs in Cairo to invest them with the supreme Muslim authority of sultans, the Ottoman rulers had called themselves sultans since the fourteenth century without bothering about the legalities of the question. It was the tremendous Islamic prestige they had gained as the conquerors of the Christian lands of the Balkans that earned them the title. When Selim I entered Cairo in 1517, the Abbasid caliph in the city – a man called al-Mutawakkil – had already invested the Mamluk Tuman Bay with the sultanate. Selim I may have seriously considered securing a formal transfer of the title to himself, to strengthen his position against Tuman Bay while the latter was still alive and offering resistance. It was perhaps for this reason that he treated al-Mutawakkil initially with some deference.

Once Tuman Bay was captured and killed, however, Selim I ceased having a rival to the sultanate, and his attitude towards al-Mutawakkil immediately changed. To begin with, the *waqf* or mortmain trusts which the Mamluks had established to support the caliphal household in Cairo were abolished, which rendered the Abbasid family in the city virtually destitute. Later, in July 1517, the caliph was taken from Cairo to Alexandria, then sent from there by sea to Istanbul. Interestingly, this happened shortly after Sharif Abu Numai arrived in Cairo. The Ottoman sultan, perhaps, chose that particular moment to send al-Mutawakkil into exile to indicate that he considered the Islamic legitimacy of the Meccan sharifs more important than that of the Egyptian caliphs. Al-Mutawakkil was later permitted to return to Cairo as caliph, but his position had meanwhile come to count for nothing. After his death in 1543, the Egyptian caliphate quietly passed out of existence, and the Abbasid family was soon forgotten.

According to an old legend, al-Mutawakkil transferred his rights as caliph to Selim I and his successors before leaving Istanbul. What gave rise to the legend was the fact that the insignia of the caliphate – most important of all, the Prophet's mantle – were confiscated by the Ottomans after their conquest of Egypt and transferred to the sultan's palace in Istanbul, where pious Muslims continue to visit them to this day. From the late eighteenth century, when Ottoman power was at its lowest ebb, the sultans of Istanbul began to make a great issue of being caliphs of Islam, explaining that the Abbasids of Cairo had passed this title to their dynasty at the time of the Egyptian conquest. But this was not so in the days of Selim I and his immediate successors. To these powerful Ottoman sultans, the most important attribute of their Islamic sovereignty was the fact that they were the 'Servants and Protectors of the Holy Places' in the Hijaz. This title they never got from the caliphs of Cairo, but from the recognition accorded to them by the emirs of Mecca: the true representatives of the Ahl al-Bayt whose claims to Islamic pre-eminence, as Alid Hashemites, had finally been vindicated against those of their discredited Abbasid cousins.

* * * * * * * * * *

After conquering Egypt, the Ottomans rapidly extended their dominion to include most of the Arab world. In many parts, however, they were unable to exercise their authority on a regular basis, and before long regional principalities began to sprout all over the area. In peninsular Arabia, only the Hijaz remained uninterruptedly under Ottoman control for nearly three centuries.

Had it not been necessary for the Ottomans to keep control of the Hijazi holy places, so as to validate their Muslim sovereignty as sultans, the sharifs of Mecca could have easily transformed their emirate into an autonomous or even independent regional principality during this period, as was happening elsewhere in the Ottoman world. In the Hijaz, however, the suzerainty of the sultans of Istanbul was re-asserted on an annual basis by the forces setting out from Damascus under the *Amir al-Hajj* to escort the pilgrims bound for Medina and Mecca. In Mecca itself, the Ottoman state continued to appoint the successors of Sharif Barakat to the emirate of the holy city. These sharifs were permitted to wield authority over Medina and Yanbu, and also to receive half the dues of the port of Jidda. To keep their local power within limits, however, the Ottomans tried their best to keep the ruling sharifian family divided, and also intrigued with other local Hassanid families against it. Furthermore, until 1635, the pashas appointed from Istanbul to Sanaa were alerted to keep careful watch on the Meccan emirs lest they extend their control southwards along the Hijazi coast to the port of Jizan, which was claimed as part of the Yemen. After the time of Selim I, the Ottomans also thought it good policy to reduce the authority traditionally exercised by the rulers of the sharifian dynasty in Mecca, by sending cadis from Istanbul to administer the Muslim judiciary in the holy city independently of them.

Meanwhile, in 1631, a quarrel over the succession divided the sharifian family into two branches: the house of Abdullah (called the Abadilah) and the house of Zeid (called the Dhawi Zeid). The Abadilah considered themselves the senior house because their ancestor, Abdullah, was the grand-uncle of Zeid. The Dhawi Zeid, on the other hand, claimed the seniority for themselves because Zeid's grandfather, Hussein, was Abdullah's older brother, both of them being the grandsons of Abu Numai. For nearly two centuries, the Dhawi Zeid succeeded in maintaining a virtual monopoly of the emirate, throwing the Abadilah into opposition; and there was constant feuding between the two sides. In the following century, the leadership of the Abadilah was assumed by Sharif Abdullah's great-grandson Aoun, who became the ancestor of the branch of the Abadilah which survived into the twentieth century as the Dhawi Aoun. A genealogical table will help illustrate this point (see opposite).

Before long, however, the feuds between the rival branches of the sharifian family were overshadowed by a serious threat from the direction of Najd. Here, in about 1745, a Sunni Muslim jurist called Muhammad ibn Abdul-Wahhab began to preach a puritan religious revival under the protection of a local chieftain called Muhammad ibn Saud, whose base was the village of Dar'iyya, north of the present city of Riyadh. These two men, in alliance, were able to mobilize the Anaza bedouins of central Arabia in

Barakat
(1497–1525)
:
Abu Numai
(1512–40, d. 1584)
:
Hassan
(1589–1602)
:

	Hussein	Abdullah	
	:	(1630–31)	
THE HOUSE	Muhsin	:	THE HOUSE
OF ZEID	(1604–28)	Hassan	OF ABDULLAH
	:	:	
	Zeid	Muhsin	
	(1631–66)	:	
	THE DHAWI ZEID	Aoun	
		THE DHAWI AOUN	

Table 1. The Divisions of the Sharifian House
(Dates indicate tenure of office for those who held it)

support of their religious movement, which continued to gain strength under their successors. The Wahhabis, as the followers of this movement were called, considerd the Islam of the Ottoman state to be corrupt, and the Ottoman state itself to be unworthy of the Muslim leadership it wielded. They condemned all Muslim practices which were not strictly in keeping with the prescripts of the Koran and the authentic sunna, or Prophetic tradition. Among these practices were the cults of holy men and the pious visits to their tombs, including that of the Prophet himself in Medina.

After gaining control over the whole of central Arabia, and also over the adjacent region of Hasa, the Wahhabis marshalled their Anaza forces to wage the first attacks on Syria and Iraq in 1801. Next they turned to the Hijaz, where they seized the town of Taif – the summer residence of the Meccan sharifs – in 1803. From Taif, they proceeded to capture Mecca, where they stripped the Kaaba of its traditional adornments. Driven out of Mecca, they went on in 1804 to take Yanbu, then Medina, where they destroyed the tomb of the Prophet. In 1806, they re-captured Mecca and seized the seaport of Jidda. The emir of Mecca, Sharif Ghaleb (1787–1813), was compelled to come to terms with the Wahhabi conquerors and agree to become the governor of the Hijaz on their behalf, thereby bringing discredit to the Dhawi Zeid, who were his house.

As already indicated in the preceding chapter, it was Muhammad Ali Pasha of Egypt who undertook the suppression of the Wahhabis in Arabia on behalf of the Ottoman state. The Egyptian forces landed at Yanbu in 1811, then proceeded to take Medina and Jidda in 1812. In Mecca, Sharif Ghaleb joined the Egyptians, whereupon the Wahhabis fled the city. What followed were the Egyptian campaigns against the Wahhabis in Najd, which ended with the capture and destruction of Dar'iyya in 1818. Thereupon the Egyptians withdrew from Najd, but they stayed on for a time in the Hijaz. Here, Sharif Ghaleb had been removed from office in 1813 and replaced first by his nephew, Yahya ibn Surur (1813–27), then by his son, Abdul-Muttalib. The latter, however, was deposed by Muhammad Ali Pasha within a month of his appointment, to be replaced by Sharif Muhammad ibn Abdul-Muin (1827–51): the first emir of Mecca of the rival house of Dhawi Aoun. Owing their original accession to power to the Egyptians, the Dhawi Aoun sharifs continued to regard Muhammad Ali and his successors in Cairo as their special friends, even after Ottoman rule was restored to the Hijaz in 1840. Opposite is an abridged genealogical table to indicate the Dhawi Aoun succession to the Meccan emirate, and the descent of the Hashemite royal family of Jordan from this branch of the sharifian house:

The return of Ottoman rule to the Hijaz coincided with the period of the Tanzimat (see Chapter 2), when the Ottoman state set out to reform and centralize the administration of its empire. In keeping with these reforms, the Hijazi territory was transformed, for the first time, into a regular Ottoman province, or vilayet, administered by a vali, or pasha, appointed from Istanbul. To strengthen the position of the vali, companies of Ottoman infantry were stationed in the main towns. This new arrangement robbed the emirs of Mecca of much of their traditional power, and their repeated protests against it went unheeded. To keep them under control, the Ottoman central government, and the valis appointed to the Hijaz, pitted the more prominent Dhawi Aoun sharifs against one another, and also played their Dhawi Zeid rivals against them. As the leading representative of the latter house, Sharif Abdul-Muttalib, who had been removed by the Egyptians from the emirate in 1827, was twice restored to this position to replace emirs of the Dhawi Aoun, first in

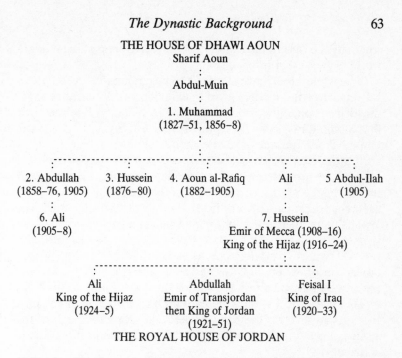

THE HOUSE OF DHAWI AOUN
Sharif Aoun
:
Abdul-Muin
:
1. Muhammad
(1827–51, 1856–8)
:

2. Abdullah   3. Hussein   4. Aoun al-Rafiq   Ali   5 Abdul-Ilah
(1858–76, 1905)   (1876–80)   (1882–1905)   :   (1905)

6. Ali   7. Hussein
(1905–8)   Emir of Mecca (1908–16)
King of the Hijaz (1916–24)

Ali   Abdullah   Feisal I
King of the Hijaz   Emir of Transjordan   King of Iraq
(1924–5)   then King of Jordan   (1920–33)
(1921–51)
THE ROYAL HOUSE OF JORDAN

Table 2. The Descent of the Hashemite Royal Family from the House
of Dhawi Aoun

1851–6, then in 1880–82. When the last appointment to the
Meccan emirate was made in 1908, Abdul-Muttalib's grandson,
Sharif Ali Haydar, was a serious contender to the Aouni candi-
date, Sharif Hussein, who actually got the office (see below).

In these circumstances, the atmosphere that came to prevail in
Mecca after 1840 was dominated by political conspiracy and
intrigue. With the appointment of each new emir, the preceding
one was sent into exile either in Istanbul or in Cairo. The same
happened to serious contenders to the emirate, regardless of
whether they belonged to the Dhawi Zeid or the Dhawi Aoun. In
some cases, it was the Ottomans who summoned politically
ambitious members of the sharifian family to Istanbul to keep them
in the Ottoman capital under close watch, ostensibly as honoured
guests. As this happened time and again, the sharifian family
became increasingly Ottomanized and attuned to the cosmopolitan
ways of Istanbul and Cairo. While many of the sharifs deliberately
maintained their parochial dress and manners, even when abroad,

some, by the turn of the century, were already men of the modern world in most other respects.

Meanwhile, the Hijazi sharifs were beginning to feel the political impact of the modern world nearer home. As early as 1819, the British, operating from their base in India, had gained their first foothold in Arabia by capturing Ras al-Khayma (today in the United Arab Emirates), at the mouth of the Arabian Gulf. In 1839 they seized Aden, and then proceeded to establish a system of Arabian protectorates which ultimately came to comprise all the southern and eastern coastlands of the peninsula. With encouragement and support from the British government in India, the Wahhabis in Najd re-established an independent principality for themselves around the town of Riyadh, which was captured by the Wahhabi chief Abdul-Aziz Al Saud in 1902. North of Riyadh, the house of Al Rashid, formerly the allies of the Saudis, had already established a principality for themselves around the town of Hail since the 1840s. While Britain backed the Saudis against the Rashidis, the Ottomans backed the Rashidis against the Saudis, and before long Austrian and German intelligence became active in Hail.

When the British occupied Egypt in 1882 (see Chapter 2), they gained direct control of the coastlands of the Red Sea facing the Hijaz. This made it possible for them to initiate secret contacts with one sharifian faction or another in the country whenever they found an opportunity to do so, the friendship between Aouni sharifs and the khedives (the successors of Muhammad Ali in Egypt) facilitating such contacts. Meanwhile, starting from 1882, the Italians began to colonize Eritrea, on the African coast of the Red Sea facing Asir and the Yemen. From Mecca, the sharifs could watch the various European powers operating all over Arabia. The more perceptive among them no doubt realized that fundamental regional changes were about to come. This could easily be observed from the developments in the neighbouring Asir.

In 1848, the Ottomans, assisted by the Meccan sharifs, succeeded in reconquering the parts of the Yemen north of the Aden protectorate which they had lost to the Zeidi imams of Sanaa about two centuries earlier; but the territory of Asir, between the Hijaz and the Yemen, remained a problem for them. Here, a certain Ahmad ibn Idris (d. 1837), originally from Morocco and claiming descent from the Prophet, had been preaching a Muslim religious revival akin to Wahhabism. After his death, his puritan preaching merged with local superstitions to produce a peculiar cult, and his descendants, establishing themselves in the town of Abha, called themselves sayyids and were revered by their followers as holy men. In the early years of the twentieth century, one of these sayyids, Muhammad al-Idrisi, made himself the ruler of Asir. The Ottomans, assisted once again by the Meccan sharifs, made war against him and occupied Abha in 1911. From their base in Eritrea, however, the Italians immediately stepped in on the side of the Idrisi, providing him with arms, ammunition and money to help him regain his lost territories, while their navy blockaded and bombarded the Asiri and Yemeni seaports held by the Ottomans. When the First World War broke out, Britain replaced Italy as the protector of the Idrisi, concluding a treaty with their leader in 1915 which secured his position in Asir for the duration of the war.

* * * * * * * * * *

As it survived into the early decades of the twentieth century, the emirate of Mecca bore no resemblance to the other autonomies that had come to exist in Arabia by that time. It was, in fact, a political institution unique in the Ottoman empire. Technically, it was neither a principality nor a province, but merely an office to which members of a particular line of Hijazi sharifs were regularly appointed. On the other hand, it represented a Muslim office of considerable antiquity, based in Islam's most holy city, and commanding general deference. Moreover, it was the only Muslim institution which continued to be the preserve of an Arab dynasty long after political sovereignty in the world of Islam had passed into non-Arab hands.

The sharifian family holding the emirate was conscious of its Arabism, and made a point of cultivating it. Young sharifs, by custom, were sent to live among bedouins, to gain direct acquaintance with the tribal customs and manners of their race. At home, on the other hand, the sharifs followed the political discipline of a ruling dynasty. Precedence between them, whether they were friends or enemies, was governed by a strict protocol. Lower-ranking sharifs addressed those of higher rank as *sidi* (meaning 'my lord'), regardless of whether they were their seniors or juniors in age. The ones who came to hold the emirate were addressed as *sayyidna* (meaning 'our lord') even by their immediate families. When one emir replaced another in office, the one who was deposed was expected to swallow his pride and defer to the wishes of his successor, agreeing to accept exile if the new emir so wanted. When members of the ruling branch of the family disputed the emirate, their more distant relatives normally stood aside, excusing themselves from getting involved in the dispute until it was settled, whereupon they accepted whatever was agreed upon.

When the idea of Arab nationalism began to gain ground among the urban Muslim classes in Syria after the turn of the century, there was no established Syrian leadership to which they could turn. The only such leadership available was the emirate of Mecca, outside Syria, with its dynastic discipline and unique historical experience. The Meccan emirs were not only Arabs, but also recognized descendants of the Prophet whose Islamic standing, as already indicated, was generally accepted as being ecumenical rather than regional or sectarian. None of the other Arab princes of the period were comparable to them in this respect. The Saudis of Riyadh, though the rulers of a virtually independent Arab principality, were essentially a Wahhabi dynasty, standing for a special interpretation of Sunni Islam which was accepted by the Arabian Wahhabis but not by others. The same applied to the Idrisis in Asir at a more elemental level. The Rashidis of Hail, who disputed the control of Najd with the Saudis, represented no more than a petty dynastic concern supported by local tribal interests. The sultans of Oman, apart from being completely subservient to the British at the time, were Ibadi Muslims. Theirs was a marginal sect in Islam which rejected both the Sunni and the Shiah traditions, and their country, historically, had lived in seclusion from the rest of the Arab world. In the Yemen, the imams who led the resistance against the Ottomans in the highlands were the leaders of the Zeidi Shiah sect, which had no followers in any other Arab country. Outside peninsular Arabia, the only leadership to be considered was that of the khedives of Egypt. But the khedives, who were probably of Turkish stock, though commonly considered Albanian by origin, could hardly be described as an Arab dynasty, and their acceptance of British tutelage discredited them politically in any case.

The first articulation of national sentiment among Muslim Arabs centred around the question of the caliphate. As already indicated, real Ottoman claims to the caliphate were made only when the Ottoman state was already losing its power. The Russians, in 1774, recognized this claim following their conquest of the Crimean peninsula, when they permitted the sultans of Istanbul to continue exercising some religious authority over the local Muslims by virtue of being their caliphs. In the course of the nineteenth century, all the European governments came to recognize the Ottoman sultans as caliphs, but learned opinion in the world of Islam maintained a quiet reserve with respect to the question. By tradition, the caliph of Islam was supposed to be an Arab of the tribe of Qureish, and he stood to be more generally acceptable to the Muslim community at large if he belonged to the Ahl al-Bayt. By the late nineteenth century, some Arabs were beginning to voice the opinion that the caliphate must be reclaimed for their race from the Turkish Ottomans. The emirs of Mecca, on all counts, were the natural Arab candidates for the office.

Of the Ottoman sultans in Istanbul, Abdul-Hamid II (1876–1909) came the closest to being generally accepted as caliph of Islam, by his Sunni Muslim subjects as well as by their co-religionists throughout the world, most notably in India. It was in his time, however, that the reclamation of the caliphate for the Arabs was first openly suggested by writers such as Abdul-Rahman al-Kawakibi (d. 1902), a Syrian Arab from Aleppo belonging to a local sharifian family. Kawakibi, like other Arab critics of the Hamidian regime, attacked the Ottoman claim to the caliphate from the political refuge of Cairo. He and others thought it best that an Arabian emir – presumably, a Meccan sharif – should be elected to the post. Such talk made Abdul-Hamid II highly suspicious of reported political activities among the sharifian family in the Hijaz. The emir of Mecca, for most of his reign, was Sharif Aoun al-Rafiq (1882–1905), who co-operated closely with the Ottoman government. But one of the chief opponents of this emir was his nephew, Sharif Hussein ibn Ali. From his earliest youth, Hussein had been eminently conscious of the moral potential of the sharifian office, which he considered to be virtually equivalent to a caliphate; and he looked forward to the day when the Islamic pre-eminence which was its right would be realized. Little wonder that the young sharif was described by one secret report to the sultan as 'wilful and recalcitrant, with a dangerous capacity for independent thought'. Naturally, the activities of Hussein became the focus of Abdul-Hamid's suspicions.

* * * * * * * * * *

Hussein ibn Ali was born in Istanbul in 1853. At that time, Sharif Abdul-Muttalib, of the Dhawi Zeid, was serving his second term of office as emir of Mecca, and his opponents of the Dhawi Aoun – among them Hussein's father, Sharif Ali – were living as honoured exiles in the Ottoman capital. When Ali's father, Sharif Muhammad, was re-appointed to the emirate of Mecca in 1856, Ali returned with his family to the Hijaz; but two years later, Sharif Muhammad died, to be succeeded in the emirate by his eldest son Abdullah. Ali then returned to Istanbul, where he died in 1861. It was then decided that his son Hussein should go back to the Hijaz to live with his uncle Abdullah and grow up among the bedouin Arabs, as was the sharifian custom.

In time, Hussein married his cousin Abdiyeh – Sharif Abdullah's daughter – who died in 1886 or 1887 after bearing him three sons: Ali, Abdullah and Feisal. Meanwhile, two of his uncles had fallen out with the Ottomans. Sharif Abdullah was deposed from the emirate, suspected of intriguing against the state with the Idrisis of Asir. Abdullah's brother Hussein, who was appointed to replace him, was stabbed by an assassin outside the British consulate in Jidda, and died of his wounds in the parlour of the British consulate. The Ottomans were convinced that his repeated visits there involved treasonable contacts. For two years, Sharif Abdul-Muttalib, the head of the Dhawi Zeid, held the emirate – his third term in the office. Then the emirate was restored to the Dhawi Aoun, in the person of Sharif Aoun al-Rafiq, Hussein's third uncle; and the new emir was careful to maintain correct relations with the Ottoman government. When Hussein, who was already deeply involved in Meccan politics, began to oppose his uncle's policies, he was summoned to Istanbul, where he arrived in 1893, followed by his three sons. Here, he married his second wife – a Circassian lady, Adleh Hanum – who bore him his fourth son, Zeid, and three daughters. In recognition of Hussein's high standing, the sultan provided him with a house on the Bosphorus and appointed him to the membership of the *shura*, the honorary high council of the Ottoman state.

The enforced stay of Hussein in the Ottoman capital lasted for fifteen years. The sharif was now in middle age, and looked extremely impressive with his Meccan turban and Arabian robes. He was a man of considerable Islamic learning, highly knowledge-able in world affairs, and his patriarchal personality, coupled with excellent manners, won him general respect. The sharif, however, had a will of iron, and was inflexible in his views. The sultan continued to be wary of his political ambitions and the exalted view he held of the paramount Islamic standing of the sharifian office, and hardly any member of the Ottoman ruling establish-ment wished to see the emirate of Mecca fall into his hands. When Sharif Aoun al-Rafiq died in Mecca in 1905, the man appointed to succeed him was not Hussein but his cousin and brother-in-law Ali, the son of Sharif Abdullah, who was on particularly good terms with Ratib Pasha, the vali of the Hijaz. Both the new emir and the vali were generally known to be corrupt.

In 1908, the Young Turk revolution in Istanbul brought a sudden change to the situation. In the Hijaz, Ratib Pasha and Sharif Ali opposed the new regime and encouraged the local units of the Ottoman army to rebel against it. The railway between Damascus and Medina had been completed in that year, and reinforcements could easily be rushed to the Hijaz to crush the rebellion and seize Ratib Pasha. Sharif Ali was deposed immedi-ately, and his uncle Abdul-Ilah – then the senior sharifian exile in Istanbul – was appointed to replace him. Sharif Abdul-Ilah, however, being already an ageing and ailing man, died before he could leave the Ottoman capital.

The choice for the Meccan succession now rested between two candidates: Hussein and Ali Haydar. The latter was the grandson of Sharif Abdul-Muttalib, of the Dhawi Zeid, and he had lived in the cosmopolitan atmosphere of Istanbul since the age of seven. A number of the Young Turks who had organized the revolution against Abdul-Hamid, and who belonged to the same Levantine circles as Ali Haidar, were his personal friends, and it appears that he was the candidate favoured by their party, the CUP (see Chapter 2). Abdul-Hamid, however, was still on the throne, and it was his privilege as caliph to have the final say in the appoint-ment of the emir of Mecca. Unwilling to accept the candidacy of Ali Haidar, he reluctantly agreed to the appointment of Hussein, who now left Istanbul to return with his family to the Hijaz.

The following year, the CUP deposed Abdul-Hamid, placing his compliant brother Muhammad Rashad – or Muhammad V – on the throne. The Young Turk officers who led the CUP were content for a time to stay on the sidelines, satisfied with having their policies pressed at the level of government by political surrogates. In 1913, however, a CUP coup finally brought these officers to power, and the Ottoman state was transformed into a Young Turk dictatorship. In the Hijaz, Sharif Hussein did everything possible to obstruct the centralizing policies of the CUP from the very beginning, clashing with a succession of Ottoman valis over the issue. Repeatedly reaffirming the prerogatives of his office, as originally guaranteed by Selim I to his ancestor Abu Numai, he was clearly set on making himself – at the very least – full master of the Hijaz. When the new military regime in Istanbul began to press its policies in the country with increased determination, the sharif's opposition to them only became more vehement. From their base in Egypt, the British followed the struggle between the sharif and the Young Turks with great interest, and they had good reason to do so.

In Istanbul, the CUP was steadily developing political and military relations with Germany. In the event of a war breaking out between the Central Powers and the Allies, Turkey seemed bound to enter the war on the German side, in which case the Ottoman sultan, in his capacity as caliph, would be prevailed upon to proclaim a general Muslim *jihad*, or holy war, against the Allies. This could spell serious trouble for the British in India, and for the French in North Africa, not to speak of other parts of the colonial world. To prepare for the eventuality, a suitable and willing Arab dignitary could be groomed for the caliphate. And what better man was there for the post than Sharif Hussein, who was already proving his mettle in the Hijaz? If matters got out of hand, he could easily be made caliph, to confound the Ottoman claim to the office and neutralize any possible Ottoman call for jihad.

In 1914, the first contacts with the sharif in Mecca were initiated by Lord Kitchener, who was then the British agent in Cairo. Shortly after, the First World War broke out, and the Ottoman state entered the war on the side of Germany, as had been expected. Also, Muhammad V solemnly proclaimed the jihad against the Allies; but this measure, the anticipation of which had given rise to so much fear, did not turn out to have much effect.

In western Arabia, however, there was a new emergency to consider. In 1915, while an Ottoman-German offensive was being attempted against the Suez canal, Ottoman forces from the Yemen entered the Aden protectorate and installed themselves firmly at two strategic points, one in the highlands and the other close to the seaport of Aden. If they expanded any further towards the coast, the Germans could get their newly invented submarine U-boats into the Red Sea, and the British had to prevent this at any cost. To keep Ottoman and German reinforcements from reaching the area, a blockade of the Red Sea was put into effect; but men and supplies could still be sent to the Hijaz by railway, to be transported overland from there to the Yemen. In Asir, the continuing revolt of the Idrisi was useful to obstruct the Ottoman lines of supply, but only to an extent. On the other hand, a revolt in the Hijaz, possibly in conjunction with an Arab uprising in Syria, could isolate the Ottoman forces in south Arabia altogether.

From their base in Cairo, British intelligence had long been in contact with the secret Arab nationalist societies in Syria. The British staff of the Arab Bureau in the Egyptian capital now immediately set to work to promote existing contacts between these societies and Sharif Hussein's sons, particularly Feisal. At the same time, Britain announced its intent to recognize an independent Arab state in peninsular Arabia after the war, as an open invitation for Sharif Hussein to co-operate.

The story of the secret negotiations between Sharif Hussein and the British, which led to his proclamation of the Great Arab Revolt in 1916, has often been told. The better documented the account, the greater the concentration on the political details: how the British set out to cheat the sharif and his family into joining the Allied war effort against the Ottomans; and how the latter, motivated by ambition, fell into the trap. The Arab essence of the story recedes further into the shadows with every fresh repetition.

In its own time, the bid for national independence which was the motive force behind the Arab revolt had a significance which went far beyond the level of political details. Underlying it were hopes and aspirations which may have been limited to Arabs of the developed urban classes in Syria and Iraq, but nonetheless represented genuine national feelings pointing to the future. As normally happens, many of the people who spoke of Arab nationalism at the time and joined the revolt were self-seeking opportunists. Others, however, were sincere in the conviction that their revolt was going to put Arab history back on the course for which it was destined, and some of those paid for their conviction with their lives. The fact that Arabian desert tribesmen joined the revolt for pay, while the common run of village and town Arabs remained loyal to the Ottoman state until it actually collapsed, is another matter. When all is said, the movement would not have been possible had it not been for the general and spontaneous Arab nationalist support it elicited. At the level of leadership, the moral commitment made to the cause of the revolt certainly transcended mere political ambition. At that particular moment, there were Arabs – both Muslim and Christian – who believed that the time had come for them to reclaim their historical position in the world. They rallied around Sharif Hussein and his family because they were convinced that they – as Hashemites representing the historical Islamic legitimacy of the Ahl al-Bayt – were the only people who could provide them with the leadership they needed. It was the failure of the revolt to achieve its set aims, and the succession of Arab political frustrations that followed, which makes it difficult today to recapture the mood of those hopeful days.

The political story of the Arab revolt nonetheless remains important; and from the very beginning, one of the leading figures behind the scenes was Sharif Hussein's son Abdullah, the man who subsequently became the founder of the Hashemite Kingdom of Jordan. Like his father, Abdullah was a firm believer in the Muslim and Arab pre-eminence of the sharifian house and its historical destiny for leadership. His political style, however, was different in a number of respects. It is to his career that we must now turn.

NOTE

1. *Ahl al-Bayt* is a term of strictly Shiah usage, referring to the Alids alone among the Hashemites. Another term of identical meaning was *Al al-Bayt*, which referred to the Hashemites in general – the Alids along with their Abbasid and other cousins. With the historical disappearance of the Abbasids, the difference in connotation between the two terms became immaterial.

4

The Founder

Abdullah, the second son of Sharif Hussein, was born in Mecca in 1882, and spent his childhood between the holy city and the summer residence of the family in Taif. Orphaned of his mother before he was five, he was entrusted to the care of his paternal great-grandmother, Saliha – an Asiri lady of the Banu Shihr tribe – and her daughter Haya, who was his great-aunt. In traditional Arab society, the exploits of the men are remembered by the women in the cosy privacy of the harem, where they are woven, generation by generation, into the tapestry of the family lore. It was at his great-grandmother's dower court that Abdullah, as a child, became familiar with this lore, learning how the different branches of the sharifian house were related by blood and marriage, and why the Dhawi Zeid were the enemies of the Dhawi Aoun. From the Asiri and Hijazi women who came to visit, he also learnt all the old stories of his Arabian homeland, embellished by the songs and verses extolling the valiant deeds of the Meccan sharifs and their bedouin followers, most of all in the wars of Muhammad Ali against the Wahhabis.

Abdullah's brother, Ali, was two years older than he was, and Feisal was four years younger, Abdullah himself being the most active of the three, which earned him the nickname *al-'Ajlan* ('the hurried one'). The three brothers started their education in the Hijaz, learning the Koran and the elements of Arabic calligraphy from private tutors. Sharif Hussein was a stern father, seeing to it that his three sons studied and behaved in a disciplined manner and got accustomed to working together as a team. In his memoirs, Abdullah recalls one occasion when his great-grandmother Saliha had to intervene personally to spare him the rod. As in all princely families, however, the children, having the social advantage over people in their service, were frequently able to get away with playing tricks at their expense. Abdullah, by his own admission, was particularly clever at devising ways and means to victimize his teachers by such pranks. Like his brothers, he retained a love of practical jokes throughout his life.

When the family moved to Istanbul in 1893, the education of Abdullah and his brothers was again placed in the hands of private tutors. This time, however, the curriculum adopted was of the modern type followed by the Ottoman military academy, their first teacher being an army lieutenant of the engineering corps who was a regular instructor at the academy. The emphasis was now on Turkish language and grammar, Ottoman and Islamic history, geography, mathematics, and military science. The social life of the family in the Ottoman capital was mostly restricted to the circle of sharifian exiles in the city, and to exchanges of visits with Turkish families of the ruling establishment. As young men, the sharif's sons wore European clothes and gained an easy familiarity with the cosmopolitan ways of the Ottoman capital, but except for the occasional fishing cruise or hunting party most of their leisure time was spent in home surroundings. Each of the three sons was given a cousin in marriage before the family returned to the Hijaz.

Among his brothers, Abdullah appears to have been the one who was closest to the older women of the family in his formative years, and perhaps for this reason he grew up to be particularly appreciative of home comforts, and also especially considerate towards his relatives. Whenever there was a delicate family mission to perform, it was assigned to him, because he had the knack of saying the right thing at the right moment and of cajoling people into accepting adversity. Those who knew the man at different stages of his life remembered him – or continue to remember him – as a person who was basically kind, exuding good cheer, and careful not to give offence by word or action. He was eminently conscious of his distinguished status as a sharif, and loved pomp and circumstance, but was able at the same time to laugh at himself, a quality rare among the Arabs of his generation. Whether in serious or playful mood, his manners were exquisite, like those of his father and brothers. Meeting him for the first time in Jidda, in 1917, T. E. Lawrence found him an extremely pleasant person, stocky and somewhat plump, but somehow giving the impression of being 'too clever':

Abdulla, on a white mare, came to us softly with a bevy of richly-armed slaves on foot about him, through the silent respectful salutes of the town. He was flushed with his success at Taif, and happy. . . .I began to suspect him of constant cheerfulness. His eyes had a confirmed twinkle; and though only thirty-five, he was putting on flesh. . . .Life seemed very merry for Abdulla. He was short, strong, fair-skinned, with a carefully trimmed brown beard, masking his round smooth face and short lips. In manner he was open, or affected openness, and was charming on acquaintance. He stood not on ceremony, but jested with all comers in most easy fashion: yet, when we fell into serious talk, the veil of humour seemed to fade away. He then chose his words, and argued shrewdly.[1]

Abdullah began to take great interest in politics from the time he was a young man in Istanbul. He was an outgoing person, congenial in company and easy in conversation, full of common sense and entertaining stories, and always ready to make his point with an Arabic or Turkish proverb. The facility he had for initiating contacts with people was remarkable. A pleasant jest or a courteous invitation to play his favourite game of chess was sometimes sufficient. He spoke only Arabic and Turkish, but was traditionally cultured and well read. His knowledge of the details of Arabian life and politics was encyclopedic, and he also possessed a vast store of historical and literary information which he could tap at will to keep a dialogue going when it threatened to come to a halt. Like his father, he held firm views on what was basically right or wrong, but he was generally resilient and prepared to give and take in argument. In this, as in other respects, he had much that was typical of the Ottoman ruling class of his generation. While taking religious tradition seriously, and observing accepted rules of social behaviour, he was basically a tolerant and unfanatical person who kept an open mind on many issues. In 1913, he returned to Istanbul as a deputy to the Ottoman parliament.

Abdullah's father, Sharif Hussein, was a hard and wilful man, which Abdullah was not, and the clash between their different personalities was too obvious to go unnoticed. The father was unshakeable in his opinions, and strongly averse to compromise, while the son accepted realities for what they were, and was always prepared to make the best out of given circumstances. He was, in this sense, an optimistic fatalist. Yet, Hussein appears to have regarded Abdullah, from the very beginning, as the most intelligent and promising of his sons, consulting him on private and public matters, trusting his judgment, and considering him 'propitious in opinion'(*maymun al-ra'y*). Abdullah, for his part, held his father in great awe, deferring to his wishes with proper filial piety even when he disagreed with him. He never wavered in the conviction that his father ultimately stood for what was right, even when he seemed set on committing tactical errors.

The young sharif, however, had some reason to be jealous of his brothers, Ali and Feisal. They always appeared to him to be closer to their father, and more visibly favoured, perhaps because they were not given to speaking their mind openly in his presence as Abdullah did. Ali could be forgiven this, because he had the natural privilege of being the eldest son. Moreover, he was by nature a retiring person, with little force of character, and his health was weak. In his middle thirties, he was already consumptive and looked sallow and weary.

With Feisal, however, it was a different matter. Apart from being favoured by his father, Feisal possessed a direct popular appeal which Abdullah lacked, and underlying this was a difference between the two brothers in looks and character. Feisal in manhood was strikingly handsome, particularly in Arab dress, and his large and dreamy eyes had a princely air about them which inspired confidence. Though only of medium height, he looked taller than he actually was because he was slender. T. E. Lawrence considered him no less skilled in diplomacy and knowledgeable in military matters than Abdullah, but he thought him a person 'fuller of wit than of humour', returning 'trust for trust, suspicion for suspicion', yet altogether 'the leader with the necessary fire' (*ibid.*, pp. 64, 98):

[He] was a man of moods, flickering between glory and despair . . . His nature grudged thinking, for it crippled his speed in action: the labour of it shrivelled his features into swift lines of pain. In appearance, he was tall, graceful and vigorous, with the most beautiful gait, and a royal dignity of head and shoulders. Of course he knew it, and a great part of his public expression was by sign and gesture. His movements were impetuous. He showed himself hot-tempered and sensitive, even unreasonable, and he ran off soon on tangents. Appetite and physical weakness were mated in him, with the spur of courage. His personal charm, his imprudence, the pathetic hint of frailty as the sole reserve of this proud character made him the idol of his followers.

Abdullah resented the fact that his younger brother was generally more popular than he was, and, typically, he would not restrain himself from asking people, now and then, why this was so. In 1913–14, both he and Feisal sat in the Ottoman parliament as representatives of the Hijaz. Together, they came to know deputies from other Arab countries who spoke of Arab national hopes and aspirations, and both the brothers were won over to the idea. They could hardly have been otherwise, faced with the offensive arrogance exhibited towards the Arabs by the more militantly nationalistic among the Young Turks: 'If we said, we and you are the people of Islam, they said, yes, but we are the masters and you are the followers; if we said, we and you, they said, you are traitors and rebels.' So Abdullah, in his memoirs, sums up the conflict that went on at the time between the two sides. Somehow, however, Feisal's commitment to the Arab national cause, as it developed, was taken more seriously than Abdullah's.

Both men were ambitious politically, but the problem with Abdullah was that his ambition always showed. The man had a transparent personality, and the openness of his character was regarded by those who later worked with him – and most of all by his British associates – as his supreme virtue. Among the political Arabs of his generation, however, he was commonly thought to be insincere in all but the open expression of his ambition, and the great show he made of his political astuteness, rather than being taken at face value, was interpreted as self-confessed deviousness.

Feisal, in this respect, was the cleverer man. His brother Abdullah, with his unaffected manners, could easily find his way among the tribal Arabs, bedouins or peasants, as well as in political circles of the traditional Arab sort. The urban effendis of the new generation – sophisticated, intellectualized and brimming with ambition and ideas – were Feisal's exclusive speciality. These effendis, full of themselves and eager to make their mark, had no patience with Abdullah's leisurely parlour talk on history, politics, religion and literature, and were repelled by the delight he took in pomp and courtly protocol. They also failed to understand his

sense of humour, mistaking it for levity, and reacted with aversion
to the great issue he made of the dynastic prerogative of the
sharifian family in Arab national leadership. Feisal, on the other
hand, seemed to them to proffer himself more as an Arab national
leader on his personal merits. Naturally cautious and withdrawn,
and tending to keep his inner thoughts to himself, he perhaps
deliberately cultivated the serious, soft-spoken manner, punc-
tuated by flares of indignant zeal, which made his followers idolize
him. While he himself shunned intellectualism, he knew how to
win intellectuals to his side by showing them trust and making
them feel important, while projecting to the romantic-minded
among them the idealized image of the Arab prince of legend.

* * * * * * * * * *

By general admission, the Arab revolt against the Ottomans was
originally Abdullah's idea. Growing up in Istanbul in the days of
Abdul-Hamid, the young sharif was impressed by the pan-Islamic
solidarity promoted in the vast Ottoman empire by this last of the
great sultans, for whom he retained a life-long admiration. The
Ottoman state in those days still seemed to be holding together
firmly, its Arab and Turkish subjects standing on the same footing
as brothers in the Muslim faith, ready to defend their sovereign
and their empire against the world. In 1909, however, Abdul-
Hamid was overthrown by the CUP. Abdullah was visiting
Damascus for the first time when the great sultan was deposed
and replaced by his weak brother, and he could hear the first Arab
murmurs against the Young Turks and their policies among the
younger generation of notables in the Syrian capital. 'The gate for
popular sedition was breached,' he wrote, reflecting on the event
in his later years. 'It was boyish play. . . . They usurped power
and came to hold the ruler and the subjects in their grip. . . .
Most of those who used to love the Ottoman sultanate became
confused by the irresponsible and despotic behaviour of the
Unionists (CUP) . . . and the fall of government prestige.' Four
years later, the 'boyish play' which had first irked Abdullah in
1909 took a turn for the worse. In 1913, the officers of the CUP
seized power directly, to establish their brash military dictatorship
in the Ottoman capital.

When he returned to Istanbul as a parliamentary deputy in

1913, Abdullah was shocked by the change which he saw. The Young Turks had become overbearing in their attitude towards the Arabs, and it seemed only a matter of time before the Ottoman partnership between the two races would reach breaking-point. From the way the CUP dictators were running the internal and external affairs of the state, Abdullah could easily surmise that the days of the Ottoman empire were nearing their end. Talk of a great war between the Central Powers and the Allies was already in the air, and there were increasing signs that the Ottomans, in the event of such a war, would be taking the side of the former. Abdullah was a regular visitor to Egypt, where the reigning khedive, Abbas Hilmi, was his personal friend; and most Arabs with Egyptian connections were convinced that if a war did take place, Britain would be the winner, and the Ottoman empire would be defeated, along with Austria and Germany. From such estimates, it was easy for Abdullah to draw his conclusions. If the Arabs, by sharifian initiative, broke with the Ottomans in time to join the British side in the war, the chances were that they would emerge on the winning side, and so gain their independence under sharifian leadership.

On his third trip to Istanbul as a member of parliament in February 1914, Abdullah stopped in Cairo, as usual, to visit his friend, the khedive. This time the British agent in the Egyptian capital, Lord Kitchener, paid him a courtesy call, which he returned. On the second occasion, Abdullah broached the subject of a possible Arab revolt against the Ottomans, and what the British attitude was likely to be in the event of this, but the response he got from Kitchener was evasive. The contact, however, was established, and Abdullah managed to keep the channels of communication open. When the war broke out in Europe later that year, and Turkey entered on the German side, Abdullah pursued the dialogue with the British authorities in Cairo, and Sharif Hussein was finally persuaded to take over the Anglo-sharifian negotiations in person. In the meantime, Feisal pressed for caution, suggesting alternatives for a compromise solution with the Turks, until the point of no return was reached in the spring of 1916. Little wonder that Abdullah was generally considered the chief engineer of the Arab revolt and the political brain behind it on the sharifian side.

Lawrence realized this when he arrived in the Hijaz from Cairo in 1917. By now, however, the revolt in the country was grinding to a halt, while the Turks prepared for a counter-offensive. Somehow, the sharifian uprising had to be re-invigorated to achieve its aims, and ultimately move forward into Syria to help beat the Ottomans there. In the judgment of Lawrence, Abdullah – 'too balanced, too cool, too humorous' – was 'a tool too complex for such a simple purpose'. Instead, he opted for his brother Feisal, who seemed to have the 'singleness of eye and magnetism', as he put it, to 'set the desert on fire'.[2] Actually, Abdullah's military performance to date had been the more creditable. He had secured the surrender of the Turkish garrison in Taif, while Feisal was failing to make a breakthrough in Medina. Nevertheless, Abdullah had now to stay behind in the Hijaz as his father's foreign minister and field marshal, while Feisal, with Lawrence at his side, proceeded northwards into Syria, and ultimately to Damascus, to receive general acclaim as the paramount Arab hero of the day.

* * * * * * * * * *

The end of the war saw Feisal established in Damascus at the head of a virtually independent Arab government recognizing the suzerainty of King Hussein in the Hijaz; but in the Hijaz itself, the king was not doing very well. His British allies were also the allies of his chief rival, Abdul-Aziz Al Saud of Riyadh, whose Wahhabi forces were beginning to press on the oases of Khurma and Turaba in the Taif region. These two positions were dangerously close to Mecca, and their tribal inhabitants were mostly Wahhabi sympathizers. When Abdul-Aziz made overtures to Hussein advocating a peaceful settlement of the Khurma–Turaba question, his letters were returned unopened. Against the advice of all those around him, the king sent the sharifian army under his son Abdullah to capture the oasis of Turaba towards the middle of May 1919. The Wahhabis, supported by their local sympathizers, struck back within two weeks. The sharifian forces were taken by surprise and butchered, and Abdullah was barely able to escape back to Taif with about 150 survivors. For the sharifian kingdom of the Hijaz, this was the beginning of the end.

Returning to Taif, Abdullah found his father adamant about pursuing the war against Abdul-Aziz and the Wahhabis. For this purpose, he entered into secret alliance with the Rashidis of Hail and the Al Sabah rulers of Kuwait. He also made approaches to Imam Yahya, the newly independent Zeidi ruler of the Yemen. Abdullah, with his intimate knowledge of the inner workings of Arabian politics, could not allow himself to subscribe to his father's policies, which stood no chance of success, but he was unsuccessful in moderating them. Hussein's alliance with the Rashidis was particularly ominous. During the war, the emirs of Hail had taken the Turkish and German side against the Saudis and the British, and they now stood doomed.

His Arabian policies apart, the king was also beginning to collide with the British on other counts. When he was proclaimed King of the Arab Countries in October 1916, the British government had recognized him only as King of the Hijaz; and after the war, it became clear to him that they did not intend to go any further than this. Their wartime promises to him about Arab independence had been studiously vague. He had trusted their good intentions, but these now seemed to be vanishing rapidly. The Arab lands were being divided between Britain and France, and there was every indication that Britain intended to honour the Balfour declaration and give Palestine to the Jews. His son Feisal, whom he had delegated to represent him at the Paris peace talks, had remonstrated against all this, but to no effect. As King Hussein saw it, his son had let him down, in return for promises regarding his personal political future. Feisal was even prepared to negotiate the subject of Palestine with the Jews. The king would have none of this, and he let the British know it. Now that his wartime alliance with them was over, he would not agree to enter into any treaty relations with them to secure his continued rule in the Hijaz, unless they went back on the Balfour declaration and committed themselves to helping him regain independence for the Arab countries of which he considered himself the rightful king. Repeated pleas made to him by his British friends to accept some compromise, in his own interest, went unheeded, even when sincerely meant. By his proud intransigence on questions of principle, the man was clearly bent on his own destruction.

Abdullah loved his father and believed in him, but he decided he could not stay in the Hijaz, awaiting the tragic débâcle which he could easily foresee. The question of timing, however, was important. On 8 March 1920, the Syrian Congress convening in

Damascus proclaimed his brother Feisal King of Syria, and the Iraqi delegates at the same congress declared Abdullah himself King of Iraq (see Chapter 2). In the Hijaz, King Hussein was furious at Feisal for agreeing to become a king in his own right, when he was technically no more than his father's viceroy in Damascus. Abdullah, for his part, was in no position to claim the throne of Iraq, as theoretically assigned to him, because this country was held firmly by the British, and its fate was still undecided.

In July of that year, however, the French entered Damascus, and Feisal had to abandon his Syrian kingdom. Moreover, as already indicated, Feisal did not hold on to what remained of his kingdom of Transjordan, but proceeded directly to Europe instead, leaving the Transjordanian territory in complete disarray (see Chapter 2). In the Hijaz, Abdullah decided that the moment had come for him to resign from his father's service and proceed not to Iraq, but to Syria. He left Mecca in October, accompanied by a force of about 2,000 men, to continue the journey from Medina by train. The Hijaz railway, dynamited at various points during the war, had just been put back into use, but its maintenance was extremely poor and the engines stood badly in need of repair. The journey of about 800 kilometres from Medina to Maan, on the Transjordanian border, took no less than 27 days to complete.

Abdullah and his party arrived in Maan on 21 November 1920. The sharif – now carrying the title of emir, by virtue of being the son of a king – was thirty-eight years old, and the father of three children. By his first wife, who was his cousin, he had a daughter called Haya, after the great-aunt who had helped raise him as a child, and a son called Talal, a name of Abdullah's own contrivance which was to gain wide Arab popularity later on. By his second wife, a Turkish lady he had married in Istanbul, he had a second son called Nayef.

Moreover, Emir Abdullah already had a rich political past. He was the veteran of many wars: against the Idrisis in Asir, the Turks in the Hijaz, and the Wahhabis in Najd. The country where he had gained his political and military experience was not much different in basic topography and social structure from the one at whose borders he now arrived. In a way, Transjordan was no more than a northward extension of the Hijaz, until the point was

reached beyond Amman where the land became more distinctively
Syrian. It was the colours, mainly, that were different between
the two countries, the dark igneous rock of the so-called Arabian
shield, which formed the Hijazi territory, giving way to the Syrian
sedimentary stone a short distance north of Aqaba. The rural
population in the two lands partook of the same tribal character,
and the bedouins had the same mores. If anything, the tribal and
bedouin character of Transjordan was the purer. The established
urban traditions of Hijazi cities such as Mecca and Jidda had no
parallel in Transjordanian towns such as Amman or Salt.

Abdullah and his party received an encouraging welcome upon
their arrival in Maan: a desert town which was still part of the
kingdom of the Hijaz at the time. The following day, the emir
issued a statement from there addressed to 'our Syrian brethren',
calling upon them all to join him in the liberation of the Syrian
fatherland from the wanton imperial control imposed on it by the
French. Alec Kirkbride, who was then the British adviser of the
'Moabite government' in Karak (see Chapter 2), tells the story as
follows:

In January, 1921, news came of the arrival at Ma'an . . . of the Amir
Abdullah at the head of a force of nearly two thousand men. . . . he
proposed to expel the French forces from Syria and to take over that
kingdom on his own account. Having told the world of his plans, which
involved the armed invasion of territory which was under British Mandate, the Amir sat back and waited to see what His Britannic Majesty's
Government would do. As the weeks passed and His Majesty's Government pursued a policy of masterful inaction, it became apparent that the
Amir really did intend to advance northwards. As my territory was the
first part of the mandated area he would reach, I sent a dispatch by
special messenger to the High Commissioner in Jerusalem asking for
instructions.[3]

Receiving no specific directives from the British government in
Palestine on the matter, Kirkbride decided to adopt the 'hat-in-
hand policy' and rode out with the other members of the high
council of the Moabite government to meet the emir at the Qatrana
railway station, about 40 kilometres downhill from Karak:

The Amir was most charming, specially when he realized that we did not
propose to make any trouble. . . . When we were ushered into his

presence, I introduced myself and presented my colleagues individually
. . . as the Council of the National Government of Moab. . . . The Amir,
with intense charm, [asked] . . . 'By the way, has the National Government of Moab ever been recognized internationally?' . . . [I answered] 'I
am not sure of its international status. I feel, however, that the question
is largely of an academic nature now that Your Highness is here.' He
leant forward and said, 'Ah, I was sure that we understood each other!'
So the National Government of Moab passed away quite painlessly, as
did the other autonomous administrations in the north, and the Amir
Abdullah set up a central administration in Amman. . . . In due course,
the remarkable discovery was made that the clauses of the mandate
relating to the establishment of a National Home for the Jews had never
been intended to apply to the mandated territory east of the [Jordan]
river. . . . In later years . . . politicians in Britain took credit for the way
they dealt with the country's future in its earliest years.[4]

Since the war years, the myth had spread in the Arab world that
an endless flow of British gold was pouring into the sharifian
coffers in Mecca and Jidda, and, once the war was over, adventurers of every sort began to converge on the Hijaz from the different
Arab countries to seek their fortunes with the sharifian house.
When Emir Abdullah arrived in Maan, it was rumoured that he
carried loads of money, or at least had ready access to the sharifian
treasury, and this whetted many appetites. When it was realized,
however, that the emir was virtually penniless, most people turned
away. This applied to the bedouins and villagers as well as to the
local civil administrators and army and police officers who had
served under his brother Feisal in the Syrian government. Abdullah noted this in his memoirs:

I wrote to the districts to say that I was the viceroy of Syria, summoning
the members of the Syrian Congress to Maan, and also all the officers
and conscripts of the Syrian army. . . . From the bedouin sheikhs in the
north, I received answers which were not encouraging. Answers also
arrived from some leading Arab officers making it a condition that their
pension rights be transferred to the Hashemite government in the Hijaz
should the movements against France in Syria fail. They said that if the
Hashemite government accepted this they would come; and if the
government in the Hijaz does not accept, then their excuse [for not
coming] would be clear. Of the well-known notables, Aouni Abdul-Hadi
and Kamel al-Budeiri joined me in Maan, while others came and went,
Kamil al-Budeiri asking me for 80,000 guineas to organize an intelligence

and propaganda department, while Nabih al-Azmeh asked for 120,000 guineas for the same purpose. I had nothing of what they asked, my financial situation being extremely difficult.[5]

As a natural optimist, Abdullah was no doubt sincerely convinced that 'the common run of the people of Syria' were with him, having a 'great enthusiasm' for what he proposed to do. This was certainly true among Transjordanian groups that had no interest in the perpetuation of the prevailing anarchy. The Circassian farmers of Amman and its vicinity, for example, had long been weary of living, year after year, under the threat of bedouin raids. The Christians of the various Transjordanian regions also looked forward to the re-establishment of a central authority in the country and, like most other Christian Arabs in Syria, they were favourably disposed towards the Hashemites, as an Arab dynasty representing the best in the political traditions of Islam. Abdullah appealed to them in a special way as a sharif and a Muslim of undoubted credentials who was, at the same time, tolerant and fair-minded, without the least hint of religious fanaticism in his character.

Among the Muslim Arabs, however, Abdullah faced strong opposition from the Arab nationalists of the urban effendi class who had always supported his brother Feisal rather than himself. These were now politically organized as *Hizb al-Istiqlal* (the Independence Party), and they derided Abdullah and his ambitions, fanning a wider opposition against him. Highly evocative of the prevailing mood among these nationalists are the political memoirs of one of their number, the Damascene Kheir al-Din al-Zirkili, who was living in Transjordan as a political fugitive in 1920. His reminiscences of that period, entitled '*Aman fi Amman* ('Two Years in Amman'), lampoon 'His Highness the Emir' and his political actions and pronouncements with sour disdain. Frustrated by the recent collapse of Feisal's Syrian kingdom, and with their political future in the balance, many Arab nationalists, like Zirkili, were becoming cynical about the Hashemite leadership in general. As the French began to set up republican governments in the Syrian territories under their mandate, while the British envisaged a similar type of government to secure Jewish–Arab co-operation in Palestine, increasing numbers among the Istiqlalis and their followers began to harbour political feelings that were distinctly republican, and no longer envisaged the Arab future exclusively in terms of dynastic monarchies.

Whatever the forces working against him, however, Emir Abdullah was determined not to fail in Transjordan, and there were three factors on which he could count to achieve success. First, the political situation in Transjordan was still fluid, the British not having yet taken the decision as to how the eastern part of their Palestinian mandate should be run. Second, the Arab nationalist administrations which had survived Feisal's downfall in the region had discredited themselves not only by remaining divided, but also by failing to run affairs properly in the areas under their jurisdiction, small as those were. Third, Abdullah had a military force at his disposal on which he could rely, while no other organized Arab force existed in the country which could resist him. His morale, moreover, was high, and he was personally convinced that what he had to offer politically was good and would ultimately prove acceptable, despite all that was being said against him. Of the legitimacy of his bid for leadership he had no doubt, and he would brook no opposition:

When I was in Maan, I received a letter from Mazhar Raslan, the governor of Salt . . . saying: 'the national government has received note that you intend to visit Transjordan. If this visit is merely for leisure, the country will receive you with welcome. If it is for political motives, the government will take all the necessary measures to prevent your visit.' I answered: 'My visit to Transjordan will be a visit of occupation. . . . Know, therefore, that your duty is to accept orders from Maan. Otherwise, I shall appoint someone else in your place.'[6]

True to his word, the emir left Maan on 27 February 1921, making a first stop to meet Kirkbride at Qatrana, then a second stop at Ziziya (close to the present airport), and finally arriving in Amman on 2 March. The sheikhs of the Karak region, where the Moabite government had disbanded without ceremony, had preceded him there, accompanied by Kirkbride, to accord him a welcome. With them were the chiefs of the Huwaytat and Banu Sakhr bedouins, and notables from the Salt and Ajlun districts. To all intents and purposes, the emirate of Transjordan was already in existence, with Abdullah at its head. Constitutional formalities did not take long to follow.

By establishing himself in Amman, and laying claim to the whole of Transjordan, Emir Abdullah had inadvertently solved a problem for the British where their Palestinian mandate was concerned. He had also pointed a way to them to 'repair the injuries done to the Arabs and the house of the Sharif of Mecca', as Winston Churchill put it. Churchill at the time was the British colonial secretary, and the affairs of the Arab world had just been removed from the Foreign Office to be placed in his hands. In February 1921, a special Middle East department had been created in the Colonial Office under his direction, and his chief adviser on Arab matters was none other than T. E. Lawrence. By this time, there was no longer any question of Feisal returning to Syria, because the French would not have him. Abdullah was welcome to have Transjordan, provided he desisted from calling for the liberation of the whole of Syria from the French. Of the territory of the Palestinian mandate, of which Transjordan formed the eastern part, Lawrence must have briefed Churchill as follows:

[The] section in the latitude of Jerusalem would have begun with Germans and with German Jews, speaking German or German-Yiddish, more intractable even than the Jews of the Roman era, unable to endure contact with others not of their race, some of them farmers, most of them shopkeepers, the most foreign, uncharitable part of the whole population of Syria. Around them glowered their enemies, the sullen Palestine peasants. . . . East of them lay the Jordan depth, inhabited by charred serfs; and across it group upon group of self-respecting village Christians. . . . Among them and east of them were tens of thousands of semi-nomad Arabs, holding the creed of the desert, living on the fear and bounty of their Christian neighbours. Down this debatable land the Ottoman Government had planted a line of Circassian immigrants from the Russian Caucasus. These held their ground only by the sword and the favour of the Turks, to whom they were, of necessity, devoted.[7]

The Middle East department of the Colonial Office had hardly been established when Churchill called a conference in Cairo, in March 1921, to draw the broad lines of British policy in the area. Abdullah was, by now, already in Amman and on 28 March he was invited to Jerusalem, accompanied by Lawrence, to meet with Churchill and Herbert Samuel, the first British high commissioner of the mandated territory. The emir was told that he could keep Transjordan on a temporary basis under British mandatory 'protection' until some more permanent arrangement was agreed upon with the French. He was also made to understand that he must renounce his claim to the throne of Iraq in favour of his brother Feisal. When he pressed for the unification of Palestine and Transjordan, he was told quite plainly that Britain had other plans for Palestine, which took Jewish national aspirations into account. Realizing that he had no power to alter matters as they stood, Abdullah conceded.

The following year, Britain took the necessary measures at the League of Nations to exclude Transjordan from the terms of the Palestinian mandate relating to the establishment of a Jewish national home in Palestine. Emir Abdullah was then invited to London for talks which resulted in the replacement of the British mandate over the Transjordanian territory by a special Anglo-Jordanian treaty. Accordingly, the Emirate of Transjordan was formally recognized on 15 May 1923 as a national state being prepared for independence under the general supervision of the British high commissioner in Jerusalem. The emir was to rule this country with the help of a constitutional government and British advisers (see Chapter 5).

*   *   *   *   *   *   *   *   *   *

When Abdullah, in 1921, agreed to renounce his claim to Iraq in favour of Feisal, he was little aware of the fact that his younger brother was actually being groomed for the Iraqi throne. Lawrence had been pressing for this all along, and Feisal must have known of the matter long before, but he made no mention of it to Abdullah in the messages he sent him from London about his work for the Arab national cause. When the referendum was finally held in Iraq towards the end of that year to make Feisal king, Abdullah in Amman could not forgive him for having acted behind his back to secure the Iraqi throne for himself. Relations between the two brothers consequently became strained.

In the Hijaz, King Hussein was extremely unhappy to learn that Feisal had accepted a British-made throne. He became more incensed when Feisal brushed aside all family considerations and proceeded to conclude a border agreement with Abdul-Aziz Al Saud in 1922. From that moment, he would have nothing more to do with him. But King Hussein was no less unhappy with

Abdullah, roundly denouncing his acceptance of the British terms for ruling Transjordan. These terms, from his strict point of view, sundered the integrity of the Arab territory and gave tacit recognition to the Jewish claims in Palestine. When the independence of Transjordan from the Hijaz was formally consecrated by the Anglo-Jordanian treaty of 1923, King Hussein's fury at Abdullah took a turn for the worse. On Feisal, who was already recognized internationally as the ruler of an independent kingdom, Hussein had given up. Abdullah, however, had stood in great awe of his father and could still be taken in hand.

In January 1924, King Hussein arrived at the Tranjordanian border, stopping for a while at Aqaba. From Amman, Emir Abdullah hastened to meet him, but the king refused to grant his son direct audience. The mayor of Aqaba, then a young man called Allawi Kabariti, was instructed to arrange for the emir and his party to encamp outside the town, where they were kept waiting for two days. When the king finally agreed to receive his son, in the presence of the mayor and the town notables, he had nothing for him but harsh words, admonishing him in particular for acceding to the terms of the British mandate concerning the Palestinian territory. A copy of the Anglo-Jordanian treaty had earlier been sent to him for ratification, and this he now took out of his pocket, unratified, and practically threw in his son's face. The king next set up camp in the Jordan valley, where he held court and proceeded to take over the direction of the affairs of Transjordan, heedless of the authority of Abdullah and his British advisers. For a while, the British feared that the emir, in filial obedience, might actually step down in favour of his father and hand the country over to him.

While King Hussein remained in Transjordan, Abdullah continued to do his bidding. Meanwhile, on 3 March 1924, the office of the Ottoman caliph in Istanbul was abolished, and King Hussein immediately made it known that he intended to assume the vacant office. He was actually proclaimed caliph in Jidda two days later, against a wave of political indignation from countries such as Egypt and India. In Arabia, the Wahhabis pounced on the issue to resume their offensive against the Hijaz with increased vigour. Probably against his better judgment, Abdullah, from Amman, exerted every effort on his father's behalf to solicit Muslim support for his acceptance as caliph, bringing discredit upon himself for his loyalty. Hardly anyone was prepared to take the suggestion seriously, let alone consider it.

Eager to assume his functions as caliph, King Hussein finally left Transjordan to return home before the end of the month, after repeated hints from the British that his continued presence in his son's territory was no longer desirable. Back in Mecca, however, he found his kingdom already collapsing before the Wahhabi onslaughts directed by his old foe, Abdul-Aziz Al Saud. In October of that same year, Hussein was compelled to abdicate the throne of the Hijaz in favour of his eldest son, Ali, and shortly after retired to Aqaba; but the British would not agree to his stay there, and it was arranged for him to be taken into exile on the island of Cyprus instead. When his health later broke down, he asked for permission to die in an Arab country, and was allowed to return to Amman, where he died in 1931. His son Abdullah, who remained by his side in his last years, arranged for his burial with due royal honours in the Aqsa mosque of Jerusalem – the third holiest place in Islam after the Kaaba of Mecca and the Prophet's mosque and tomb in Medina. Feisal, who was never reconciled with his father, did not attend the funeral, on the grounds that he was too busy with affairs of state.

Once King Hussein had left the Hijaz, Hashemite rule there was all but completely ended. Within a short time, his son and successor, King Ali, found himself hopelessly besieged in Jidda by the Saudis. Taif and Mecca had already been lost. In May 1925, the hapless king was persuaded by his brother Abdullah to cede the Aqaba and Maan districts of the Hijaz to Transjordan, and the British brought some pressure on him to do so. The transfer was made just in time to save these parts of the Hijaz from imminent Saudi occupation. Unable to carry on with his resistance any further, Ali handed over power in Jidda on 20 December 1925 to a provisional government, which subsequently arranged for the peaceful surrender of this last Hijazi outpost to the Saudis. Leaving the Hijaz directly after his abdication, Ali spent the remaining years of his life in Iraq.

* * * * * * * * * *

So far, the focus has been mainly on the early life and career of Emir Abdullah as a person. After 1921, however, Abdullah became the founder of a state, and a prominent figure on the broader Arab political scene. When he first arrived in Transjordan, the country – if it was a country at all – was in disarray: an 'unallocated area', as it was euphemistically put, which was conceded to Abdullah because nobody else really cared to have it. The place was considered ungovernable, and one gets a vivid picture of the social disorganization that made it so from the pages of Zirkili's memoirs: bedouin sheikhs riding with cavalier nonchalance in the desert, as if they owned the place, wearing their Arab headdress at a rakish slant, and expecting privileged hospitality wherever they chose to stop; merchants and townsmen moving cautiously from place to place, and hoping to keep out of trouble by putting on the appearance of grave respectability and maintaining a modest profile; helpless peasants, trying to hold on to what they had and avoid predation by staying invisible and pretending they had nothing; regional governments that were present only in name, preoccupied with the problem of survival, and having little time or ability to spare for anything else. To Zirkili, the arrival of Abdullah in the country promised little more than the intrusion of a new element into the general anarchy, an element which seemed to him more comic than serious. In Transjordan, and in Arab political circles outside Transjordan, many people appear to have shared Zirkili's cynicism.

Hardly had Emir Abdullah arrived in Amman, however, than things began to change. The established regional governments somehow vanished from existence by themselves; and within a relatively short time the general unruliness of Transjordan began to give way to the sort of organization that inaugurated its transformation into a country. How this was achieved, considering all the internal and external odds that were originally against it, is a story that deserves treatment by itself.

NOTES

1. T. E. Lawrence, *Seven Pillars of Wisdon* (London, 1955) pp. 64, 67.
2. *Ibid.*, p. 68.
3. Alec Kirkbride, *A Crackle of Thorns* (London, 1956), pp. 25–28.
4. *Ibid.*
5. *Al-Athar al-Kamila* (The Complete Works of King Abdullah, Beirut, 1985), pp. 158–9; author's translation.
6. *Ibid*, p. 160.
7. T. E. Lawrence, *Seven Pillars of Wisdom*, p. 340.

5

Putting the Country Together

By 1921, the broad lines of the present political map of the Arab world had already been drawn by the victorious Allies, yet Emir Abdullah still publicly maintained that all the Arab countries were essentially one. As a key participant in the Arab revolt, this was the only position he could reasonably take. In theory, his father, as the generally accepted leader of this pan-Arab uprising, was not simply king of the Hijaz, but king of the Arabs. In 1916, he had actually been acclaimed *Malik al-Bilad al-'Arabiyyah*, meaning 'King of the Arab Countries', the reference being, collectively, to Arabia, Syria and Iraq as the original historical homelands of the Arab people.

From Abdullah's point of view, his brother Feisal, as King of Syria, had actually been no more than a viceroy in a key province of his father's pan-Arab realm; and he himself had finally arrived in Syria to assume the same Arab vice-regency as a deputy for his brother, recognizing his father as his legitimate overlord. True, the Allies had meanwhile brushed aside Arab national aspirations to divide the northern parts of the Arab countries first into 'occupied zones', and then into British- and French-mandated territories, and these were already being subdivided into different states. Abdullah was compelled to take this fact into political consideration; but to allow it to confuse the issue at the level of principle meant the willing sacrifice of the ideals of the Arab revolt, of which the Hashemites considered themselves the natural guardians. There was no room for permissiveness on this crucial issue, as that would amount to nothing less than the complete surrender by the Arabs to the dictates of the Allies.

The emir went out of his way to make his opinion clear on the question of the fundamental unity of the Arab homeland in his farewell speech at Maan station, before boarding the train for Amman. His words on the occasion must have been directed as much to the ears of the British in Jerusalem, and the French in Damascus, as to those of the small Arab crowd he was in fact addressing. The emir wanted it understood that, although he was an Arab from the Hijaz rather than a native Syrian, he did not consider himself an alien to the Transjordanian territory he intended to take over and rule. On the contrary, in this territory, soon to be redeemed for the cause of the Arab revolt, no Arab was to consider himself an alien:

I do not wish to see any among you identify themselves by geographical region. I wish to see everyone, rather, trace his descent to the Arabian peninsula, from which we all originate. All the Arab countries are the country of every Arab.[1]

It was in accordance with this principle that Abdullah organized his first government in Amman on 11 April 1921, shortly after receiving the six-month option from Winston Churchill to assume the rule of the 'unallocated' parts of mandatory Palestine east of the Jordan river. In strict terms, Transjordan was not yet a state on its own, so the government in question was simply called a 'Council of Consultants' (*Majlis al-Mushawirin*), a name changed shortly afterwards to the 'Central Authority' (*al-Hay'a al-Marka-ziyya*). This provisional cabinet was composed of eight 'consult-ants' (Arabic singular *mushawir*), three of them Arab nationalists of the Istiqlal party, and most of them men who had served in different parts of Syria under Feisal. Of these eight ministers, only one – Ali Khulqi al-Sharayiri, of Irbid – was Transjordanian. The head of the government, who was styled 'Administrative Sec-retary' (*al-Katib al-Idari*), was a gentlemanly Druze from Mount Lebanon: Rashid Tali', who had been mutasarrif and military governor of Hama, acting minister of the interior, and military governor of Aleppo in Feisal's time. Of the remaining six members of the cabinet, three were Syrian, two were Hijazi, and one was Palestinian. The members of the Istiqlal party in the group included the premier, Rashid Tali', and two others: the Syrian, Mazhar Raslan, from Homs; and the Palestinian Amin al-Tamimi, from Nablus. Of the two Hijazi ministers, one – Shakir ibn Zeid – was a Hashemite sharif and a close relative of the emir.

What applied to the government also applied to the security forces, where the officers, for the most part, were not Transjordanians, but veterans of the Arab revolt from different parts of Syria, Iraq and Arabia who had formerly served under Feisal or Abdullah. Of the commanders of the various security units, not one was a native Transjordanian. The chief of gendarmerie, Aref al-Hasan, and the commanding officer of the cavalry, Fuad Slim, were both from Mount Lebanon: the first a Sunnite Muslim from the mountain hinterland of Tripoli, and the second, like Rashid Tali', a Druze from the Shuf. The commander of the infantry unit, Ahmad al-Istanbuli, was originally from Beirut; and the chief of the camel corps, Ibn Rumeih, was a tribal partisan of the Hashemites who came from Najd.

Clearly, what Abdullah had in mind at the time was not a Transjordanian administration, but a nuclear pan-Arab government for the whole of Syria based in the available territory of Transjordan, with elements representing the central Arab government of King Hussein in the Hijaz. Actually, the emir had no liking for the name Transjordan (Arabicized as *Sharqi al-Urdun*), now introduced by the British to denote the territory placed under his rule. He preferred to refer to this territory, initially, by a vaguer term, *al-Sharq al-'Arabi*, meaning the 'Arab East', which left the pan-Arab option theoretically open. When a unified security force was finally created for the country in 1923 (see below), it was pointedly not called Transjordanian. The name it was given, *al-Jaysh al-'Arabi* ('the Arab Legion'), remains the official name of the Jordanian army to this day.

To Abdullah's disappointment, the British saw things differently. From their point of view, the Arab revolt and its ideals were matters of the past, and it was mainly the issues of the moment that counted. All they were prepared to grant Abdullah was the rule of Transjordan: a buffer zone between the British and French mandated territories, and also between Iraq and Palestine, Syria and peninsular Arabia. Somehow, this buffer zone – with or without Abdullah – had to be transformed into a buffer state, or the closest possible approximation to one. Most important, the anarchy prevailing in the country had to be brought under control; otherwise, it threatened to disrupt the delicate relations between the British and the French in the area. Since the collapse of Feisal's regime in Damascus, Transjordan had become the main refuge of Arab nationalists fleeing the Syrian capital, and a leading base of anti-French activity. In response, the French, from their new base in their Syrian mandate, angled for support among disgruntled or self-seeking village sheikhs and tribal chiefs in the northern parts of Transjordan, taking advantage of the fact that the exact frontier line between the French and British mandates in the area was not yet settled. In the southern parts of the country, the tribal situation was equally fluid, threatening to invite Wahhabi incursions into a territory dangerously close to both Syria and Palestine.

Initially, however, it was the situation in the north which was most pressing. Before agreeing to allow Abdullah to take over the rule of Transjordan on a provisional basis, the British had made the matter clear to him: if he were to keep the country, he had to make certain not only that it was made governable, but also that it ceased to be a base for anti-French activity which embarrassed Britain. The emir, as a political realist, understood the need to follow the British directive; but he equally realized that he could not go all the way in doing so, because this might easily rob him of political credibility in Arab nationalist circles. The Arab nationalists who formed the main body of the emir's political entourage were doubtless aware of the delicacy of his position and of the need to compromise, but few among them were willing to temper their principles or abandon their rhetoric, and offer help. Some, in fact, appear to have persisted in pushing the hard Arab nationalist line on purpose to discredit Abdullah and keep him perpetually embarrassed, in full knowledge that the British were pressurizing him in the other direction. As a way out, the emir was compelled to resort to half-measures and play for time, which earned him criticism from both sides. A British intelligence report of 1 July 1921 sums up his predicament in his own words:

I came over to Trans-Jordania determined to make a bid for Syria; in Jerusalem I agreed to Mr Winston Churchill's policy, because I did not wish to do anything to cause trouble to Great Britain. . . . I pointed out that six months' inaction in Trans-Jordania after going there and telling the whole Arab world that I intended to make a bid for Syria, would mean the loss of Syria and the alienation of the Arabs. . . . I have now lost everything. . . . I have had enough of this wilderness of Trans-Jordania where I am surrounded by these hateful Syrians who think of themselves only.[2]

In the British Foreign Office, there was considerable debate in 1921 as to whether or not Abdullah should be allowed to continue ruling Transjordan, and not all the views expressed concerning his character and ability were charitable. Negative intelligence reports received from the area described him to the authorities in London as a 'fraud'; 'indolent, pleasure loving'; 'unscrupulous, extravagant'; 'languid and ineffectual'; 'idle and very lazy'. The more positive reports spoke of him patronizingly as the 'most intelligent of Hussein's sons', pointing out that he was a 'cleverish fellow', certainly 'cleverer than his brothers', except that he was 'very ambitious'. Ironically, it was the more negative reports that recommended the emir to the British government as 'the ideal man' to rule Transjordan – a man who would at least do 'tolerably well' if Britain could find 'the right man to control him'. One such report stated the matter quite baldly: if Abdullah was essentially indolent, yet clever, he would make 'a presentable titular ruler . . . intelligent enough to grasp real facts and conform to them'. The more positive reports, on the other hand, sounded a note of warning. Being a man who was essentially 'ambitious', Abdullah was 'not likely to be content for long as a mere figurehead', which was what Britain wanted him to be. If he was to be permitted to remain in Transjordan, it was essential to select a British officer with the proper qualifications to be his adviser and keep his ambitions under proper control.

The first of these, Albert Abramson (April–November 1921), was detailed to Amman from Palestine, where he had served first as military governor in al-Khalil (Hebron), and then as president of the land commission. Abramson was subsequently dismissed as 'not the best possible man' for the job, to be replaced by the competent and wilful H. St John Bridger Philby (November 1921–April 1924), a member of the Indian civil service who arrived in Amman from Iraq. Philby – who later converted to Islam and attached himself to Ibn Saud – was a man of many talents, with an excellent knowledge of Arabic and Arabic folk culture; but he was also contentious and highly opinionated, and could be extremely petty. Initially, the relations between the emir and his new adviser were friendly. The business of the day over, they would play chess together, or engage in easy conversation on subjects of common interest: Arab history, Arabic literature and tribal lore, or Arabic proverbs. With time, however, Philby's pettiness became so insufferable that the emir lost patience with him. The two men ultimately ceased to be on speaking terms, which meant that Philby had to go. He was replaced by the stern and hard-nosed Lieutenant-Colonel Henry Fortnam Cox, the district governor of Nablus in Palestine, who had served before the war in the Sudan. Cox appears to have conceived of his position as being essentially that of a colonial governor.

Abdullah was uncomfortably saddled with Cox for thirteen years, from April 1924 until March 1939. It was only then that a British adviser was finally assigned to Amman who admired Abdullah and appreciated his style of rule: Alec Kirkbride, for whom the emir had retained a special liking ever since their first meeting at the Qatrana railway station in 1920 (see Chapter 4). Kirkbride was to remain in Amman, close to Abdullah, to the very end. After 1946, he became the first British minister (then ambassador) to the independent Kingdom of Jordan, and only left the country in 1951 after the king's assassination.

* * * * * * * * * *

It is hard to imagine that Abdullah did not surmise, from the very beginning, what the British in Palestine – and ultimately in London – thought of him, and what sort of local Arab potentate they wanted him to be. Being the 'clever' man everyone was convinced he was, he knew that the British in the final analysis needed the co-operation he could offer them, no less than he needed the support they could give him. Certainly, he was able to 'grasp real facts and conform to them', but he invariably did so in his own manner, to the discomfiture or admiration of his British advisers, depending on who they happened to be.

While his father remained king in the Hijaz, Abdullah made a point of publicly deferring to his instructions, on the theoretical basis that it was he and nobody else who exercised the ultimate authority over him. This naturally annoyed the British, and he knew it; but as they remained determined to keep him guessing about their plans regarding his political future in the region, he no doubt felt that they deserved to receive, in return, some deft needling on his part. Abdullah fully realized, however, that Arab demands anywhere, if pressed to the extreme, were bound to clash with British or French imperial interests backed by naked power. The experience of his brother Feisal with the French provided ample demonstration of what could happen in such cases. For any Arab success to be achieved, it was necessary to discover ways and means to make Arab demands somehow compatible with the standing imperial interests. To Abdullah, moreover, appearances also counted. To pre-empt open prescription from Jeruslaem or London on issues which he knew were vital to British regional policy, the emir often acted as he guessed he was expected to act before he was plainly told to do so. This earned him much castigation from nationalist circles in the Arab world for being 'more British than the British', but he was quick to develop immunity to such criticism from people who, in his opinion, refused to recognize the validity of the dictum that politics was the art of the possible. It was by succumbing to the influence of such people, after all, that his brother Feisal had lost his Syrian throne.

Not all issues connected with Transjordan, however, were of fundamental importance to the British, and on such issues the emir invariably found a way to behave independently, taking little notice of received instructions. The repeated references in the British records to his 'indolence' and 'languidity' suggest this. When 'advice' with which he did not agree was pressed on him, the emir apparently procrastinated and studiously dragged his feet, until his British advisers let him do what he pleased out of sheer exasperation. The alternative for them was to take matters into their own hands and deal directly with an assortment of extremely difficult and intractable people better left in the hands of a fellow-Arab who had the patience for them.

To transform Transjordan into a country, Abdullah needed three things from the British: money, military assistance and goodwill. The rest he was confident he could attend to by himself, all the better without British advice or interference. No matter how competent or experienced, none of the British officials appointed to Amman from Jerusalem knew how to handle parochial Arab situations better than he. More important, none of these officials could really understand – let alone tolerate – the elusive attitudes and ways of the Arab nationalists of the Istiqlal party who helped the emir run the country during its formative years. The emir himself had problems with these nationalists, Syrians and others, as already indicated. He was convinced of the sincerity of some, and had good reason to doubt the sincerity of others. Until 1926, however, he could not do without them: first, because he wanted to maintain the image of Transjordan under his rule as 'the country of every Arab'; second, and equally important, because educated Transjordanians who were fit for public office were hard to find at the time. To make up for the paucity of the Transjordanian element in the administration, he had to search for candidates among the Palestinian families from Safad, Acre, Nablus, Jaffa or Jerusalem who had been arriving to settle in Irbid or Salt since the 1880s, or in Amman since 1920.

Ultimately, however, the original Transjordanians had to be reckoned with if their country was to be organized into a state. Before anything else, the influential bedouin chiefs and village sheikhs among them had to be prevailed upon to help rather than hinder the process. Some of these could only be made to do so by force (see below). The less recalcitrant, however, could be persuaded to moderate their doubts about the new order and co-operate with the emir and his government by other means.

Abdullah's thorough understanding of tribal Arabs was based on long experience. More than anyone else, he knew that what counted most for them was their highly sensitive *amour propre*: their exaggerated sense of individual and collective self-esteem. As long as one heeded this in dealing with them, one was on safe ground. The emir also appreciated the fact that tribal Arabs were staunchly egalitarian. The most lowly individuals among them considered themselves the social equals of the highest potentates. At the same time, the abstract concept of the state was not alien to them, and no matter how much they stood to gain from continuing anarchy, they realized that orderly government offered a better way of life, provided their rugged sensitivities were taken into account. In the final analysis, they were prepared to accept the legitimacy of political authority and recognize people wielding such authority as political – though not social – superiors. What was vital was the initial approach. If a ruler, from the beginning, behaved towards his tribal subjects as a political superior but a social and human equal, there was no end to the concessions he could exact from them in return.

From the moment he arrived in Amman, Abdullah made it clear that he intended to establish his rule firmly over the whole territory of Transjordan, calling upon all the tribal chiefs in the country and on everybody else to recognize his authority and pay him obeisance. For the time being, however, he did not stand on ceremony. Until the construction of Raghadan palace was completed in 1925, the emir had no permanent residence, but lived modestly in temporary homes made available to him by local notables: the Christian Sukkars and Abu Jabers of Salt, or the Circassian Muftis of Amman. This manner of living earned Abdullah the enduring friendship of the families who felt honoured to be his hosts, and of the town notables of the Balqa region in general. The emir, however, also spent much of the year camping in the open country, in the manner of the bedouins. In winter, he would pitch his tents outside the village of Shuna, in the Ghor valley downhill from Salt. In summer, he would move camp uphill to the plain of Madaba, or the hilltop of Marka outside Amman. Wherever he camped, Abdullah held court in the traditional tribal manner, setting little store by courtly ceremony, and sometimes joining the tribal sheikhs who came to visit him in outdoor games – rough-and-tumble local versions of 'blind-man's-buff, tug of war, wolf and lambs and the like', according to one confidential report received by the Foreign Office in London in the late summer of 1921. To British observers, no less than to the urban Arabs of the Istiqlal party who formed the emir's political *Équipe*, such behaviour on his part seemed to stop little short of outright levity. At best, they were at a loss what to think of it. It was by such informalities, however, that Abdullah rapidly succeeded in winning the hearts of his tribal subjects, before proceeding to the more arduous and complicated task of teaching them to appreciate the benefits of orderly government.

As a first step in this direction, the emir had to train the tribal sheikhs to defer to princely authority. What was important, to begin with, was to get the sheikhs to realize the advantages of princely favours, by withholding favours from the recalcitrant. A sheikh in this position was ignored and left to sit on his pride and face mounting problems, until he was finally compelled to apply for a formal audience with the emir. The response to the application would normally be delayed long enough to bring the applicant to the point of despair, whereupon the audience would be granted at very short notice, the time for it being fixed at some improbable hour – for example, shortly after sunrise. Not to miss his appointment, the sheikh in this case had to set out on his trip to Amman,

Madaba or Shuna in the small hours of the morning, or perhaps the evening before, depending on the distance he had to cover; and travelling by night over rugged desert country, he naturally arrived at his destination sleepy, dusty, dishevelled and looking his worst. By this time, the emir, having had a good night's rest, and having performed his morning ablutions and completed his prayers, was looking his radiant best in his spotless white robes and elegantly plaited turban. The mere contrast in appearance between placid host and harried guest was enough to put the latter in his place. Confident that he had made his point, the emir would forthwith proceed to accord the visiting sheikh a most friendly and courteous reception, listening to his complaints, and promising to attend to all his reasonable wishes or grievances. Chastened by the encounter, the sheikh, for his part, would return home after the audience praising the emir and extolling his bounty and consideration.

Such stories about the emir and the ploys and pleasantries he devised to temper the overbearing conduct of his more arrogant tribal subjects made him a legend when he was barely in his forties. During the early years of Abdullah's rule, however, the internal situation in Transjordan was far too complicated to be handled by such methods alone. In the summer of 1920, rebellion had been rife in some parts of the country since the downfall of the Feisal regime, and there was a strong suspicion that the mandatory authority in Jerusalem secretly encouraged it. Whatever pretence they made to the contrary, the British certainly did not wish to see Abdullah succeed in pacifying the country without their active participation. They were jealous of every success he achieved on his own, even when such success was in their own interest.

Apart from grudging Abdullah the least thing that enhanced his independence, the British, in particular, were not happy with the emir's reliance on the Arab nationalists of the Istiqlal party in manning his administration and (more important) his security forces, as this threatened to keep their own influence in Transjordan to a minimum. The British interest, at this level, coincided with the interests of the most obstructive elements in the country: the village sheikhs and bedouin chiefs who refused to yield to political discipline and persisted in fomenting trouble. The story of the Kura rebellion illustrates this point well.

Geographically, the Kura district comprises the hilly eastern parts of the Irbid region, which descend in steep and rugged slopes to end in the northern Ghor. Here, the most powerful of the local sheikhs, Kulayb al-Shurayda, had established himself since 1920 as an autonomous rural potentate, with French support and encouragement from Damascus; and Kulayb showed no intention of relinquishing his autonomy. When the first central government was organized in Amman in April 1921, and the Kura was declared to be part of the administrative region of Irbid, Kulayb refused to accept this arrangement. One reason for this was purely personal: the standing feud between Kulayb and Ali Khulqi al-Sharayiri, who had been the head of the government of Ajlun in Irbid when the Kura rebellion first started. Sharayiri, who actually came from Irbid, was now the minister in Amman in charge of security, and he was no doubt the member of the central government who urged most that Kulayb's ambitions as the strong man of the Kura district be forcibly curbed. In the Kura, however, Kulayb enjoyed strong backing from the local villagers who shared his hatred not only of Sharayiri, but of the Irbid townsfolk in general. What Kulayb and his followers asked for was that the Kura be separated from Irbid and established as an administrative district on its own, answerable directly to Amman.

The central government, naturally, could not accept such an irregularity, particularly as it opened the way for ambitious chiefs in other Transjordanian regions to claim similar privileges. If the country was to be properly run, the Kura had to be subordinated to Irbid, even if this meant an armed confrontation. Having only recently been organized, the government in Amman was badly in need of money, which meant that taxes had to be collected right away. To make certain that the Kura people did not resist the tax-collectors sent from Irbid, these tax-collectors were escorted to the district by a contingent of the local gendarmerie, the orders to this effect being issued from Amman.

The gendarmerie force had hardly arrived in the Kura, however, when its deputy commanding officer – a tribesman from the vicinity of Shawbak, south of Karak – was killed in a skirmish with local villagers, whereupon the force retreated back to Irbid, leaving the Kura taxes virtually uncollected. The central government promptly issued orders to Fuad Slim, the commander of the cavalry, to advance in person against the rebels with a mounted force, seize Kulayb al-Shurayda and his chief aides (one his son, the other his nephew), and round up all the men suspected of having had a hand in the killing of the officer from the Irbid gendarmerie. Alerted to the cavalry advance, the Kura people caught the attacking force in an ambush, inflicting on them a humiliating defeat. No fewer than fifteen of the attackers – many of them tribesmen from different parts of the country – were killed, and among the prisoners taken was Fuad Slim himself.

Unable to reduce Kulayb by force, the central government was now compelled to negotiate for the release of the cavalry prisoners, to which Kulayb readily agreed. When the government, however, proceeded to demand the surrender of the Kura rebels held responsible for the killings, it was roundly refused. After much give-and-take, it was finally decided to follow tribal custom and arrange for the Kura people to return the horses and armaments they had taken from the government forces as booty, and pay the *diyyah*, or blood money, to the relatives of the officers and men they had killed in the fighting; but even this arrangement did not really work. While part of the booty was indeed returned, the blood money was not forthcoming.

To save appearances for the time being, Abdullah decided to resort to personal diplomacy and announced his intention to pay a formal visit to the Kura. The inability of the central government to reduce the local rebellion by force had been amply exposed, and it was useless to pretend the contrary; but the emir was confident that he could still use his personal prestige to patch up matters temporarily. His judgment turned out to be correct. Flattered by the prospect of dealing directly with the emir, the rebel Kura leader hastened to meet him directly upon arrival, promptly declaring his surrender and submission. In return, the emir granted the sheikh and his followers a general amnesty, and the matter for the moment was considered settled. At about the same time, a government reshuffle in Amman removed Ali Khulqi al-Sharayiri from the cabinet: a matter which no doubt added to the sheikh's satisfaction.

In the country at large, however, the scandalous failure of the central government to subdue the Kura rebellion encouraged similar rebellions in other areas, which made the collection of taxes impossible in many parts, and, unless taxes were properly collected, the treasury in Amman was doomed to remain empty.

It was, in fact, a chicken-and-egg situation: for proper taxation to be possible, the country had first to be completely pacified, and for this purpose adequate military forces were needed; but while taxes remained unpaid, it was impossible for adequate military forces to be organized and maintained. By the summer of 1921, many elements in the Transjordanian security units were resigning their commissions or deserting the ranks because of arrears in pay. The only way to solve the problem was to ask the British for money, or at least for the Transjordanian share of the Palestinian customs revenue. But the British would give money only if they were given control over expenditure. They also wanted the final say in military matters, which effectively meant that they wanted to run Transjordan themselves, with the emir and his government as no more than a liaison with the local population.

To make Abdullah comply with their wishes, the British were in a position to tighten the screws on him from another direction. The most serious threats to the emir's position in Transjordan, between 1921 and 1925, were the repeated Wahhabi incursions from Najd into the southern parts of his territory, which the emir was powerless to repel by himself. The British maintained a military base – including a small air force – at Marka, close by Amman, which they could easily use to secure the country's southern frontier against the Wahhabis. Initially, however, they seemed in no hurry to do so, and deliberately ignored Abdullah's repeated appeals for help. Before they would agree to intervene, there was a price to be exacted. Abdullah had to start disengaging himself from the nationalists of the Istiqlal party who ran his administration and commanded his security forces, and accept an increasing measure of British control.

To meet the British at least halfway, Abdullah persuaded Rashid Tali' to resign from office as premier, and appointed Mazhar Raslan, a member of the Istiqlal who was less objectionable to the British, to replace him at the head of the new cabinet. He also agreed to accept a British officer, Captain Frederick Peake, as the supreme commander and financial comptroller of his armed forces.

In addition to the existing military units, whose structure was left unchanged, Peake was to raise a reserve of 750 men; and it was only by the following year, when the training of this reserve force was complete, that attention could be turned again to the rebellion which continued to simmer in the Kura district. This time, the British were willing to use their air force to bomb the stronghold of Kulayb al-Shurayda in the village of Tibna, while Peake led his newly organized reserve force in a successful all-out attack on the district. Unable to offer further resistance, Kulayb fled the Kura to seek refuge in the Balqa with the Banu Sakhr bedouins, while a number of his henchmen were seized and brought to justice. Abdullah did not intervene in the trials until they were over and the prisoners received the sentences they deserved. But it was important, from his point of view, that the ugly affair should not leave behind a legacy of permanent bitterness. Now that Kulayb and his followers had been chastened, it did more good than harm to have them pardoned. On 25 May 1923, Britain formally announced 'the existence of an independent government in Transjordan under His Highness Emir Abdullah', and the emir deemed it the right moment to issue a general pardon for the Kura rebels in honour of the occasion.

* * * * * * * * * *

The Kura affair was hardly over when trouble began to loom from another direction. Since his arrival in Amman, Abdullah had been showing special favour to Mithqal al-Fayez, the chief of the Banu Sakhr bedouins, who had long been locked in a feud with the Adwan bedouins of the Salt and Shuna regions on the other side of the Balqa water divide. As the chief of the latter tribe, Sultan al-Adwan resented the attentions paid by the emir to his Banu Sakhr rival, and this naturally deepened the political rift between the two men. Moreover, Sultan al-Adwan was not satisfied with being simply the chief of his own tribe, as he also claimed to be overlord of other bedouin groups in the Balqa, such as the Daaja and Banu Hasan of the Amman and Zarqa regions. By so doing, he challenged the ascendancy of the Banu Sakhr on their own home territory.

Abdullah set great value on the friendship of Mithqal al-Fayez, who had been the first bedouin chief of the Balqa to welcome him upon his arrival in Amman. While the Wahhabi threat from the Najd continued, it was also important for the emir to cultivate the loyalty of the Banu Sakhr bedouins whose territory, surrounding Amman and bordering the inland desert in the direction of central

Arabia, was dangerously exposed to Wahhabi incursions and influence. Abdullah certainly had no wish to keep the Adwan alienated by the special attentions he paid to the Banu Sakhr; but when he attempted to conciliate their chief by paying him a formal visit, the emir reportedly met with a rude rebuff. Sultan al-Adwan, it is said, broke the cup in which Abdullah was offered the ceremonial coffee of welcome, so as not to be second to drink from it.

As he became set on opposing Abdullah and his tribal policies, Sultan received support from an unexpected direction: the educated members of the younger generation in the larger towns of Irbid, Salt and Karak who were beginning to criticize Abdullah's personal style of government and press for democratic rule. When the British government in 1923 recognized the existence of an 'independent government' in Transjordan, the stipulation was made that this government had to be 'constitutional', with representative institutions. The new generation of urban intellectuals had meanwhile been growing increasingly envious of the Lebanese, Syrians and Palestinians who monopolized the most important positions in the government and administration. Sensing some underhand encouragement from the British, these intellectuals – among them Mustafa Wehbeh al-Tall of Irbid – began to voice strong opposition to the emir and his government, in some cases in the Arab press outside Transjordan. The demand was for the immediate promulgation of a constitution and the election of a Transjordanian parliament, which was seen as the ideal way for true nationals of the country to replace the *ghuraba'*, or 'aliens', in public office. Some of those who pressed these demands actually held administrative office. Mustafa al-Tall, for example, was the district governor of Wadi Musa, near the ruins of Petra. In the absence of direct evidence, one cannot really be certain how these urban intellectuals – in their time, the pick of Jordan's intelligentsia – became the chief allies and supporters of Sultan al-Adwan. It seems undeniable, however, that this redoubtable chief, whose quarrel with the emir derived from the most archaic motives, found it useful to adopt the progressive programme of the intellectual front in all its details, providing it with the full backing of his bedouins and their tribal confederates.

Thus, in August 1923, Sultan arrived in Amman at the head of an armed demonstration. This was ostensibly in order to place the popular demand for a constitutional, parliamentary government before the emir and press for the redress of some urgent fiscal grievances, but was actually designed to show who were the real masters of the Balqa region (i.e., the Adwan, and not the Banu Sakhr). At the time the government was not prepared for a showdown, so Abdullah had no recourse but to receive the bedouin chief, listen to his demands, and promise to give them due consideration. To stem the tide of opposition among the people in general, the standing government which had ordered the collection of tax arrears dating back to 1918 was dismissed, and a new government was formed which promptly rescinded these fiscal orders.

The defiance of established authority by the Adwan, however, could not be allowed to go unpunished, as it could easily be repeated. As a first measure, Mustafa al-Tall and two other Transjordanian officials who were known to be in close contact with the Adwan were arrested and brought to trial, accused of conspiracy against the state in connivance with Sultan. Fearful of the consequences to himself, the bedouin chief decided to strike first and advanced on Amman in full force, occupying the two gendarmerie outposts which controlled the western entrances to the capital. This time, however, the government troops under the command of Peake were fully prepared for the encounter, defeating the Adwan forces in a fierce battle outside the town and putting them to flight. The prisoners taken from among the attackers were banished to the Hijaz, while Sultan al-Adwan and his sons fled the country to seek refuge in Syria, in Jebel Druze. By March 1924, a general pardon permitted all the Adwan exiles to return home, now that they had learnt the limits of what the government was prepared to permit.

What the Kura and Adwan rebellions drove home to Abdullah was the basic need for an effective armed force to be employed as the state's coercive instrument, even if such a force was under British rather than Arab command. Without power, the state could have no authority. Some tribal restiveness continued to simmer in the country for a few years after the suppression of the Adwan insurrection. In 1926, for example, the government had to send a force with armoured cars to suppress a rebellion in Wadi Musa, where the villagers, refusing to pay arrears of taxes, had seized and looted the local gendarmerie post and government house. Otherwise, law and order, after 1924, had come to be generally established.

Hostile critics – die-hard Arab nationalists from one side, and ambitious Transjordanians of the urban elite from the other – lost no opportunity to belittle the success of Abdullah in bringing the country under proper control, on the grounds that this success had been achieved only at the price of increased subservience to the British. This, to a great measure, was true; but what Abdullah's critics persisted in overlooking were the remarkable gains the emir had meanwhile managed to secure in his territory at the grass roots, sometimes in spite of the British rather than with their help. By 1924, or at the latest 1926, Transjordan had been transformed by imperceptible stages from the 'unallocated territory' originally entrusted to the emir on a provisional basis, into something that could legitimately be called 'Emir Abdullah's country'. While the urban intellectuals continued to be generally critical of his policies, the emir had been successful where success really counted: he had secured recognition of his authority by the established regional and tribal leaderships which alone, at the time, were in a position to make or break his political aims. True, Abdullah had depended on the British to crush the more obdurate of these leaderships. Once this was done, however, it was by his special skills in handling people that the emir pacified his former enemies and turned them, one after another, into loyal friends and political associates.

* * * * * * * * * *

Constitutionally, the history of Transjordan between 1921 and 1946 passed through different stages. Contrary to Winston Churchill's frequently quoted boast, the country was not really created by a stroke of his pen on a Sunday afternoon in 1921. As already indicated, Abdullah in that year had already established himself in Amman by his own initiative, when the British agreed to grant him a six-month option to demonstrate his ability to govern the Transjordanian territory as part of their Palestinian mandate. This initial option – Churchill's vaunted stroke of pen – was subsequently extended until 1923: not because the British authorities in Jerusalem and London needed more time to observe Abdullah in action, but rather because Abdullah was quick to make himself the effective master of Transjordan, while the British remained undecided as to whether they really wished to keep him there. As Alec Kirkbride saw it, Abdullah became ruler of Transjordan from the moment he arrived in Amman, while the British, slow to make up their minds about what they really wanted, continued to dally and play for time:

Amir Abdullah set up a central administration in Amman with which to govern the Amirate of Transjordan, and ultimately, the Hashemite Kingdom of Jordan, as it is known today. . . . The Amir . . . actually took over control of the whole country in March, 1921, and it was not until the following July that His Majesty's Government decided to follow its usual policy of accepting a *fait accompli* and announced that they were prepared to recognize Amir Abdullah's rule over that part of the mandated territory which lay east of the river Jordan, provided (a) he recognized the validity of the mandate in question and (b) renounced his avowed intention of attempting to conquer Syria. Whether his bellicose intentions against Syria had ever existed was a moot point. In due course, the remarkable discovery was made that the clauses of the mandate relating to the establishment of a National Home for the Jews had never been intended to apply to the mandated territory east of the river. In later years, when Jordan proved the staunchness of its friendship during the bad years of the Second World War, politicians in Great Britain took credit for the way in which they dealt with the country's future during its earliest days.[3]

An invitation to Abdullah to visit London for talks in October–November 1922 marked the beginning of the second stage of his rule of Transjordan. It was in consequence of this visit that Britain, in May 1923, recognized an 'independent government' in the country – the occasion which Abdullah celebrated by issuing a general pardon for the Kura rebels. Abdullah's father was still king of the Hijaz at the time, claiming suzerainty over Transjordan as a *mintaqa* (territory, region) of his kingdom, while the British regarded this same *mintaqa* as part of their mandated territory. Anxious not to offend his father, Abdullah did not press for a clear definition of the independence of Transjordan from the Palestinian mandate, as this would have equally implied the end of his father's claimed suzerainty over this territory. At the same time, the British wanted to retain as much control as possible over Transjordanian affairs. The outcome was that Abdullah, in 1923, was officially recognized by the British as emir of Transjordan, while the country continued to be referred to vaguely as a *mintaqa* rather than as an *imara* (or 'emirate'). Hence the studied wording of the British official statement:

Subject to approval of the League of Nations, His Britannic Majesty's Government will recognise the existence of an independent Government in Trans-Jordan, under the rule of His Highness the Amir Abdullah ibn Husain, provided such government is constitutional and places His Britannic Majesty's Government in a position to fulfil their international obligations in respect to the territory by means of an agreement to be concluded between the two Governments.

In dealing with Abdullah, the British high commissioner in Jerusalem was now to act as the representative of the mandatory power rather than as the head of the Palestine administration, which implied a change in the political status of Transjordan. Technically, the territory was no longer to be considered an integral part of the Palestinian mandate. This, of course, made little difference in practice. In the course of the London talks, however, Britain promised to help establish proper and secure frontiers for Transjordan with Syria in the north, and the realm of Ibn Saud in the south. Also, Britain undertook to provide the government in Amman with an annual subsidy, fixed at £150,000, this being subject to financial and political conditions, the most important of which related to the military. Among other things, the different Transjordanian armed units were to be merged into one force under the command of Frederick Peake, ostensibly to limit expenses. This effectively meant that the dependence of Transjordan on veterans of the Arab revolt to officer its armed forces would be gradually reduced. When the required military merger was finally effected in October of that same year, the unified security force was called the Arab Legion (see above) – a last, nominal British concession to the emir's pan-Arabism.

Peake, who organized the Arab Legion and retained its command until 1939, had no liking for Abdullah. He disapproved of his personal style of rule, and tried his best to influence the British mandatory authorities against him. In 1924, he even pressed to have Abdullah removed from Transjordan. The emir, at the time, only managed to foil the plan for his removal by accepting further British restrictions on his powers.

What further complicated matters for Abdullah during the first two stages of his rule in Transjordan were the difficulties he had with his British advisers. The first, Abramson, was recalled from Amman within seven months of his appointment, essentially because he was not considered forceful enough. He failed to turn the emir into the 'mere figurehead' the British wanted him to be. Abramson appears to have been somewhat favourably disposed towards Abdullah, though not without reserve. He sympathized with Abdullah's predicament to some extent, and was reluctant to give him offence. He spoke of him in one of his reports as 'loveable, considerate and generous, possibly simple and frank, but more probably extremely deep and purposeful' (although, in another, he had described him as 'very often depressed and at other times very impatient').

Abdullah's second British adviser, Philby, held strong opinions of his own as to how Transjordanian affairs should be run, and therefore ended up clashing with the emir on a number of issues, great and small. He accused the emir of financial mismanagement, and was determined to purge the Transjordanian administration and security forces of Arab nationalists, on the grounds that they were foreigners. With his excellent command of Arabic, Philby could easily intrigue with the emir's adversaries – most readily, with the educated class in the towns – to make things difficult for him. (For example, he was generally believed to have been instrumental in bringing about the alliance between the urban intellectuals and the Adwan bedouins, which resulted in the Adwan uprising of the summer of 1923.)

Philby's successor, Lieutenant-Colonel Cox, arrived in Amman in April 1924 determined to curb the emir's power, or else have him removed from Transjordan, as Peake was then suggesting. The government in Amman, at the time, was headed by Hassan Khalid Abul-Huda: an old and trusted friend of Abdullah's, whom the emir had known since his boyhood in Istanbul.[4] Cox immediately saw to it that Hassan Khalid was removed from office, and imposed in his place a Damascene called Ali Rida al-Rikabi, who was known to dislike Abdullah, and whom Abdullah equally disliked in return. Rikabi had headed an earlier government in Amman in Philby's time (1922–23), and what recommended him to the British – judging by the highly negative official reports about him – was not so much his reputation for administrative competence as his political usefulness.

The mutual dislike between Abdullah and Rikabi was an open secret. Abdullah had first come to know Rikabi in 1910, when the latter was serving in the Hijaz as Ottoman *muhafiz*, or governor, of Medina. In that year, the Young Turk government had decided to put an end to the authority traditionally wielded by the emirs of Mecca over Medina. Acting on behalf of his father, Abdullah had gone to Medina to protest against the new policy, and he had clashed with Rikabi over the issue. He makes it abundantly clear in his memoirs that, on that first meeting, he found Rikabi a most unsatisfactory person. In those days, Rikabi, although an Arab, refused to speak anything but Turkish. Underlining this fact, Abdullah adds wryly: 'This is Rikabi Pasha, who later became our prime minister in Amman twice.'

When the Arab revolt broke out in the Hijaz in 1916, Rikabi was serving the Ottomans as head of municipality in Damascus; but when the Ottomans were defeated and left, he lost no time in shifting his loyalty to Feisal, to become a leading member of the Arab nationalist society *al-Fatat*. Feisal thereupon appointed him military governor of Damscus. But unlike other members of Feisal's political and military entourage, Rikabi stayed on in Damascus after Feisal was ousted by the French. Obviously, he was shifting loyalty again, this time to the French side. To keep his political options open, Rikabi also maintained contacts with the British in Palestine, who apparently made some hesitant use of his services for native liaison with the French in Syria.

An incident which occurred in June 1921 made the need for such native liaison between the British and the French a matter of great urgency. The French high commissioner for Syria and Lebanon, General Henri Gouraud, was visiting the southern parts of Syria at the time, when he drove into an Arab nationalist ambush near the Transjordanian border, and one of the French officers who accompanied him was killed. The French held Abdullah's government responsible for the incident, and this triggered a crisis between Damascus and Jerusalem which lasted until the following year (see below). As the crisis was approaching its final settlement, Rikabi suddenly appeared in Amman; and the British authorities in Jerusalem, apparently with an eye to appeasing the French, got Abdullah to appoint him head of the Transjordanian government for the first time. Both Philby and Peake considered him the right man for the job. After his first term as premier was over, Rikabi resumed his political angling with the French in Damascus, and with the British in Jerusalem. There was actually some speculation at the time that he would make a more suitable ruler for Transjordan than Abdullah.

Anxious to keep Abdullah's wings clipped after Philby's departure, Peake was quick to persuade Cox to re-appoint Rikabi as the head of the Transjordanian government, leaving Abdullah to smart under the arrangement for over two years. While he remained in office (April 1924–June 1926), Rikabi was successful in discrediting Abdullah in every way. The British, at the time, were determined to tighten the financial and administrative screws on the emir. Rikabi showed readiness to agree to all they wanted, making it appear as if all obstinacy came from Abdullah. Meanwhile, with remarkable subtlety, he managed to project the image of himself, in Transjordan as in the wider Arab arena, as the 'strong' prime minister who was resisting British pressures on Amman as best he could, while the 'weak' emir, anxious to keep himself in power at any cost, was set on turning himself into a British puppet. At that time, the Transjordanian administration and armed forces were being finally purged of the last 'alien' Arab nationalist personnel by Cox and Peake in connivance with Rikabi, and in the face of remonstrances from Abdullah. Yet, somehow, Rikabi effectively managed to escape direct blame for his role in the purge. Arab opinion outside Transjordan, already mobilized against Abdullah by his political adversaries, was all too ready to lay the principal blame for the purge on the emir.

* * * * * * * * * *

The third stage in the constitutional history of Transjordan began with the Anglo-Transjordanian agreement negotiated in Jerusalem and concluded on 20 February 1928. From being a *mintaqa*, which implied that it was still no more than a 'region' of the mandated territory, Transjordan was now to be officially an *imara* on its own. In the course of the Jerusalem negotiations, the official title of the British adviser in Amman – now Sir Henry Cox – was changed from 'chief British representative' to 'British resident', but his powers remained virtually the same. By the terms of the

1928 agreement, Britain was to retain extensive control over the country – most important, in the areas of foreign affairs, armed forces, communications and state finances – in return for continuing to provide an annual subsidy. The only gain achieved for Transjordan from the agreement was that the stipulations regarding relationships with Britain were put down on paper, so that they became fixed, whereas formerly they had been arbitrary and subject to British whim. These stipulations still left much to be desired, but they set the rules of the game; and, as in any game with set rules, the room for manoeuvre, no matter how narrow, remains open.

One point the 1928 Agreement pressed was the need to provide a constitution for the country – a stipulation already made by Britain in 1923, as a condition for recognizing an 'independent government' in Transjordan. At that time, the government in Amman was still dominated by the Istiqlal party, and the popular demand for a constitution, mainly limited to the intellectual class, was strongly coloured by the Transjordanian hostility to the non-Transjordanian Arabs in power. Abudullah, moreover, must have rightly feared that, given the circumstances, the introduction of representative institutions at that early period would have provided a focus for political opposition to his rule which any interested party – British or non-British – could exploit. It was doubtless a combination of these two factors that caused early plans to promulgate an organic law for the country to fail, or to be deliberately left to stall. The blame for this, though, had been laid on the British.

By 1926, however, the men of the Istiqlal party had lost power and influence in Amman. The army, under British command, had been effectively purged of non-Transjordanian Arab elements, and Transjordan, contrary to Abdullah's original wish, had ceased to be 'the country of all Arabs'. In March of the following year, the first Transjordanian political party (*Hizb al-Sha'b*, or the 'Party of the People') was organized, pressing for representative institutions at the very time when the Anglo-Transjordanian agreement was being negotiated. The party – a coalition of urban intellectuals and traditional notables – declared itself for pan-Arabism, and emphasized its opposition to Jewish ambitions in Palestine, but its programme was otherwise completely parochial. Its leaders hoped that the talks in Jerusalem would result in a declaration of independence for Transjordan; and when no such independence was declared, nor even mentioned once in the text of the agreement, they unleashed a wave of demonstrations in the capital and the larger towns. For the first time, schoolboys responded to the call of political leaders and went out on to the streets, clamouring against Abdullah and Britain.

The emir was greatly angered by what he considered a blatant show of disloyalty to his person. On the other hand, he was quick to understand the significance of the signals which the opposition leaders in the country were giving out. These leaders were clearly demanding a role in the new Transjordanian order. This was acknowledgement enough on their part of the emir's political achievement to date. Obviously, the time had come for Transjordan to have representative institutions, for political responsibility to be shared with the emir and his government, as well as the blame for unpopular decisions dictated by necessity. Thus, on 16 April 1928, a constitution was finally promulgated, providing for a parliament called the Legislative Council whose powers were mainly advisory. Of the twenty-one members of this parliament, fourteen were to be elected, while the rest – the prime minister, four members of the government, and two tribal representatives, one for the north and one for the south – were to be appointed. The government was to remain responsible to the emir, who appointed prime ministers and dismissed them. In keeping with this constitution, elections were held in February 1929 which brought the first Legislative Council to power. Efforts on the part of the opposition to boycott the elections only served to ensure a victory for the partisans of Abdullah. But the leading members of the opposition, having gone back on their attempted boycott, were also elected. Now that they had gained a say in decision-making, these opposition leaders joined in ratifying the Anglo-Transjordanian agreement which they had originally denounced. It was the only thing they could reasonably do.

Peake, as already indicated, remained in command of the Arab Legion until 1939. After the conclusion of the Anglo-Transjordanian agreement, however, his attitude towards Abdullah began to mellow. In the end, the emir was actually sad to see him go. Meanwhile, in 1930, a Desert Force (*Quwwat al-Badiyah*) was created as part of the Arab Legion, to suppress tribal raiding in the country. A British officer, John Bagot Glubb, was summoned from Iraq to organize and head this force, and Abdullah found him a man after his own heart. More than any other Englishman of his time, Glubb loved the tribal Arabs and knew how to win their affection and trust. At the same time, he was a professional soldier who served Abdullah with loyalty, using his influence with the tribes to marshal support for the emir rather than to intrigue against him, as other British officers who had influence with the tribes often did. When Peake finally resigned the command of the Arab Legion, Glubb was appointed to replace him. He recalls the occasion in his memoirs as follows:

His Highness the Amir Abdulla was sitting behind his desk. . . . 'You are English,' said the Amir, motioning me to sit down, 'and this is an Arab country, and an Arab army. Before you take over command, I want you to pledge me your word, that, as long as you remain in this appointment, you will act always as if you had been born a Trans-Jordanian. I know you would not wish to fight your own countrymen. If it should ever come to fighting between us and the English, I will hold you excused. You may leave us then and stand aside. But if, by God's will, this does not happen, I want you to be one of the people of Transjordan.' 'Sir,' I answered, 'I will give you my word of honour. From now on, I am a Trans-Jordanian, except under the conditions you mentioned, and which I pray may never come.'[5]

By the end of the first decade of his rule, Abdullah was already in a position to boast of his achievements. As he later said in his political memoirs:

We entered Transjordan to find four governments, each one separate from the other. . . Our first aim was to put the country together and secure its need to achieve unity. And here it is today . . . enjoying the complete . . . unity to which sister countries in its neighbourhood still aspire.

The political unity Abdullah brought to Transjordan was achieved at a cost. The many concessions the emir had to make to Britain to secure his position in the country had left his pan-Arab reputation badly tarnished. In an Arab world where nationalist sensitivities and frustrations were at their peak, few were willing to admit that Abdullah's concessions to the British had been made by necessity rather than by choice. What proved most damaging to the emir, after 1924, was the break with the men of the Istiqlal party, the officials and officers of the first Arab nationalist generation who had converged on Amman to form his original political entourage.

From the very beginning, these nationalists had expected from Abdullah more than he could deliver. They wanted Transjordan to remain a hotbed of nationalist activity against the French in Syria, at a time when the British were not prepared to allow this. As already mentioned, when General Gouraud, the French high commissioner in Syria and Lebanon, was ambushed near the Transjordanian border in 1921, the organizers of the ambush were mainly Syrian political refugees in Transjordan. Pressed by the British to deliver them to the French authorities, Abdullah, after much protest, went through the motions of having a search made for the suspects, while making certain that none were actually caught. Rather than have any of the men delivered, he tried to relieve the British pressure on him by persuading the Arab nationalist head of his government, Rashid Tali', to leave office and make way for the formation of a new government under Mazhar Raslan (see above). Tali' graciously agreed to do so, stayed on quietly in Amman for two more years, and then retired to his village in Mount Lebanon. By this time, General Gouraud had been replaced in Beirut and Damascus by General Maxime Weygand, and the matter was forgotten. As far as Abdullah was concerned, the way in which he had handled this delicate question was the best that could be done in the circumstances. In this, as in other incidents of the kind, however, most Arab nationalists maintained that the emir sacrificed principle for expediency with unwarranted readiness. They felt that, in the Gouraud affair, he should never have agreed to the search for the organizers of the ambush in the first place. The fact that he had no choice but to do so was a poor excuse from their point of view.

The 'foreign' Arab nationalists were phased out of the government and armed forces in Transjordan partly as a result of the tightening of British control over the emir, and partly because of local Transjordanian pressure. Starting in 1923, tribal chiefs such as Mithqal al-Fayez, no less than urban intellectuals such as Mustafa al-Tall, made more and more issue of the principle that 'Transjordan was for the Transjordanians', and that the 'foreigners' must go. After the last of these 'foreigners' had gone, many

Transjordanians, once they happened to be out of political office or favour, began to criticize the emir and his government on points of Arab nationalist principle, including those individuals who had formerly toed the particularist line. Meanwhile, most of the Arab nationalists who lost their administrative or military posts in Amman held Abdullah personally responsible for what had been done to them, and lost no opportunity to deprecate him in private or in public from outside the country.

Between 1925 and 1927, when a local uprising in Jebel Druze sparked off a general insurrection against the French in Syria, Abdullah gave refuge to many Druzes fleeing Syria in the oasis of Azraq, where a Druze community survives to this day. The leader of the Druze uprising himself, Sultan al-Atrash, sought refuge in Amman for a while, as he had done once before in 1922. When Peake, answering to British rather than Transjordanian orders, tried to arrest him there, his safe escape could not have been arranged without the connivance of his host. As the French at the time saw it, Abdullah was once again turning Transjordan into a base for rebellion in the territory of their mandate, and had to be stopped from doing so. The Arab nationalists, however, expressed outrage at the fact that Abdullah did not intervene actively in Syria itself to help the insurrection. They also blamed him for failing to stop French troops from entering his country to join the local British forces in driving the more belligerent Druzes out of the Azraq oasis into the territory of Ibn Saud. What Abdullah's critics on this issue did not take into account was that the emir could hardly have done more at the time. With Cox as his adviser, Rikabi as his prime minister, and Peake as the commander of his armed forces, his hands were all but completely tied.

Abdullah, in any case, never entertained the criticisms directed against him by his Arab nationalist deprecators. These nationalists, for the most part, had never been prepared to comprehend or accept responsibility for the consequences of the policies they pressed. Had Abdullah listened to them, it is doubtful that he would have succeeded in securing the establishment of a state. In any case, as far as he was concerned, Transjordan under his legitimate Hashemite rule remained, in principle, an outpost for true pan-Arabism, regardless of what was said to the contrary. As he wrote in the introduction to his memoirs:

I hope that our brethren in the sister Arab countries acknowledge the measure of what their brethren in the Jordanian sister country have achieved, so that when the time of [pan-Arab] unity comes, Transjordan would provide [this unity] with a fast mainstay.[6]

For all practical purposes, however, Transjordan for the remaining years of the mandatory period was an Arab country of marginal importance to other Arabs, barring those of Palestine. Throughout this time, the Anglo-Transjordanian agreement of 1928 remained in force, as originally concluded, except for an amendment introduced in 1934, whereby Transjordan was permitted to have consular representation in neighbouring Arab countries. Demands for further measures towards political independence were unheeded for the time being. Internally, however, the Transjordanian house had been put in proper order, to produce what remained until 1948 a cosy, 'happy little country', as it was described in those days. All but Abdullah's harshest critics were prepared to concede that it was largely the influence of the emir's personality that had made it so.

NOTES

1. *Al-Athar al-Kamila* (The Complete Works of King Abdullah, Beirut, 1985), p. 161; author's translation.
2. This citation from the British intelligence reports of the period, and the ones that follow, are taken from Mary C. Wilson, *King Abdullah, Britain and the Making of Jordan* (Cambridge, 1987).
3. Alec Kirkbride, *A Crackle of Thorns* (London, 1956), pp. 27–8.
4. Hassan Khalid's father, Muhammad Abul-Huda al-Sayyadi, had held the honorific post of *naqib al-ashraf* (syndic of the Prophet's descendants) in Aleppo, and was a powerful figure in Istanbul during the reign of Abdul-Hamid II, because of the special influence he wielded – as a sufi and a practitioner of divination – over the religious and superstitious sultan.
5. John Bagot Glubb, *A Soldier with the Arabs* (London, 1957), p.19.
6. *Al-Athar al-Kamila*, p. 36.

6

Abdullah and the Palestinians

If Transjordan in 1920 was still 'unallocated territory' with unde-
fined boundaries, the opposite was the case with Palestine. By the
Balfour promise of 1917, the British government had formally
allocated this territory to the Jews as a 'national home'. Its
borders, fixed in consultation with biblical scholars, were supposed
to be those of the ancient land of Israel: 'exactly as in the Bible,
from Dan to Beersheba', as Lloyd George once explained. The
terms of the Palestinian mandate, as articulated in 1922, endorsed
the British promise of this land to the Jews, and points of dispute
regarding its boundaries with Lebanon and Syria were settled
between the British and the French in that same year.

The facts of the arrangement were made clear to Abdullah from
the very start. While the territory east of the Jordan river, as
placed under his rule, was to remain purely Arab, the land of
Palestine, west of the river, was to be open to Jewish settlement.
What was not clearly spelt out at the time was the motive behind
this arrangement. By keeping Transjordan purely Arab, it was
obviously hoped that this territory could serve one day as a place
where Arabs from Palestine would go to settle once the growth of
the Jewish population in Palestine made this necessary.

Like most other Arab countries, Arab Palestine had always had
a native Jewish community: Jewish families who had lived for
centuries side by side with Muslim and Christian neighbours,
mainly in the towns, sharing their language and day-to-day culture. Since 1882, however, and more particularly since the World
Zionist Organization was formally set up by the Basle congress in
Switzerland in 1897, foreign Jews from central and eastern Europe
had been arriving in small bands to settle in the land, which the
Zionist movement planned to turn into a Jewish state.

To liberal-minded Muslim Arabs, the Jewish attachment to Palestine as their holy land was perfectly understandable on religious grounds. The Muslims had never stopped Jews from visiting the country on pilgrimage, nor had they ever objected to any number of them staying there. It was no doubt for this reason that the first Zionist settlements in the country did not attract much notice. In actual fact, Jews throughout the Arab world had generally fared well under Islamic rule. By and large, they had historically been more favoured than the Christians, because their presence in the territory of Islam, unbacked by an external power, had never been considered a threat. Barring the occasional flare-up of anti-Jewish feeling, the Muslims in the Arab world, unlike the Christians in Europe, had never subjected the Jews to systematic blackmail, persecution or humiliation. In fact, it was under Muslim Arab rule that Jewish learning, in medieval times, had known its golden age, using the Arabic language as its principal medium of expression. When the Crusaders captured Jerusalem in 1099, the Jews were massacred or expelled along with the Muslims, and were able to return only when Muslim control over the holy city was restored. After the Christian reconquest of Spain in the late fifteenth century, it was in Arab and Muslim countries such as Egypt and Turkey that Spanish Jews fleeing the Christian inquisition had found safe refuge.

Arabs who retained this traditional Muslim attitude towards the Jews took some time to grasp the fact that the Zionists who had been arriving to settle in Palestine since the last decades of the nineteenth century represented a different Jewish breed. They were tough-minded Jewish nationalists for whom Palestine was not only their holy land as a religious community, but also their rightful national homeland as a people. From their point of view, it was incumbent on the Jews of the world to do nothing less than reclaim this land for themselves, by whatever means and at whatever cost. Once they had re-gathered themselves there, they were to turn the page on the long centuries of their diaspora and re-constitute themselves as a nation in their own right, entitled, among other things, to use their own national language, biblical Hebrew, which Jewish scholars in Europe were set on modernizing so that it could be revived for spoken and literary use.

Historically, the Jews, wherever they happened to exist, had always shared a sense of common peoplehood. With the emergence of Zionism, this sentiment became the basis for a nationalist ideology with a set political programme. As far as the Zionists were concerned, Palestine was the biblical land of Israel, and it legitimately belonged to the Jews of the world, rather than to its Muslim or Christian Arab inhabitants. The fact that, in 1920, Arabs resident in the country still outnumbered Jews by about nine to one was not allowed to confuse the issue.

While the Zionists were aware that their ambitions in Palestine were bound ultimately to clash with local Arab interests, not all the early Zionist settlers in the country followed the hard doctrinaire line. As individuals, many among them felt that Zionist ambitions and Arab interests could possibly be reconciled, to the satisfaction of both parties. This was in the days before the Jews in Palestine had developed the military muscle which ultimately enabled them to realize the Zionist dream by force. Among the earlier Zionist settlers were Jewish Arabists and Arabophiles who eagerly sought to fraternize with Arabs, bearing in mind the racial affinity between Arabs and Jews as sibling peoples. While most Arabs suspected ulterior motives behind such Jewish advances, not all Arabs rejected them outright. To the very end, many remained prepared to talk things over, albeit to different degrees. The Jews, some Arabs argued, arriving from Europe and financially well backed, were introducing money and sophisticated modern skills into the country which promoted its development, making it the secret envy of its neighbours. If they were prepared to integrate with Arab society, they should be welcome to settle wherever they wished.

Zionist policy, however, was geared to confrontation rather than integration. Therefore, as the British mandate over Palestine was established, and as it became obvious that the Balfour promise was going to be officially incorporated into the terms of the mandate, a militant Arab reaction to Zionism set in. To the accompaniment of a first outburst of violence in 1920, repeated in 1921, then again in 1929, the Arabs of the country declared their opposition to the British mandate, denouncing in particular the right of Britain to give away to the Jews a land which was not her own. What they demanded was an immediate ban on Jewish immigration and purchase of land, and complete independence for Palestine as an Arab state.

To meet the Arabs half-way, the British were willing to regulate and limit Jewish immigration and land purchase. As a step towards Palestinian independence, they were also prepared to introduce some form of constitutional government for the country in which the Arab majority and the Jewish minority would more or less take equal part. The Arabs, however, would not consider sharing a Palestinian state with the Jews on an equal basis. The Jews, while pretending to the contrary, were happy it was the Arabs rather than themselves who were turning down British proposals for a shared Palestinian state, because they wanted Palestine for themselves. Consequently, Palestine remained under direct British government until 1948, while a Jewish Agency, formally established in 1929, was permitted to operate as a sort of parallel government attending to Jewish interests. The Arabs, in 1923, had in fact been offered an agency similar to the Jewish Agency; but they had refused the offer, since its acceptance would have implied a recognition on their part of the Jewish claims in Palestine. What they had instead was an Arab Executive Committee, which had already been serving since 1920 as a forum for the co-ordination of policy among the various Arab leaderships.

The Nazi persecutions in Germany and other parts of Europe, which began in the 1930s, drove larger numbers of German and other European Jews to flock to Palestine, where they were smuggled or helped to force their way in when the British tried to stop them. As friction between Jews and Arabs intensified, a full-scale Arab insurrection broke out in the country, lasting from 1936 until 1939.

In those days, few Arabs thought that the Jews would succeed in acquiring Palestine for themselves. Even with the increased immigration of the 1930s, the Jewish population of the country – estimated in 1939 at 475,000 – did not yet amount to much more than a third of the total population. Meanwhile, only 9 per cent of the cultivable land of Palestine, and 5 per cent of the total land area, had actually passed into Jewish hands. More important, the Arabs remained convinced that history was on their side, and that Jewish ambitions in Palestine could ultimately be contained. Some even believed that this could be achieved by peaceful means. Ethnic and religious minorities had always existed in the Muslim world, where they had normally been allowed a considerable degree of autonomy in the management of their internal affairs.

Under the Ottomans, this traditional arrangement had been formalized in the so-called *millet* system.

Abdullah, in Transjordan, was one man who believed the Jewish–Arab conflict in Palestine could be resolved on this basis, granting that a re-interpretation of the Balfour promise would be required for the purpose. If the Jews were prepared to accept the extension of his rule over Palestine, which he conceived to be possible, they could be left to enjoy their autonomy as they pleased, with all their legitimate civil rights guaranteed. The Jews naturally scoffed at the idea. What they wanted to achieve for themselves in Palestine was far more than mere autonomy as a *millet* under Arab rather than Ottoman rule. Abdullah, however, saw no harm in trying to persuade them to modify their set concept of the Jewish national home by acceding to the sort of arrangement he suggested.

Such an arrangement, Abdullah argued, would not only secure the position of the Jews in Palestine at minimum cost to existing Arab rights, but would also make it possible for Jews to settle and acquire land in Transjordan, where they could contribute to the country's development. The emir ventured to try some experiments. Transjordan, for example, had no electricity. In 1927, the Palestine Electric Corporation, which was a Jewish concern, was allowed to buy a tract of land east of the Jordan river for the construction of a Transjordanian plant, and Abdullah himself ceremonially started the turbines at the official opening. In that same year, Amman and Salt were badly hit by an earthquake. The emir welcomed Jewish colonists from Palestine to help in the work of reconstruction.

Some argument could be made for such demonstrably useful experiments in Arab–Jewish co-operation. However, one could not safely go further than this type of venture. Nevertheless, there were economic temptations to proceed beyond this acceptable limit. The principal economic asset in Transjordan was land, but this remained undeveloped because of lack of capital and skills. The principal landowners were tribal sheikhs and town notables who, like the emir, stood desperately in need of cash. For them, as for Abdullah, the prospect of Jewish settlement east of the Jordan river had a strong appeal. The Jews, for their part, were interested in extending their settlements to Transjordan, and therefore intensified their contacts with willing Transjordanian parties. In the 1930s, a number of options for Transjordanian land sales or leases to Jews were signed, and down-payments were made. But the British, who remained opposed to Jewish settlement outside Palestine, would not allow the transactions to go ahead. Moreover, the popular denunciation of the land deals was so strong, both in Palestine and in Transjordan, that the options were finally allowed to lapse.[1]

* * * * * * * * *

Initially, Abdullah's credentials as a Hashemite prince and a leader of the Arab revolt had stood him in good stead with the Arabs of Palestine. It was principally after the affair of the Transjordanian land deals that Palestinian reservations about him began to gain ground. On his first visit to Jerusalem in the company of Lawrence, to meet Winston Churchill, villagers from the Jerusalem district had assembled to greet him at the approaches of the city, and were greatly offended when he did not stop to respond to their greetings. According to Lawrence, who habitually denigrated Abdullah, the emir was too engrossed in conversation regarding his political future to notice the cheering crowd. According to Abdullah, it was Lawrence – in connivance with a British sergeant on local duty, and despite the emir's remonstrations – who would not permit the British driver of the car carrying the party to stop, suggesting that security considerations prevented this.

The British, clearly, had no wish to promote Abdullah's popularity in a territory he was not supposed to rule. The terms imposed on the emir, starting in 1921, distinctly precluded any intervention on his part in Palestine. Little could be done, however, to prevent Abdullah from developing Palestinian political contacts from his home base. For example, the emir's modest court in Amman remained open to Palestinian leaders who regularly arrived to visit and discuss the situation in their land. Also, Arab political activists who got into trouble with the British in Palestine could always count on the emir to provide them with safe refuge. Whatever the British terms imposed on him, Abdullah continued to regard himself as a legitimate pan-Arab leader who was entitled to concern himself with Arab national causes.

Even if he had tried to remain uninvolved in Palestine,

Abdullah was bound to be drawn into such involvement in the long run. Transjordan, after all, was Palestine's twin. The culture of the two countries was virtually identical, and the movement of people from one side of the Jordan stream to the other was continuous and normally unrestricted. There were also fundamental administrative, economic and social connections that had always tied the two lands together. Under the mandate, the British high commissioner in Jerusalem, who directly headed the Palestine government, was also responsible for Transjordan. When the Palestinian pound was introduced in 1927 to replace the Ottoman and Egyptian currency in general use, the same pound was made the legal tender in Transjordan. Families from the leading Palestinian towns – Muslim as well as Christian – had close relatives in Transjordan, where educated Palestinians formed the mainstay of the professional class, taught in the schools, and served in administrative posts. Similarly, many Transjordanian villagers went to work as seasonal labourers in Palestine. Moreover, during the mandatory period, the politically conscious middle class in the Transjordanian and Palestinian towns shared the same social and political orientation, and Transjordanian sympathies for the Arab cause in Palestine were naturally strong. Whenever trouble broke out in Palestine, the repercussions were immediately felt in Transjordan; and with every fresh outbreak of trouble, Abdullah's involvement in Palestinian affairs increased.

In Palestine, however, there were indigenous Arab leaderships to reckon with, and some of these leaderships were no less eager than the British to keep Abdullah away from the scene. Particularly important were the Husseinis, who had been established in Jerusalem for several centuries as a family of *sayyids*, tracing their descent from the Prophet. In 1745, the head of the family, Sayyid Abdul-Latif, had become the *mufti* (jurisconsult) and *naqib al-ashraf* (syndic of the Prophet's descendants) of Jerusalem – the two highest positions of the Muslim institution in the city to which local Arabs were normally appointed. These two positions – of which the first carried more weight – remained the exclusive preserve of the family thereafter. At the start of the twentieth century, the mufti of Jerusalem was Taher al-Husseini, who was succeeded in office by his son Kamel. When Kamel died in 1922, he was succeeded in turn by his younger brother Amin.

Born in 1897, Amin al-Husseini – popularly known as Hajj

Amin[2] – was a young man of twenty-five when he assumed office as mufti. As a boy, he had received his education partly in Ottoman government schools, and partly in the Roman Catholic missionary school of the *Frères de la Salle* in Jerusalem, after which he was sent to Egypt to pursue religious study in the Islamic university of al-Azhar. There, by his own account, he was influenced by the pan-Islamic political ideology preached by Rashid Rida (d. 1935): the ideology from which radical Islamic movements such as that of the Muslim Brethren subsequently proliferated. In 1914, however, the young man's religious education at al-Azhar was interrupted by the outbreak of the Great War, when he was recruited for Ottoman military service as a junior officer and stationed in Smyrna.

The war over, Amin al-Husseini, now aged twenty-one, returned to Jerusalem, where he became involved in the burgeoning Arab resistance to the newly established British rule. His political activism first attracted the attention of the British authorities in 1920, when a warrant was issued for his arrest because of the role he played in the anti-Jewish riots of that year. The young man, however, managed to escape arrest, and also a ten-year prison sentence passed upon him *in absentia*, by seeking refuge with King Feisal in Damascus. After the capture of Damascus by the French, he fled to Amman, where Emir Abdullah accepted him as his guest, then interceded with Herbert Samuel, the British high commissioner in Jerusalem, to secure his pardon. Typically of the mores of the Arabs of that generation, the man who was to spend most of the years of his active career locked in bitter conflict with Abdullah never forgot the emir's kindness to him on that occasion. In his later years, he recalled the event as follows:

Herbert Samuel arrived to visit Emir Abdullah, and in the course of the lunch which Emir Abdullah prepared for him, the high commissioner said to the emir: 'I have heard that Amin al-Husseini is in Amman!' The emir answered: 'Yes, this is true!' Herbert Samuel pursued the question: 'And what is he doing here?' 'He is my guest,' the emir answered; 'his father was a friend, and his brother is one of our best men of religious learning, so I cannot refuse him hospitality. He is entitled to my respect.' Then the high commissioner said: 'And why does he not return to Palestine?' 'You know as well as I,' the emir answered, 'that he has been condemned to ten years with hard labour.' 'I shall pardon him. We, for our part, are appreciative of the qualities, enthusiasm and patriotism of this young man.' 'I cannot but thank you'. . . . The emir realized, as he later made clear to me, that the high commissioner Herbert Samuel wanted to win my affection. . . . After that pardon was issued, I returned to Jerusalem, and some of the high commissioner's friends suggested that I pay him a visit to thank him, but I refused.[3]

It was shortly after Amin al-Husseini's return from Amman that his brother Kamel died, and he was elected to succeed him as mufti of Jerusalem. As it happened, however, his choice for this important post was contested, ostensibly on the grounds of his youth and his dubious competence in the fields of Muslim learning. The real reason why his candidacy was opposed, however, was political. The Husseinis in Jerusalem belonged to a local urban aristocracy – the so-called *afandiyyat* – which included a number of other families; and the more ambitious among these families naturally coveted the prominence the Husseinis had long enjoyed under the Ottomans, and saw in the coming of the mandate the opportunity for a change. The leaders of this party of *afandiyyat* were the Nashashibis, whose rise to local prominence was relatively recent, dating to no earlier than the middle decades of the nineteenth century. The death of Kamel al-Husseini in 1921, which left the post of the mufti of Jerusalem vacant, seemed to the Nashashibi party the ideal moment to turn the tables against the Husseinis, so they presented a candidate of their own – Sheikh Hussam Jarallah – for the post. It was generally believed at the time that the British mandatory authorities supported Jarallah's candidacy. As it turned out, however, the apparent British support for Jarallah was no more than a ploy. What they were actually searching for in Palestine was a potential Arab leader with enough political credibility to serve as a valid Arab spokesman, and Amin al-Husseini, it seems, appeared to them to be the right man for the job.

A visit by Emir Abdullah to Jerusalem in December 1921 provided the British with the ideal opportunity to establish contacts with the promising young man. Herbert Samuel, at Government House, was to entertain Abdullah to lunch, in company with Philby, who had recently been appointed to be the emir's British adviser. The only other guest was to be Hajj Amin. Considering that Abdullah had only recently been his host in Amman, Hajj Amin could not refuse the invitation. In actual fact, he must have been happy to come, because the occasion provided him with an excellent opportunity to press his strongly contested candidacy for the post of mufti directly with the high commissioner.

Impatient to have a private moment with Samuel after the lunch was over, Hajj Amin, according to Philby, suggested that Emir Abdullah take a nap, so that he and Samuel could talk alone. Such a pointed slight could not have failed to offend Abdullah, especially as it came from a man who was his junior in rank and age, and who also owed him a debt of gratitude. The emir may perhaps have explained away the slight as the impertinence of a novice who had still to learn better manners. Most probably, however, the slight was calculated. Suspecting that Abdullah might have ambitions in Palestine, the young Husseini wanted the emir to understand from the very start that intervention on his part in Palestinian affairs would not be welcome.

* * * * * * * * *

As mufti of Jerusalem and president of the Supreme Muslim Council, Hajj Amin became the paramount Arab leader in Palestine, and the dominant figure in the Arab Executive Committee. In physical appearance, he was red-haired, with eyes light hazel to green in colour; and though not a tall man, he had an athletic build, and made a point of maintaining his physical fitness by regular exercise. 'I am a veteran officer', he would explain, 'and the blood in my veins is not only the blood of men of learning.' Socially, he was mild-mannered, soft-spoken and exquisitely polite. What was most remarkable about him, however, was the imperturbable serenity of his countenance, and the benevolent, seraphic smile, behind which lurked a strong, unbending will. To the chagrin of the British, who had originally pinned their hopes on him and probably helped him come to office, Hajj Amin proved not only to be politically inflexible, but also incorruptible. Once installed as mufti, Hajj Amin, most probably in complete sincerity, came to conceive of himself as the caretaker and champion of a sacred Muslim Arab cause which he held in popular trust, and on which no compromise was possible under any circumstances, not even by way of manoeuvre. On two points, he was unquestionably right. He was convinced that the Jews were no more willing to compromise than he was. They simply pretended moderation, for the time being, as a political tactic, because they were not yet strong enough to get all they wanted from the Arabs by force. He was also convinced that the British counselled moderation on the Arabs because they wanted to have done with the Palestine problem as soon as they could. Whatever they officially said to the contrary, their chief concern was to honour their commitment to the Jews, with the least possible trouble to themselves.

It was certainly not the mufti who initially unleashed the Arab reaction to the British mandate and Jewish colonization in Palestine. Even as late as 1936–39, this reaction remained diffuse rather than centralized. Outbursts of Arab violence in different parts of the country were organized by a host of different local leaders whose names have long been lost to memory: village chiefs or religious sheikhs with peasant followings, or urban gang leaders, most of them acting on their own, without regular reference to any central direction. What set the Arab resistance in motion was certainly not the nationalist rhetoric of the upper- and middle-class urban leaderships, but rather the accumulation of unsettled grievances and frustrations at the grass roots: most of all, the apprehensions of tenant peasants who lived in constant fear of losing their lands, and the helpless anger of those who had been evicted from their villages to make way for alien Jewish colonists. Coupled with these grievances and frustrations was the staunch attachment of the Palestinian peasantry to its Muslim faith, which gave the general revolt of the 1930s, in particular, the character of a holy war.

Unlike Transjordan, where the tribal system cut across social class, blurring distinctions between the townsfolk and the villagers, the rich and the poor, Palestine was a country where the Arab townsfolk and the peasants lived, socially, in two different worlds. For this reason, the urban political leaderships – the old-established as well as the emergent – were generally out of touch with the villagers who formed the bulk of the population. Whatever these leaderships thought or said had little, if any, impact on the country at large, where their nationalist rhetoric often rang hollow. As for their political activities, they were mostly limited to intrigues and mutual recriminations, which took a further toll of their credibility among the people. As head of the Husseini family in Jerusalem, Hajj Amin was no exception to the general rule. Throughout his political career, much of his energy was directed towards the weakening or destruction of actual or potential rivals. He had, however, another side to his character. Unlike the other Jerusalem notables, he was able to communicate with ordinary folk and get them to accept him as the champion of their cause. By virtue of his office as mufti, and more so as president of the Supreme Muslim Council, he could readily appeal to the elemental sentiments of the Palestinian peasants and ordinary townsfolk by a simple Muslim rhetoric which they could understand. Meanwhile, the traditional good relations between the Husseini family and the Christians of Jerusalem, which he was careful to maintain, won him considerable Christian support in the rest of the country.

As his paramount leadership of the Arabs of Palestine became established, Hajj Amin rapidly gained recognition throughout the Arab and Muslim worlds as the only valid spokesman for the Palestinian Arab cause. At the same time, the wide popularity he came to command among the Palestinian Arab masses made it increasingly difficult for any rival to compete with him on home ground. In the circumstances, Palestinian politicians who remained bent on opposing Hajj Amin began to veer towards Amman, to seek support from Emir Abdullah. Foremost among these were the Nashashibis, whose political stand with respect to the British and the Jews was not much different from Abdullah's. Like the emir, the Nashashibis and their partisans argued that the Palestinian Arabs could not hope to achieve much unless they cultivated the goodwill of the British. They also agreed that Jewish ambitions in Palestine could be contained only if the Arabs were willing to offer some concessions on particular issues, provided these did not involve any sacrifice of fundamental principle.

The Nashashibis had been close to Abdullah ever since he first arrived in Transjordan. Starting in the 1930s, however, they and their followers began to urge the unification of Palestine with Transjordan under British auspices, with Abdullah as king. Other Palestinian leaders converging on Amman at the time were more reserved in their approach, yet did not rule out a possible role for Abdullah in the future of Palestine. Among them were the Arab nationalists of the Istiqlal party (see Chapter 5), now reconstituted as a Palestinian political front by Awni Abdul-Hadi, a leading notable from Nablus. While this party opposed Abdullah's moderate policy towards the Jews, and frequently joined the Husseinis in denouncing it, Abdul-Hadi and other Istiqlal leaders were personal friends of the emir. Moreover, the party retained enough of the old Istiqlal leanings towards the Hashemites to keep the contacts between Nablus and Amman open.

By the 1930s, Abdullah himself was in a better position to respond to Palestinian political overtures than before. The Anglo-Transjordanian agreement, as concluded in 1928, had finally made it possible for him to put his Transjordanian house in order, so he could now broaden the sphere of his political activities. Meanwhile, the British who had originally precluded any role for the emir in Palestinian affairs were beginning to have second thoughts about the matter. At the time, the arrival in Palestine of the first bands of Jewish refugees fleeing persecution in Germany was beginning to intensify the Arab–Jewish conflict in the country, leaving the British at a loss what to do.

In the summer of 1929, anti-Jewish feeling among the Arabs, which had been building up since the start of the decade, had come out into the open on an unprecedented scale in the so-called Wailing Wall riots. The troubles began when Jewish demonstrators in Jerusalem marched to the old city in solemn procession to plant the Zionist flag at the Wailing Wall: the last remnant of the temple of Herod, which survives as the western wall of the Aqsa mosque, the third most holy sanctuary of Islam.[4] When the Arabs arrived to remove the flag, a clash ensued in which twenty-eight Jews were reportedly killed. This incident triggered a wave of Arab attacks against Jews in other parts of Palestine which lasted for five days, bringing the total of Jews killed to 133 by the official count. The British had to use force – in some cases with great harshness – to restore order. The perpetrators of the troubles were then arrested and tried; the Arabs among them receiving severe punishments, including the death penalty, while Jews, whom Arabs alleged to be equally guilty, were left virtually unpunished. Justifiably or not, the outcome of the trials following the Wailing Wall riots confirmed most Arabs in the belief that the British were conniving with the Jews against them.

Immediately following the trials, a special parliamentary commission arrived from London to investigate the underlying causes of the troubles. Its findings, which resulted in the publication of an official statement of policy known as the Passfield White Paper, indicated that the root of the problem was the justified Arab apprehension elicited by increasing Jewish immigration and purchase of land, which was rendering many Arab villagers homeless and destitute. The White Paper therefore ruled that immigration and land sales be subjected to strict mandatory control, and that immigration, in particular, must be made dependent on the capacity of the economy of the country – Arab as well as Jewish – to absorb new immigrants. Hajj Amin and other Arab extremists were not satisfied with the White Paper because it did not question the Jewish claim to Palestine, which to them constituted the heart of the matter. The Jews, for their part, would not agree to any restrictions on immigration, and the British government in London was subjected to strong Zionist pressure to have the White Paper revoked.

With the coming of the Nazis to power in Germany in 1933, larger numbers of German Jews began to arrive in Palestine as refugees, which further compounded the problem. The British mandatory authorities found it extremely embarrassing to deny the Jewish refugees admission to the country in keeping with the stipulations of the White Paper. The Arab reaction was not long in following. In what were initially sporadic eruptions of violence, bands of armed Arabs resumed their attacks on Jewish settlers and British security outposts in different regions. The British at the time still hoped that a compromise settlement between the Arabs and the Jews in the country could be reached, if only Hajj Amin could be persuaded to co-operate. But the mufti was unwilling to agree to any compromise. The Arab Executive Committee, acting under his command, would settle for nothing less than the complete and effective stopping of Jewish immigration and land purchases, and the cessation of all British support for the Jewish national home project. In addition, the committee demanded the immediate promulgation of a Palestinian constitution, as a first step towards the termination of the mandate and its replacement by special treaty relations between an independent Palestine and Britain.

By persistently taking the same uncompromising stand, Hajj Amin might well have appeared to have been acting from sheer obstinacy. The plain fact, however, was that he did not hold as much personal power as his reputation suggested. Consequently, what was expected of him was invariably more than he could, or was prepared to, deliver. From the very start, as already indicated, the Palestinian Arab resistance to British rule and Jewish colonization had been too diffuse for any one man or party to direct; and by the 1930s, the movement had already developed a momentum which was extremely difficult to keep in check. Hajj Amin, as its accepted leader, could speak for it, articulate its demands, and exercise some influence over it now and then. Regardless of the degree to which he was inwardly convinced of the wisdom and effectiveness of the intransigent policies he pursued, Hajj Amin was ultimately a politician who could ill afford to alienate his constituency, if he was to remain the paramount leader of Arab Palestine and keep political rivals away from his turf. The British sought his co-operation because they valued his political credentials, but Hajj Amin apparently felt that he could keep these credentials only for as long as he continued to behave exactly as his followers expected.

* * * * * * * * * *

In Amman, Emir Abdullah was in a far stronger position. To begin with, he was the ruler of a state, which Hajj Amin was not. Despite the British financial and other restrictions under which he functioned, the emir was in command of a regular government, with administrative and military machinery sufficiently effective for the control of his home ground. Starting in 1933, he began to appoint men of Palestinian origin to head his government, which signalled the fact that he stood ready to play a Palestinian role. More important, the emir was known to possess a dogged determination, coupled with a political resourcefulness which never seemed to fail him. Once he had set himself an objective, it was extremely difficult to deter him from moving to achieve it. From the moment Abdullah began to concern himself with Palestine, Hajj Amin recognized him as a serious political competitor: the more so because Abdullah did not play the game according to accepted Arab rules.

From the very start of his political career, Abdullah had been a practical man. He was also a person with an independent mind, and nothing restrained him from speaking it. While he certainly cared about what people thought of him, he did not allow this to influence his judgment or stop him from making his convictions known. From his point of view, Arab aspirations, no matter how justified, stood no chance of being even partly achieved unless they were made somehow compatible with British interests, in a part of the world where Britain was in a position to dictate her will. With respect to Palestine, he had no illusions about the ability of the Arabs to prevent the Jews from achieving their aims in the country by using force against them. The Jews, after all, though still vastly outnumbered by the Arabs, enjoyed an international support which the Arabs lacked, and which made them the stronger party politically. Abdullah saw continuing Arab opposition to the British as a serious tactical error. He also believed that the persistence of the Arabs in refusing to talk with the Jews served no useful purpose, and was proving harmful to the Arab interest.

In the charged political atmosphere of the period, Abdullah could not easily express such pragmatic views without raising popular doubts about his sincerity as an Arab leader, especially as he had many political enemies who stood ready to encourage such doubts. By 1934, Hajj Amin and his partisans were already passing the word around that the emir was not to be trusted as a *bona fide* spokesman for the Palestinian Arab cause. Abdullah, so the whisper went, was essentially a political opportunist and a British stooge whose relations with the Jews, moreover, were highly suspect, particularly as they involved land dealings with the Jewish Agency.

In that year, Abdullah was to visit London in response to an official invitation, and he proposed to use the occasion to present the Palestinian Arab case before the British government. Except for his Nashashibi friends, none of the Palestinian leaders would give him a mandate to speak on their behalf. Nor did the British government, at that time, consider Abdullah qualified to negotiate the Palestinian problem, considering that he had no 'body of opinion' behind him (as the high commissioner in Jerusalem, Sir Arthur Wauchope (1931–38), had written to London). Abdullah, however, did not give up. If he was to be denied a speaking role on the Palestinian stage, he could still make his voice heard from the wings. On the day after his return from London, according to his memoirs, he wrote to Wauchope to press on him the urgency of the problem:

The Balfour promise states that the Jews should have a national home in Palestine, but the actual state of affairs indicates that the Jews have managed by various means – and without being opposed – to formulate another plan which would make of all Palestine a national home for the Jews. Anyone who objectively considers their condition when they first began to immigrate to the country, and the great extent to which they have managed to colonize it since, would realize that their success is almost complete, and that their aims would be achieved in a few years. . . . The Jews have attempted, and continue to attempt to go beyond what the promise to them says. By this, they have caused the Arabs to develop the fixed idea that a Jewish state is going to be established in Palestine disguised under the name of the national home. The fears are such that they will permeate Arab countries beyond Palestine.[5]

Abdullah warned of the consequences to be expected if affairs were left to drift:

The Jews have not come forth with a single indication that they can integrate with the original Arab population. I would have wished, with all my heart, that they would have behaved otherwise. Experience leads me to conclude that if the situation persists unchanged with respect to unrestricted immigration, and other matters of which the Arabs complain, evil and terrible results will appear in the near future.[6]

To avoid this catastrophic eventuality, the emir urged the need to promote mutual understanding and co-operation between the Arabs and the British – a matter in which he was prepared to play an active role:

I do not deny that the interests of Great Britain have expanded in Palestine and in other Arab countries after the war. Would you not agree with me, considering all this, that the maintenance of the true affection which the Arabs feel for your noble nation is a matter of central importance, worthy of due attention and care? I have continuously attempted, with all the ability with which I have been endowed, to strengthen these links between the two nations, being firmly convinced that their consolidation is in the interest of the Arabs, as it is in the interest of the British. I do not contest that my Arab people, in Palestine, have committed many political errors. In my opinion, however, this has been entirely due to the fear that has overcome them with respect to their threatened existence.[7]

Wauchope did not have to wait long to see the 'terrible results' of the British inaction in Palestine which Abdullah had predicted. In the early months of 1935, troubles erupted in the hill country north of Nablus, where an organized band of about sixty armed Arabs, training in the forests of Jenin, clashed with British security forces. The leader of the Arab guerrillas was a Muslim religious preacher of Sufi background called Sheikh Izzuddin al-Qassam. Born in 1882 in the Syrian seaport of Jabala, south of Latakia, and educated in al-Azhar, Qassam had first attracted public notice by leading the Muslims of his native town in armed resistance to the French. In 1922, he arrived as a refugee in Palestine with six of his veteran followers, whereupon Hajj Amin – as head of the Supreme Muslim Council – secured for him an appointment as a mosque orator and religious instructor in Haifa, while his companions worked in the docks. In Haifa, Qassam's zealous pan-Islamic preaching attracted many Palestinian followers, most of them villagers who worked as day labourers in the city and its port. From among them, Qassam and his fellow Syrian veterans ultimately managed to organize a body of armed and trained *talamidh*, or 'disciples', who stood ready to fight under the sheikh's command.

In the latter months of 1935, Qassam arrived in the Jenin vicinity to proclaim a general Palestinian revolt against British rule and to fight alongside his disciples in person, but he was killed in action before the end of the year. The Arab Executive Committee then stepped in to adopt the revolt he had started. Having little ability to control the guerrilla fighters, who rapidly lost their discipline after the death of their original leader, the committee decided to call a general strike in the spring of 1936, demanding a ban on Jewish immigration and on the transfer of land from Arabs to Jews, and calling for the introduction of self-governing institutions. Meanwhile, the armed insurrection spread rapidly throughout the country, independently of the strike. Observing the developments from Amman, Abdullah correctly estimated that Hajj Amin and his committee in Jerusalem had inadvertently bitten off more than they could chew. They had made themselves politically responsible for a movement of popular rebellion over which they exercised no real authority.

Having called the general strike and articulated its aims, the committee had no clear idea what to do next. What they needed was a mediator between themselves and the British, who did not seem in the least prepared to agree to their demands; and the only possible mediator was Abdullah himself. Thus, for the first time, delegates of the committee representing all the Palestinian parties arrived in Amman to enlist the emir's support. Abdullah strongly advised them to call off the strike which was worsening their relations with the British to no purpose, and to send a delegation to London instead to negotiate the Palestinian Arab demands. However, his advice was turned down.

Next, from London, the British government proposed to send a Royal Commission to study the situation, provided the strike was called off. Again, Abdullah urged the Arab Executive Committee in Jerusalem to comply with the British demand, so the Arab case could at least get a hearing. As a minimum condition for stopping the strike, the committee asked that Jewish immigration be stopped at least for the duration of the Royal Commission's visit. Abdullah exerted every effort to get the British or the Jews themselves to concede this reasonable Arab demand. From the Jews, he could get nothing. The British, for their part, were prepared to modify their position and consider putting a temporary stop to Jewish immigration while the Royal Commission did its work, provided the strike was first stopped. In repeated meetings with the Arab Executive Committee in Amman and Jerusalem, Abdullah urged that the British conditions be met, and that the strike be called off. As a way out, he offered to make a public appeal to the committee to do so in the Arab interest, and so take upon himself the moral responsibility for ending the strike. Hajj Amin and his partisans, however, were not prepared to allow Abdullah such direct personal involvement in their affairs. Meanwhile, as the split within the committee between the partisans and the opponents of Hajj Amin widened over the issue, the majority, which supported Hajj Amin, decided to dispense with Abdullah's mediation efforts. The emir was sent a curt letter thanking him for all he had done to help.

The Palestinian Arab leaders had become convinced by this time of the necessity of bringing the strike to an end. The only way they could do this without losing face was to call off the strike in response to a prestigious external Arab appeal, as Abdullah had suggested. The appeal, however, could not be accepted if it came from Abdullah alone, because of the special sensitivities felt against him by Hajj Amin and his party. Ultimately, an acceptable solution was worked out. The British government announced its intention to end the strike by force, whereupon the Arab Executive Committee agreed to call it off voluntarily in response to a joint appeal by the kings of Saudi Arabia and Iraq, the imam of the Yemen and the emir of Transjordan. Shortly afterwards, in November 1936, the long-awaited Royal Commission, chaired by Lord Peel, arrived in Palestine to begin its work, without the Arab pre-condition of a temporary ban on Jewish immigration being met. The Arab Higher Committee consequently decided to boycott the proceedings of the British commission, which they did for two months, until the kings of Saudi Arabia and Iraq finally persuaded them to end this boycott in their own interest.

* * * * * * * * *

It was largely at the initiative of Hajj Amin that King Abdul-Aziz Ibn Saud – the inveterate enemy of the Hashemites – was brought into the Palestinian picture at this juncture as a counterpoise to the emir of Transjordan. By 1932, Ibn Saud had already consolidated his conquests in peninsular Arabia into a Saudi kingdom, and stood ready to confront his old Hashemite foes on the Arab regional scene. Hajj Amin was to become his chief ally among the Palestinian leaders; but the Saudi king also managed to gain some support within the ranks of the Istiqlal party, whose stronger pro-Hashemite leanings, in any case, were geared more towards Baghdad than towards Amman. This left Abdullah with only the Nashashibis for support among the Palestinian leaderships.

Hajj Amin, however, wanted to get Abdullah out of the Palestinian picture altogether. When the Peel Commission decided to begin its work with an official visit to Amman, the mufti published an article in the Jerusalem newspaper *al-Liwa* warning Abdullah not to meddle in Palestinian affairs by attempting to speak with the members of the British commission on behalf of the Arab Executive Committee. For the first time, the hitherto silent conflict between the mufti and the emir came out into the open. Abdullah, according to his memoirs, responded to Hajj Amin by writing him a personal letter:

Your Lordship, I have read an article in *al-Liwa* alerting me as to how I should behave . . . that I should not say any word on behalf of the Arab

Executive Committee, and so on. . . . You and I, Your Lordship, have been in complete agreement that I would not object to anything you decide. Yet I have made it clear to you that I am not the sort of person who keeps his views to himself. . . . This being the case, was it necessary to hurt my feelings by attacking me on the pages of *al-Liwa*, assuming that I intended to meddle with the affairs of the committee and speak on its behalf? . . . All I want from Your Eminence is an explanation as to how matters stand. Are there any points of disagreement between us, or cause for suspicion or dissatisfaction? For my part, I only think well of you, and harbour good intent. . . . I await your early reply, so that I . . . can be enlightened.[8]

Contrary to what the mufti thought, Abdullah was no ordinary politician who could be easily intimidated by a negative press statement. Public attacks on him could certainly give great offence, but they could not make him retreat. As already indicated, Abdullah, unlike the Palestinian leaders of the Arab Executive Committee, operated from a home base over which he exercised firm control. He was also fully aware of what lay in store for Palestine. In his view, the worst could perhaps be prevented from happening by the sort of judicious compromise he counselled. By refusing to consider his advice, Hajj Amin and his followers, in his opinion, were signing the death warrant of the Palestinian Arab cause, which would be much better off without them. As he once stated plainly in a letter to the president of the Young Men's Muslim Association in Egypt:

O Brother in Islam, the pillars of Zionism in Palestine are three: the Balfour promise; the European nations that have decided to expel the Jews from their lands and direct them to Palestine; and the extremists among the Arabs who do not accept any solution, but simply weep and howl, calling for help from those who cannot do them any good. So behold Palestine, breathing its last![9]

The Arab Executive Committee was able to put a temporary stop to the popular revolt in Palestine while the Peel Commission did its work. In July 1937, however, the publication of the findings and recommendations of the commission provoked the resumption of armed rebellion in the country. According to the Peel Commission report, the Palestine problem involved an 'irrepressible conflict between two national communities within the narrow bounds of one small country', and the only workable solution was the partition of the country between 'an Arab state consisting of Transjordan and the Arab part of Palestine, and . . . a Jewish state'. Abdullah, in defiance of expressed public opinion in Palestine and the rest of the Arab world, declared his acceptance of this recommendation. The fact that he personally stood to gain by the partition, as officially proposed, was capitalized upon by his political enemies, who unleashed a loud public outcry against him. Abdullah subsequently advanced an alternative proposal in twelve points, suggesting that the whole of Palestine be united to Transjordan under his rule, with a guarantee of autonomy for the Jewish areas. In one of the twelve points, Abdullah audaciously suggested that the whole territory of the united Arab state could be open to additional Jewish immigration at the discretion of the Arabs 'should they be satisfied with respect to Jewish good faith and willingness to integrate'.

As it turned out, the effect of the emir's alternative proposal was further to inflame Arab public opinion against him. Abdullah, it was commonly believed, had advanced his twelve points under British directives. Awni Abdul-Hadi, his old friend of the Istiqlal party, wrote to tell him so, expressing concern about the harm the emir was bringing upon his personal reputation. Abdullah answered:

The proposals have been contrived by no one except myself, as I believe that the present situation, if it continues, will be a disaster to Palestine and the Arabs. I would agree to withdraw them if you can convince me that the perpetuation of the present situation can keep the Jews away from Transjordan, after Palestine. . . . Dear friend, I thank you very much for your concern about my reputation. Thank God, it is safe and spotless. Moreover, I do not lack the capacity to defend my good name, as I have not forfeited a single span's stretch of territory, nor a single right. Had the policy pursued by the Arabs for twenty years been truly effective, there would not have been today nearly half a million Jews in Palestine, while not a single one is to be found in Transjordan. The protection of Transjordan against the Jewish promise has been due to God's providence and my own work. As for Palestine, prepare yourselves to say its requiem, as it has been left without management or direction.[10]

At the time that Abdullah was writing this to Abdul-Hadi, the Arab Executive Committee had already been disbanded by the

British, who held its leaders responsible for the resumption of armed rebellion in the country. Hajj Amin, as its president, had fled Palestine in disguise to escape arrest, and was living under French protection in Lebanon. Other members of the committee had fled to Cairo, Damascus or Baghdad, making Damascus, in particular, the centre of their political operations. From there, they managed to keep the Arab insurgents in Palestine supplied with arms and ammunition, without otherwise exercising much influence over them. Meanwhile, the rebellion began to simmer down, until it finally came to a halt in 1939 out of sheer exhaustion.

As far as any observer could tell, all that Abdullah had earned from his involvement in the Palestinian problem by that time was considerable damage to his Arab political standing. The emir himself, however, remained convinced that he alone was ultimately destined to get the Palestinian Arabs out of the predicament in which their own leaders had left them. Some Palestinians were prepared to agree that he was right on this count, although few dared to say so openly. The story of the emir's Palestinian involvement, however, was not yet over. It was only the first episode that petered out with the outbreak of the Second World War, an episode in which Abdullah's role remained peripheral. The second episode, which finally brought the emir to the centre of the stage, had to await the end of that war.

NOTES

1. For the details of this affair, see Avi Shlaim, *Collusion across the Jordan: King Abdullah, the Zionist Movement, and the Partition of Palestine* (Oxford, 1988), pp. 50–54.
2. A Muslim earns the title *hajj*, meaning 'pilgrim', by performing pilgrimage to Mecca. By custom, however, this title is also used to address or refer to people of age or social eminence, to indicate respect coupled with familiar affection. Strictly, the title of address for a mufti was *shaykh*.
3. The last sentence of this passage is originally related in the third person by Husseini's interlocutor, who recorded his memoirs. See Zuhayr Mardini, *Falastin wa'l-Hajj Amin al-Husseini* (Beirut, 1986).
4. Muslims hold this wall sacred, calling it *al-Buraq*, after the name given by Muslim tradition to the mount which the Prophet Muhammad rode on the celestial voyage which took him from Mecca to Jerusalem and back in one night (Koran 17:1). The wall is believed

to mark the point where al-Buraq alighted in Jerusalem, then left the ground for the return to Mecca.

5. *Al-Athar al-Kamila* (The Complete Works of King Abdullah, Beirut, 1985), pp. 333–5; author's translation.
6. *Ibid.*, p. 335.
7. *Ibid.*, p. 336.
8. *Ibid.*, p. 336.
9. *Ibid.*, p. 381.
10. *Ibid.*, pp. 371–2.

7

A Kingdom at a Price

The resurgence of Germany as a European power under the Nazi dictatorship had been viewed by Britain and France with concern from the very start. This concern, however, reached the point of alarm in 1938, when Germany annexed Austria, and then proceeded to invade and occupy Czechoslovakia in complete disregard of the Paris peace settlement. By the autumn of that year, it had become clear that nothing short of a new world war was going to stop the Germans from further territorial expansion in Europe. Britain, in the circumstances, felt compelled to prepare for the eventuality by securing her position in the Middle East: an area which commanded vital land routes and waterways, and whose oil was a strategic asset of the first importance.

To achieve this purpose, Britain had to mend her fences with the Arabs – first and foremost, over the crucial Palestinian question. In 1937, the Peel Commission, as indicated in the preceding chapter, had recommended the partition of Palestine between the Jews and the Arabs, despite strong Arab objections. Subsequently, a special commission of inquiry, the Woodhead Commission, had been sent out to discover how the recommended partition could best be carried out. The Woodhead report, which was completed in the late spring of 1938, offered three partition plans, suggesting which of these it thought preferable, and why. The report warned, however, that none of the three suggested plans would result in viable states. It further recommended that none of these plans should be put into effect in the event of a world war. By November of that same year, as the outbreak of war became virtually certain, the idea of going ahead with partition was dropped altogether, and the British government invited Jewish and Arab representatives – in the latter case

Palestinians, along with delegates from Egypt, Iraq, Transjordan, Saudi Arabia and the Yemen – to discuss the future of Palestine at a special conference in London. The British, at this conference, offered independence for Palestine as a federal state by the end of five years, with restrictions on Jewish immigration and land purchases during the transition period.

The Jews were naturally dismayed by this sudden switch in British policy to the Arab side. To everyone's surprise, however, the Arabs failed to take advantage of the British offer which was so plainly in the Arab interest. From his exile in Lebanon, Hajj Amin al-Husseini, as the acknowledged leader of the Palestinian Arabs, pressed his representatives at the London conference not to accept the offer as presented, and to insist on a shorter transition period. As he explained in his later years:

The decision to convene this conference was made by the British government in consultation with the Arab states of Egypt, Saudi Arabia, Iraq, the Yemen and Transjordan. The Arab Executive Committee was ignored by the British. It was important for them that I should not personally participate in the conference. I felt honoured by this slight. I realized that they were afraid of the objections I would raise. . . . I saw no use in the dialogue. . . . The fact that the London conference ended in failure proved me right.[1]

Losing patience with the Arab delegates, none of whom seemed able or willing to stand up to Hajj Amin's directives, the British government finally decided to resort to unilateral action. On 17 May 1939, a White Paper was issued reiterating the terms of the British offer at the London conference, and conceding all the basic demands of the Arabs: a unitary state, to be granted independence after ten years; severe limitations on land transfers from Arabs to Jews; the restriction of Jewish immigration to 75,000 during the first five years of the transition period, after which any further immigration would be dependent on Arab readiness to acquiesce. The Jews rejected the White Paper as an abrogation of the Balfour promise which they were prepared to fight. Emir Abdullah applauded it from Amman as the best deal the Palestinian Arabs could ever hope to get. He was the only Arab leader to do so. Privately, many Palestinian Arabs were prepared to agree with him that the deal which the British were finally offering was not one to be missed. Hajj Amin, however, denounced the White Paper as a devious British ploy, and his opinion, as usual, carried the day on the Arab side.

* * * * * * * * *

As Hajj Amin persisted in obstructing the British effort to pacify Palestine, his continued presence in Lebanon became a serious embarrassment to the French. The Palestine Government had been pressuring France to extradite Hajj Amin from the very start. The mufti had originally fled to Lebanon to escape banishment to the island of Mauritius, at a time when a number of his associates in the Arab Executive Committee were being successfully rounded up for banishment to the Seychelles.

The British demand for the surrender of Hajj Amin began to be pressed with increasing urgency after 1 September 1939, when Germany invaded Poland and the Second World War broke out. While the French, even now, remained reluctant to surrender their political guest to the fate that awaited him, they no longer had any excuse to continue hosting a man whom their British allies regarded as their chief enemy in the Arab world. A few pointed hints to this effect, however, sufficed to make Hajj Amin leave Lebanon of his own accord before the middle of October and flee to Iraq. About 200 of his guerrilla followers had already arrived in that country shortly before, as the last pockets of Arab rebellion in Palestine were being subdued.

Iraq in those days was the only Arab state which could provide Hajj Amin and his party with safe refuge under the very nose of the British. The kingdom had been formally independent since 1922, subject to special treaty relations with Britain; and a revision of the terms of these treaty relations in 1930 had been followed two years later by the admission of Iraq to full-fledged membership in the League of Nations – the first Arab country to achieve this privileged status. After 1930, the only rights officially reserved by Britain in Iraq related to the maintenance of British military outposts in specified locations, the most important being two airforce bases, one of them at Habbaniyya, near Baghdad. In practice, Britain continued to wield considerable influence on Iraqi decision-making where issues touching vital British interests were concerned; but this influence could only be exercised with Iraqi consent.

The British hated the thought of being saddled with Hajj Amin in Baghdad for the duration of the war, but, for the time being, there was nothing they could do about the matter. The man was idolized as a national hero throughout the Arab world, and the Iraqi government could not refuse him hospitality without exposing itself to general Arab censure. Hajj Amin had hardly arrived in Baghdad, however, when he ceased to behave as a mere political fugitive. He showed himself determined to cross swords with the British in whichever Arab country he happened to be, and the political situation in Iraq in the early years of the war provided him with the ideal opportunity.

After the death of King Feisal I (1920–1933), the throne of Iraq had passed to his son Ghazi: an impetuous young man, and a staunch Arab nationalist, whose youthful zeal made him the idol of his people. Ghazi, however, was killed in a car crash in March 1939, at the age of 27, leaving the throne to his son Feisal II, who was barely six years old at the time. The regent for the throne became Abdul-Ilah, son of the late King Ali of the Hijaz. He was Ghazi's first cousin and also his brother-in-law, which made him the maternal uncle of the boy king. Unlike the outgoing Ghazi, Abdul-Ilah was secretive and aloof, which made him generally unpopular as regent. Among Arab nationalist hard-liners, he was classified as pro-British, which added to his unpopularity. The chief of his court, however, was Rashid Ali al-Gaylani: one of the few leading figures in the Iraqi administration whom the hard-line nationalists considered fully trustworthy.

Under the prince regent, the dominant figure in Iraqi politics was Nuri Pasha al-Said (d. 1958), a veteran of the Arab revolt of 1916 who had been serving the Hashemite royal family in Iraq since the days of Feisal I. Like Emir Abdullah in Transjordan, Nuri Pasha, in 1939, was firmly convinced that the British were going to win the Second World War, as they had won the first, and that the Arabs stood the best chance of achieving their legitimate national aspirations of independence and unity by lending full support to the British in their hour of need. In Transjordan, Abdullah had placed the modest resources of his Arab Legion at the disposal of the British from the moment the war had started. Nuri would have liked to have done the same, had it been in his power.

In Iraq, however, there was no question of the country entering the war on the side of the Allies, because public opinion was not prepared to accept such a course of action. Moreover, Nuri al-Said, in Baghdad, had to reckon with political opposition from Arab nationalist hard-liners, among them high-ranking officers in the army whose views, in essence, were no different from those of the Palestinian followers of Hajj Amin. By 1939, many of these nationalists had come to harbour pro-German sentiments, not so much from love of Germany as from hatred of the British. When the government of Nuri Pasha broke off diplomatic relations with Germany on 13 September, then proceeded to have the German nationals living in Iraq arrested and handed over to the British government in India, there was enough of a public outcry in the country to prevent the government from going any further in its show of support for the Allied cause. Hajj Amin arrived in Baghdad on 15 October, just in time to throw his considerable political weight on the nationalist side. His home in the Iraqi capital became the unofficial headquarters of the nationalists and other critics of Nuri's policy – among them Rashid Ali al-Gaylani, the chief of the royal court.

To Nuri Pasha in Baghdad, as to Emir Abdullah in Amman, Hajj Amin appeared as a 'devil straight from hell'. Both men regarded Hajj Amin as a mischief-maker whose obstructive tactics against the British served no useful purpose, and were in fact damaging to the Arabs. At the time when Abdullah was having his problems with Hajj Amin, however, Nuri had failed to come to the emir's rescue; and when he did intervene on one occasion, his intervention had proved a hindrance rather than a help.[2] Now it was the turn of Nuri to be harassed, and Abdullah, with everything under control in Transjordan, could afford to sit back for the moment and watch the Pasha squirm.

In the summer of 1940, however, the war was brought into the very heart of the Middle East by the fall of France and the defection of the Vichy regime to the side of Germany. From being the allies of the British, the French in Lebanon and Syria were suddenly transformed into potential enemies. The British, as a result, were faced with an emergency in the Middle East which they were unable to handle without first securing adequate control over Iraq, where the latent pro-German feelings among the nationalists were rapidly coming to the surface in response to the unexpected turn in the war's fortunes.

Earlier in that year, Nuri al-Said, sensing difficulties ahead, had given up the Iraqi premiership to keep a lower profile as foreign minister in two successive coalition cabinets: the first under Rashid Ali al-Gaylani; and the second under Taha al-Hashimi, another leading figure in the nationalist camp. Without Nuri Pasha at the helm, Abdul-Ilah, as regent, could do little more than temporize to maintain the precarious balance in the Iraqi government between the moderates and the hard-liners. Hence, during the difficult period that followed, Abdullah, in Amman, remained the only Arab on whom Britain in the Middle East could safely rely as an ally.

Hashimi replaced Gaylani at the head of the Iraqi government in January 1941, at a time when the war fortunes of Britain were reaching their lowest ebb. The German army in North Africa was beginning to push towards Egypt, while the Vichy French were still in control of Lebanon and Syria. For Britain, the ability to move troops from India to Palestine and Egypt by way of Iraq now became a matter of urgent necessity, and the first British troop-carriers from the sub-continent soon began to arrive in the waters of the Gulf. In Baghdad, however, the nationalist officers in the army command, who were in close touch with Hajj Amin, would not permit the government to grant Britain the right of military passage through Iraqi territory. This meant, in effect, that they wanted to see Britain lose the war. On 1 April, the Hashimi government resigned, having been pushed to do so by a military clique composed of four of these officers. The day before, Nuri al-Said had fled to Amman in anticipation of the troubles ahead. On 2 April, Gaylani was called upon to form an emergency government of national defence. Actual power, however, fell into the hands of the four officers who had organized the coup; and if these men answered to anyone at all, it was to Hajj Amin as their political mentor. Frightened by these developments, Abdul-Ilah fled Baghdad for Basra on the following day, to seek refuge on a British warship. About two weeks later, he managed to join Nuri al-Said in Amman. Sharif Sharaf, a distant relative of the royal family who shared the views of the new government, was forthwith appointed to replace him in the regency.

After a month of negotiations with the Gaylani government which broke down at every turn, the British decided to resolve the issue by force. On 18 April, a naval and military expedition from India landed in Basra, but the Iraqi army was able to hold up its advance. As it remained bogged down on the outskirts of the town, the British air force at Habbaniyya went into action on 2 May, attacking Iraqi military positions outside Baghdad. Meanwhile, a detachment of British troops from Palestine began to advance in the direction of Iraq, and Emir Abdullah, from Amman, ordered his Arab Legion to join them. The Iraqi command, finding itself in serious difficulty, called on the Axis powers for help, and the Germans and Italians responded by sending war planes to Mosul and Kirkuk, in the northern parts of the country. By then, however, Abdullah's Arab Legion had arrived outside Baghdad to cut the Iraqi lines of communication north of the capital. At the same time, the British troops from Palestine took up positions to the west and south, so that the city was besieged from all but the eastern side, in the direction of Iran. The attack on Baghdad was finally launched by the British and Transjordanian forces on 27 May. Two days later, the fighting ended with the capture of the city and the flight of Gaylani, Hajj Amin and their supporters to Iran. From there, they ultimately made their way to Germany, where they remained for the duration of the war.

* * * * * * * * * *

To many people, though not necessarily to military historians, the turning point in the Second World War was the battle of Alamein, in October 1942, when the German advance into Egypt was halted. What paved the way for the British victory at Alamein, however, was the capture of Baghdad sixteen months earlier. By braving Arab public opinion and sending his forces to fight alongside the British in Iraq, Abdullah had made a major contribution to the Allied cause. Alec Kirkbride, who was the British resident in Amman during the war years, recalled the mood of the moment in his memoirs:

The military situation was grim. . . . The French Army in Syria . . . had turned from allies to enemies, almost overnight, and were now co-operating actively with the Axis command. The civil population of Jordan had decided that Great Britain had lost the war and that it was only a matter of time before the German Army would arrive to take over control. King Abdullah himself was in a state bordering on despair, and he had twice walked into my house unannounced and said 'I am sorry, but you must tell me that all will be well in the end!' . . . Tribal leaders came and told me openly that they would not make any difficulties so long as the British remained in their posts, but that they would not oppose the enemy forces when they arrived. . . . In these conditions it was obvious that unless the situation in Iraq was restored quickly our position in Jordan would become untenable. His Majesty's Government decided to use force in Iraq, but at first matters did not go well. . . . I found myself left in Amman . . . radiating a confidence which I did not feel to a king and a government who no longer had faith in our future victory. . . . There were some nasty riots and demonstrations in the streets of Amman at a time when there was not very much left in the way of forces to deal with the mobs. The worst feature was the evidence that some of the Arab officers of both the local forces had been disaffected and could no longer be depended upon. Full credit was due to King Abdullah and to his Prime Minister of the time, Tewfiq Pasha Abdul Huda, who, though sure in their hearts that we were losing the war, backed us up through those black days and kept a precarious situation from becoming desperate. . . . The Arab Legion detachment had covered itself with glory. . . . From then onwards, in spite of three more years of ups and downs in the fighting, our ultimate success was not doubted, and I no longer needed to bother about looking cheerful as I drove through the town of Amman.[3]

Obviously, Abdullah had to be rewarded for his gallant stand on the side of Britain in her hour of direst need. What the reward was to be was a different matter. Abdullah himself expected that he would be made king of a Greater Syria, with Damascus as his capital. This had been his dream ever since he had first arrived in Transjordan; and he now felt that the moment had finally come for this dream to be turned into reality. To achieve his dreams of a Greater Syria, however, Abdullah had to convince the Syrians and the Lebanese to accept it, which was not possible; nor was it possible for the British to impose this dream upon them. Having thrown the Vichy French out of the two countries by the autumn of 1941, the British were keen to win the Syrians and the Lebanese to their side, and were pressing the Free French to grant them their full independence for this purpose. Moreover, Abdullah's Greater Syria scheme was opposed from other directions – most of all, by the king of Saudi Arabia, who had no wish to see a second strong Hashemite kingdom established on his northern borders. Britain, like the

United States, was anxious not to do anything to annoy Ibn Saud. His territory was known to contain major oil reserves, as yet largely unexploited. Little wonder that Winston Churchill and other Britons and Americans at the time considered him the 'greatest living Arab'.

Certainly, Abdullah could not be made king of a Greater Syria. He could be rewarded by being given the Arab part of Palestine, should Palestine one day be partitioned; but this was a matter for the future. One thing he could be given immediately was independence for Transjordan, but the emir had to wait even for this. His problem was that the British took his trust for granted, at a time when they were busy bargaining with other Arabs for their friendship. In the summer of 1941, Abdullah's Arab Legion, having just returned from Iraq, was willingly sent to help the British and the Free French drive the Vichy forces out of Syria. Two years later, both Syria and Lebanon had been granted complete political independence, while Transjordan remained under British mandate. The status of the country was still unchanged when the Arab League was formally constituted in Cairo in May 1945, with Transjordan as a founding member. The formation of the League had been engineered by Nuri al-Said of Iraq and the Egyptian premier, Mustafa Nahhas, in co-operation with the British foreign minister Anthony Eden. Its charter emphasized the individual sovereignty of the member states at the expense of the idea of unity, which was seen by Abdullah as a blow to his Greater Syria scheme. As he later put it in his memoirs, the Arab League was no more than 'a sack into which seven heads had been speedily thrust'.

* * * * * * * * *

It was only after the war was over in both Europe and the Far East that Abdullah was finally invited to Britain by the new Labour government for treaty talks. An Anglo-American committee had been sent to the Middle East towards the end of 1945 to try to work out an acceptable solution for Palestine, and the British foreign minister, Ernest Bevin, thought it appropriate to attend to the question of Transjordan at the same time. Abdullah arrived in London at the end of February 1946, and his negotiations with the British government ended with the conclusion of a new Anglo-Transjordanian Treaty on 22 March. By the terms of this treaty, Transjordan was finally to become an independent country, maintaining perpetual peace and friendship with Britain. In a special annex to the treaty, Transjordan agreed to provide Britain with military facilities on her territory in return for continued British subsidy and support for the Arab Legion. On 15 May, six weeks after the return of Abdullah to Amman, the Transjordanian cabinet took the decision to change his title from Emir to King. This decision was approved by the parliament on 22 May. At the same parliamentary session, the name of the country was officially changed from Transjordan to Jordan.

Abdullah's detractors in the Arab world scoffed at the independence he had finally managed to achieve, belittling its importance, and treating the emir's assumption of the royal title as a joke. The Syrian government of the time was particularly petty in its attitude: on the day of Abdullah's coronation, it tried to spoil the occasion by stopping a truckload of fruit for the official luncheon from crossing the border. More serious difficulties, however, came from other directions. In Palestine, Zionist leaders who stuck to the doctrine that Transjordan was part of the historical Jewish homeland were opposed to the country's independence in principle, and their lobby in the United States pressured the American government into delaying recognition. The Soviet Union, which regarded Abdullah as a bulwark of western imperialism in the Middle East, raised strong objections regarding the military annex to the Anglo-Jordanian treaty, arguing that its terms consecrated Jordan as a permanent British military base in the area. Consequently, the Soviets not only withheld recognition of the country's independence, as the Americans did, but also blocked the admission of Jordan to the United Nations.

Although the borders between the different Arab states of the Middle East had hardened considerably by this time, talk of Arab political unity was still in the air. Different unification schemes – unitary or federal – were advanced, some backed by the British, others by the Americans. At a time when Soviet propaganda had become a factor to reckon with in the Middle East, both London and Washington had come round to the idea that the encouragement of pan-Arab nationalism was the best way to check the spread of communism in the Arab world. Bids for pan-Arab leadership were made from different directions, and money was invested in the competition by the parties concerned. Ibn Saud, from Riyadh, had his eye on Syria, and did not consider the Hashemite monarchy in Transjordan a serious obstacle in his way. Nuri al-Said, from Baghdad, proposed the unification of the countries of the Fertile Crescent under the leadership of the Hashemites of Iraq. When the Arab Cultural Club was founded in Beirut in 1945, to propagate the idea of pan-Arab nationalism at the intellectual level, the Saudis and the Iraqis vied with each other in offering to provide this club with material and moral sponsorship, which left the founders of the club at a loss as to which of the two offers to accept.[4] Egypt was yet another serious contender for pan-Arab leadership, especially after the Egyptian capital became the seat of the Arab League: King Farouk, in Cairo, grew a beard, to enhance his chances of being accepted as an Arab caliph.

Given the political atmosphere of the period, the Greater Syria scheme which King Abdullah continued to press from Amman was no more quixotic than other Arab unity proposals. Had it not been for the highly personal manner in which Abdullah advanced it, it would have been the least quixotic. What further militated against it was the marginal significance of Jordan as an Arab state, and also the fact that Abdullah lacked the money to back his scheme against other, better-funded, pan-Arab schemes. Also, the Lebanese and the Syrians, as already indicated, were not in the least prepared to accept the Jordanian king as their ruler, losing their newly acquired sovereignty in the process, along with their cherished status as republics. Royalist and pro-Hashemite sentiments were not entirely lacking among the Syrians and the Muslims in Lebanon, but where such sentiments still existed, they were clearly geared towards Iraq rather than Jordan. The only significant body of people in Syria and Lebanon who actually veered in the direction of Amman were the members of a relatively small pan-Syrian party known as the PPS (*Parti Populaire Syrien*). The weight of this party in Syrian and Lebanese politics was too slight to really count. The PPS, moreover, was republican rather than monarchist in sentiment, and its Syrian nationalism, apart from being staunchly secularist, was also particularist rather than pan-Arab. The party, therefore, co-operated with Abdullah only because his concept of Greater Syria was geographically identical with its own, and for no other reason.

All that Abdullah achieved by continuing to press for his Greater Syria scheme was the further alienation of the Lebanese and

Syrians, who opposed the plan, and the Egyptians and Saudis who had no wish to see the Jordanian king expand his dominion and enhance his bid for regional leadership. With the Iraqis, Abdullah could reach a minimum of political understanding through the Hashemite connection, although his relations with Nuri al-Said continued to be somewhat strained. Otherwise, the king found himself isolated in the Arab world, with the Syrians, the Lebanese, the Egyptians and the Saudis aligned against him. Abdullah, however, remained undaunted. In the summer of 1947, he went to the extent of actually calling for a pan-Syrian conference, to lay the grounds for setting up a Greater Syria government as a first step towards an Arab union of Greater Syria with Iraq. The call was loudly denounced as a breach of the Arab League covenant by the four states aligned against Abdullah. Even Iraq distanced herself from the project. There was talk at the time of the Arab League censuring the king, or even expelling his country from its ranks.

In the Middle East, however, international attention after the war was focusing not so much on the details of inter-Arab relations, as on the unresolved problem of Palestine. On 20 April 1946, about a month before Abdullah's coronation, the Anglo-American committee on Palestine had completed its report, suggesting that the country remain under British mandate pending arrangements for a trusteeship by the United Nations. Jordan had joined the other members of the Arab League in opposing this recommendation. The Jordanian prime minister, Ibrahim Hashim, chaired an extraordinary session of the Arab League council in the Syrian summer resort of Bludan, on 18 May, where the Anglo-American report was unanimously condemned. Jordan also joined the other Arab states in rejecting a subsequent plan to introduce federal government to Palestine while the Anglo-American report was being implemented. Arab opinion demanded the immediate independence of Palestine as a unitary Arab state; and although the Arab governments were fully aware that this was not possible, they felt constrained to abide with the popular will. The Jordanian government, for its part, realized that the rejection of the Anglo-American proposals could only lead to partition. Amman, however, had been receiving repeated intimations that, should partition take place, the Arab parts of Palestine would go to Jordan.

At the same Bludan conference where the Anglo-American report was condemned, the Arab League took the decision to form a new Arab Executive Committee to represent the Palestinians, with Hajj Amin as its chairman. Since the end of the war, Hajj Amin had been stranded in France as a fugitive; but he had left France a week before the Bludan conference was convened, and his whereabouts at the time of the conference were unknown. He ultimately arrived in Egypt towards the end of May, but his arrival was kept a secret for three weeks, and it was only on 20 June that his presence in the Egyptian capital was dramatically announced by the press. King Abdullah, in Amman, had to brace himself for a new encounter with his old adversary.

Having failed to persuade the Arab League to accept the Anglo-American proposals, the British government invited the Arabs and the Jews to London once again to discuss the future of Palestine. As in 1938, the British had to negotiate with each side separately, since the Arab delegates – now as before – made it a point not to sit in open session with the Jews. When this second London conference failed, Britain referred the problem to the United Nations, where a special international body was organized to deal with it: the United Nations Special Committee on Palestine, or UNSCOP, as it was called. The findings of UNSCOP, which were published at the end of August, were divided between a majority report recommending partition, and a minority report recommending federalization. The Arab governments were in no position to favour either recommendation, so that the UNSCOP findings were unanimously rejected, part and parcel, by the Arab League. The Jews, for their part, naturally favoured the majority report, and pressured Washington to help force it through. On 29 November 1947, the United States secured the adoption of the UNSCOP recommendation to partition Palestine by a narrow margin, with Britain abstaining. Once the partition resolution was passed, Britain announced her intention to end her civil administration of Palestine on 15 May 1948 and evacuate her military forces from the country. The message was clear. On the day assigned, nothing would stop the Jews from proclaiming their state in Palestine. The Arabs had that much time, and no more, to prepare for the eventuality. King Abdullah of Jordan was the only one already prepared.

* * * * * * * * * *

According to the United Nations partition plan, Palestine was to be divided more or less equally between the proposed Arab and Jewish states, but the lines of division were complicated. In the north, the Arabs were to have the western sector of Galilee, including the adjoining strip of coast, while the inland sector, bordering Syria and Jordan, was to go to the Jews. In the central parts of the country, it was the other way round: the Jews were to have the coastal parts, from the north of Haifa to the south of Jaffa, while the inland highlands were to go mostly to the Arabs, except for a United Nations zone comprising the city of Jerusalem and its environs. In the southern regions, which were mostly desert, the division was to be the same as in the north, with the coastal parts around Gaza going to the Arabs, and the inland parts to the Jews. Thus, the proposed Jewish and Arab states were each to consist of three alternate stretches of territory, unconnected one to the other except at the points of juncture. The Arabs were opposed to the partition altogether, and thought they could prevent it by war. The Jews were unhappy with the partition plan itself, which denied them Jerusalem, and left the territory allotted to them lacking in compactness.

The decision of the United Nations to partition Palestine was met with a loud public outcry in the Arab world, with demonstrators taking to the streets in every Arab capital, calling upon Arab governments to stir themselves into action. Ordinary Arabs were convinced that the Jews stood no chance of getting away with their allotted share of Palestine if the Arab states made the necessary military effort to stop them. During the autumn and winter of 1947–8, the Arab League was in virtually continuous session, trying to agree on a concerted strategy for this purpose; but mutual suspicions among the member states made such agreement difficult to reach. What further complicated matters was that the established regimes in Egypt, Syria and Iraq – the three Arab states which were most vocal in opposing the partition – each faced serious internal problems. This left their respective governments unable to decide whether it served them better to send adequate forces to Palestine, and thereby redeem their questioned reputations as nationalists, or whether to keep their best forces at home for internal security purposes. The Jordanian government, by contrast, was in firm control of its home ground, and could therefore afford to deploy the full force of the Arab Legion in Palestine.

Since 1941, Jordan's Arab Legion had been built up into an effective fighting force of nearly 7,500 officers and men, composed of three mechanized regiments and sixteen infantry companies under the experienced command of Lieutenant-General Glubb (see Chapter 5). While Egypt and Iraq had larger armies, the Arab Legion, with its mixed British and Arab officer corps, was a far more disciplined body, with the additional advantage of superior training and equipment. The Arab League, however, was only willing to accept a Jordanian military intervention in Palestine within the context of a joint Arab intervention. The Palestinian Arabs, moreover, following the directives of Hajj Amin from Cairo, were opposed to Jordanian intervention. Just before the partition of Palestine was decided by the General Assembly of the United Nations, King Abdullah had actually proposed to send his Arab Legion to take charge of the defence of the Arabs of Palestine in the event of a British withdrawal, but the Arab Executive Committee in Jerusalem had bluntly turned down his offer. The Palestinian Arabs were willing, and in fact anxious, to receive disinterested Arab help from whatever direction it came, but they were resolved, for better or for worse, to keep their destiny in their own hands.

From the Palestinian Arab point of view, what counted at that decisive moment was the principle rather than the details. They considered the United Nations decision to partition their country a gross injustice which must not be allowed to pass. In any case, the Arabs of Palestine, unlike the Jews, were poorly prepared to establish an independent state on their allotted share of the Palestinian territory. Their Arab Executive Committee had none of the attributes of the Jewish Agency which had been acting as a parallel government in Palestine since 1929. Moreover, the Arab Executive Committee lacked a defence force comparable to the Jewish Haganah, whose ranks were swelled after 1945 by veterans of the war-time Jewish Legion of the British Army. The Palestinian Arab forces which did exist were the remnants of the guerrilla groups which had fought the British and the Jews in the 1930s; and while these were brave men who could gather around them new recruits of equal mettle, it was inconceivable that they could be transformed with the required speed into disciplined troops answering to a central command. As the committee made an effort in this direction by formally organizing these Palestinian fighters into what was called the 'Army of Holy War' (*Jaysh al-Jihad al-Muqaddas*), the Arab League sought to abort the committee's move by sponsoring the creation of a special 'Army of Deliverance' (*Jaysh al-Inqadh*), a ramshackle body of about 5,000 volunteers from different Arab countries, including some Palestinians, which so discredited itself from the moment it went into action that it came to be referred to as the 'Army of Ruination' (*Jaysh al-Anqad* – literally, the 'army of ruins').

More important, however, was the fact that neither the British nor the Americans wanted the Palestinian Arabs to establish an independent state in the parts of the country allotted to them. Under the leadership of someone like Hajj Amin, such a Palestinian state, it was believed, would be a hotbed of trouble if it survived, and a cause of serious embarrassment to Western relations with the Arab world if it collapsed, leaving its territory to be absorbed into the Jewish state. The reasonable alternative, it was thought, was to have King Abdullah take over the Arab parts of Palestine, especially as he had the military means to do so. The British government had already been sounding him on the matter before the partition of Palestine was decided by the United Nations. At a closed meeting held in February 1948, in London, between Ernest Bevin and the Jordanian prime minister Tewfik Abul-Huda, the British foreign minister virtually invited Jordan to take over the Arab share of Palestine.[5]

Abdullah, for his part, was hesitant to send his Arab Legion into Palestine unless the Palestinians invited him, or the Arab League agreed that he should do so. Privately, he was convinced that partition was the best solution to the Palestinian problem; but he was resolved this time to go along with the Arab League and openly oppose the partition, until the futility of this negative stand was amply demonstrated. In 1937, he had exposed himself to general Arab castigation by declaring his approval of the partition proposed by the Peel commission, on the grounds that he had done so because he stood to benefit by it. This time, he thought it better to wait until his intervention was solicited by the other Arab parties concerned.

Given the speed of developments, however, the king did not have to wait long. In January 1948, the Arab League's Army of

Deliverance entered the Arab parts of Palestine in the region of Nablus, Tulkarm and Jenin; but when it proceeded to attack two Jewish positions nearby, its forces were so badly routed that the local Arab villagers had to come to their rescue. The Palestine Army of Holy War, which had gone into operation in the preceding month in the Jerusalem and Jaffa regions, had held its ground much better; but this was at a time when the Jews were still preoccupied with consolidating their positions within their allotted share of the Palestinian territory. By March, the situation suddenly changed when Jewish forces began to seize strategic positions in territory which was supposed to go to the Arabs. In April, Jewish terrorists of the Irgun and Stern groups began to attack Arab villages to frighten their inhabitants away, the worst of these attacks being the one launched by the Irgun group on Deir Yasin, along the road from Jerusalem to Jaffa, where 254 unarmed villagers were indiscriminately massacred. While the Jewish Agency disclaimed responsibility for these attacks, the fear that they would become a regular feature of Jewish tactics drove streams of terrified and helpless Arab villagers in the direction of Jordan – the nearest place where they could find refuge. By now, the Arab League's Army of Deliverance had so discredited itself that the Arab states no longer had any excuse to stay away from direct involvement.

King Abdullah now took the initiative, offering to rescue Palestine on his own, or else take charge of a concerted Arab intervention. Units of his Arab Legion were already in Palestine at the time, guarding British supply lines to facilitate the British withdrawal which had already started. Hajj Amin and the Syrians would not agree to the suggested Jordanian intervention, but the Arab League overruled their objections and agreed to have Abdullah take charge of the situation, provided he was prepared to reject partition and declare his intention to take over the whole of Palestine – an aim which all the Arab countries combined proved ultimately unable to achieve. When the Arab Legion finally did intervene, the British warned that its deployment should be restricted to areas assigned to the Arabs; otherwise, the British subsidy and detailment of officers for the Legion would be subject to reconsideration. Even in the areas where it was free to operate, the Legion had to take into account the vast military superiority of the Jewish forces, already numbering 74,000. Its command, as well as Abdullah himself, had to negotiate with the Jewish authorities time and time again to limit Jordanian losses in threatened areas.

* * * * * * * * * *

The British mandate in Palestine came to an end on 15 May, as planned, whereupon the Jews immediately proclaimed the birth of their state, which they called Israel. By this time, they had captured the key towns of Tiberias, Haifa, Safad and Jaffa within the areas assigned to them by the partition; but they had also cut the road between Hebron and Jerusalem in an area assigned to the Arabs. In their declaration of independence, they made a point of not indicating the borders of their state, which they hoped to expand beyond the limits set for them by the United Nations, should circumstances permit. The units of the Arab Legion which had been assisting in the British evacuation had meanwhile returned home, except for one infantry company which was left behind, isolated in Hebron, within the territory allotted to the Arabs.

By the terms of the partition, Jerusalem was to be the centre of a United Nations zone, as already indicated, and its Arab inhabitants trusted that the place would be inviolate. As the last British troops were evacuating the city, however, Jewish forces made a thrust through Arab quarters in an attempt to capture the historical walled town. This provided the signal for the immediate return of the Arab Legion to Palestine in full force. The Jordanian troops, commanded by Glubb, took up positions in the hills around Nablus and Ramallah, in the Arab areas north of Jerusalem. Considering that the Jews had started an offensive in Jerusalem in defiance of the special status assigned to the holy city, and that the United Nations did not hasten to stop them, there was nothing to restrain the Arab Legion from sending its own forces to push the Jews back. On the orders of Abdullah, the Legion started its counter-offensive in earnest on 19 May, entrenching itself in the walled town, and taking up a strong defence position at Latrun, west of Jerusalem, to cut the main road to the city from Jaffa and Tel Aviv. By the end of the month, when the United Nations finally intervened to impose a cease-fire, the battle for Jerusalem had ended in stalemate, leaving the

Jordanian forces in full control of the historical parts of the holy city and the adjacent Arab quarters.

Two days before the termination of the mandate, a meeting of the Arab League political committee in Amman had confirmed that Lebanon, Syria, Iraq and Egypt would send troops to Palestine to join forces with the Arab Legion under the supreme command of Abdullah; but when these troops began to arrive from their different directions, each army took its orders from its own commanders, and there was no co-ordination among them. Iraq alone co-operated with Jordan by sending troops to hold the Nablus region, while the Arab Legion concentrated on the defence of Jerusalem. Meanwhile, one column of the Egyptian army advanced along the Palestinian coast to Isdud, north of Gaza, while another column advanced inland to Hebron and Bethlehem, where the Egyptian forces became engaged in a petty contest with the Arab Legion for the control of these positions. The refusal of the Egyptians to co-ordinate properly with the Jordanians in this area was later to facilitate the Jewish takeover of all the territory assigned to the Arabs south of the Hebron region, leaving the Egyptians by the end of the war with no more than a narrow strip of coast terminating just north of Gaza. In the north, attempts by the Lebanese and Syrian armies to make an advance into Palestinian territory met with little success, and were repulsed beyond the international borders in the later stages of the fighting, leaving the Jews with the whole of Galilee.

Of the Arab armies deployed in the war for Palestine, the one that lost least ground in actual fighting was Jordan's Arab Legion. With some help from Iraq, the Legion succeeded in saving for the Arabs a major part of their share of the country – the territory subsequently called the West Bank – along with the historical sector of Jerusalem, which the Jews had tried but failed to seize. The Jordanian intervention, however, was beset from the very start with political difficulties, not least of them the fact that the highly creditable performance of the Arab Legion in Jerusalem made Palestinian opinion, and Arab opinion in general, expect far more from it militarily than it could in fact deliver. Apart from being a relatively small force, trying to hold its ground against Jewish forces which were far superior in number and better equipped, the Legion had no reserves of troops on which it could depend in cases of emergency, and a United Nations embargo which was strictly observed by Britain left its forces perpetually short of ammunition. Its war strategy in the circumstances had to be pursued with great economy. In the second round of the war, when the Legion was unable to defend Lydda and Ramla, between Jaffa and Jerusalem, the fall of these two towns was attributed by Arab opinion to alleged collusion between Glubb and the Jews; and Glubb was compelled to accept public reprimand from Abdullah for his failure to defend them, in order to protect the king from the public outrage. Towards the end of the hostilities, when Abdullah, in his anxiety to secure a quick armistice, agreed to abandon a strategic strip of Arab territory to the Jews in the north, in return for a minor gain of territory in the south, this action, which Glubb considered unnecessary, was loudly protested not only by the inhabitants of the abandoned strip, but also throughout the Arab world. Abdullah, it was generally believed, had acted purely in self-interest. He had been in such a hurry to add the Palestinian territory under Jordanian occupation to his kingdom that he was ready, it was said, to make any sacrifice of principle to hasten the process.

Abdullah's Arab neighbours were unhappy with the credible presence he was able to establish for himself in Palestine during the course of the war. After the capture of Old Jerusalem, when Jordan's standing with Arab opinion was at its highest, the king travelled to Egypt, Saudi Arabia and Iraq to allay Arab fears regarding his aims. While in Egypt, he had a private meeting with Hajj Amin. It was the only occasion after 1936 when the two men met, and there were no reports of what exactly was said between them. Most probably, it was a polite exchange of diametrically opposed political views, ending with some sort of *entente*, on the basis of 'may the better man win'. Shortly after Abdullah's return to Amman, however, the Arab League created a Palestine Administrative Council answerable to Hajj Amin, which was transformed by September 1948 into a Government of All Palestine, with its seat in Gaza. At least one Arab statesman, the Lebanese foreign minister Hamid Frangieh, frankly admitted that the chief aim of creating this nominal Palestinian government in Egyptian-occupied Gaza was to thwart Abdullah's ambitions to absorb Arab parts of Palestine into Jordan. With the help of Egypt, the Gaza government began to sponsor and arm guerrilla fighters in the parts of Palestine under Jordanian occupation, to create problems for Abdullah and his Arab Legion.

Abdullah, in Amman, responded forcefully to the creation of the Government of All Palestine. He broke the Arab League consensus by refusing to recognize it, and convened a conference of his Palestinian supporters in the Jordanian capital to denounce it and demand the unification of Arab Palestine with Jordan. Hajj Amin and his partisans scoffed at the Amman conference, which they did not consider in the least representative of true Palestinian Arab opinion; but they were not able to do so for long. The month after the Government of All Palestine was formed, it was forced to withdraw to Cairo, as the Egyptian defeat in southern Palestine in October 1948 brought the Israeli forces to the outskirts of Gaza. Having lost its only foothold in the land over which it claimed legitimate jurisdiction, the Government of All Palestine rapidly lost its effectiveness and ceased to be a serious political obstacle in Abdullah's way. By December, the king was able to convene a conference, in Jericho, of Palestinian notables of the Jordanian-occupied areas to acclaim the absorption of these areas into Jordan in principle.

In the long, drawn-out contest between King Abdullah and Hajj Amin, Abdullah by now was clearly emerging as the winner. In his moment of triumph, however, the king made a point of being gracious to his defeated rival, and Hajj Amin acknowledged this fact in his reminiscences:

There were no personal differences between King Abdullah and myself; only differences in point of view and political principle. The private relations between us were marked by affection and friendship. . . . His Majesty . . . wrote me a very kind letter towards the end of 1948, expressing his desire that I return to the country, and his readiness to give me any post I wanted. I replied to thank him . . . and assure him that I have no interest in any post, nor any personal demand. All I asked was that His Majesty attend to the fortification of the mountain areas of Palestine, now under the administration of the Jordanian government, from Hebron in the south to Jenin in the north . . . and that he get the people of the land organized, trained and armed to defend it. . . . Then, I could return to the country as an ordinary citizen.[6]

The war in Palestine came to an end in March–April 1949 with a succession of armistice agreements negotiated and signed in

Rhodes between the different Arab parties and Israel. Iraq alone refused to go to Rhodes, so as not to acknowledge defeat. It could afford such a position, because it had no common boundary with Israel. The armistice agreement between Jordan and Israel was signed on 3 April, leaving Jordan in unchallenged occupation of what remained of the Arab parts of Palestine west of the Jordan river and the Dead Sea, while the Egyptians retained control of what remained in their hands of the Gaza strip.

In the spring of 1950, a year after the Jordanian–Israeli armistice, elections were held for a new Jordanian parliament in which the Palestinians of the West Bank were represented. At the first business meeting of the new parliament, on 25 April, the expected motion to unite the 'two banks of the Jordan' was presented by a Palestinian deputy and passed unanimously. The Hashemite Kingdom of Jordan, having been constitutionally expanded to include the West Bank, now had a total population of nearly a million and a half people, of whom less than half a million were Transjordanians, the rest being Palestinians. More than half a million of the latter were refugees, living for the most part in camps: about 400,000 among the Palestinians of the West Bank, and 100,000 among the Transjordanians on the East Bank. All, however, automatically became Jordanian citizens, the majority accepting the fact grudgingly. The right to Jordanian citizenship was also offered at the time to all Palestinians who wished to claim it, wherever they happened to be. No other Arab government made a similar move.

The Arab League had in fact ruled that Palestinians should not be granted citizen status by the Arab countries which hosted them as refugees, lest they lose their claim to their lost homeland which the League, in theory, was going to help them redeem. Jordan had acted against the League consensus by turning the resident Palestinians of Transjordan and the West Bank into Jordanians, and, even more blatantly, by accepting other diaspora Palestinians as Jordanian citizens. By acting against the League directives, however, Jordan offered the possibility of normal life for many people who would otherwise have remained stateless refugees. While agreeing with the Arab League that the Jordanian action in this regard was wrong in principle, even members of the Arab Executive Committee outside Palestine – including leading partisans of Hajj Amin – converged on Amman to become citizens of Jordan, where a number of them entered the government service to become leading members of the Jordanian ruling establishment. Hajj Amin himself was among the few who preferred to stay in exile. He ultimately moved to Lebanon, where he remained until his death in 1974.[7]

In Jordan, however, most Palestinians continued to nurse negative feelings about King Abdullah. They held him chiefly responsible for their plight as a people, and no argument could convince them to the contrary. In their eagerness to dissociate themselves from any blame for the loss of Palestine, other Arab rulers encouraged the Palestinians to point to the Jordanian king as the prime culprit, making great issue of the fact that he alone had ended up as a real gainer. Consequently, every move he had made with respect to the Palestine question since 1929, and more particularly since 1947, was analysed down to the last detail and given the worst possible interpretation. With every passing day, the conviction that King Abdullah had deliberately betrayed the Palestinian Arab cause to achieve personal ambitions became more deeply ingrained in the Palestinian mind. Palestinian extremists believed that the King of Jordan was one Arab ruler who richly deserved to be singled out for punishment.

Ever since the capture of Old Jerusalem by the Arab Legion, King Abdullah had made it a point to visit the city on Fridays as regularly as possible to join in the prayers in the Aqsa mosque. Friday, 20 July 1951, was one such occasion, but on that day Abdullah was strongly urged to make an exception and stay at home. One person who actually went to the palace to warn the king against going to the mosque was the United States ambassador in Amman. Shortly before, the Lebanese prime minister Riyad al-Solh, who had been on an official visit to the Jordanian capital, had been shot dead on his way to the airport.[8] The reason why Solh was assassinated had nothing to do with Jordan, but the event was nonetheless considered ominous.

Ignoring all warnings, King Abdullah arrived in Jerusalem on Thursday, accompanied by his grandson Hussein, and proceeded the following day to the Aqsa as usual – first, to visit the tomb of his father; then to join in the Friday prayers. As he was about to enter the mosque, a young Palestinian armed with a pistol stepped out of the crowd of worshippers at the entrance and moved swiftly towards the king, killing him instantly with one shot in the head.

NOTES

1. Quoted by Zuhayr Mardini, *op. cit.*, pp. 112–13.
2. Nuri al-Said, in 1936, intervened to replace Abdullah, rather than to reinforce his position, as the chief intermediary between the Arab Executive Committee and the British administration in Palestine over the question of the general strike (see Chapter 6); but his efforts at mediation, like Abdullah's, ended in failure.
3. Alec Kirkbride, *A Crackle of Thorns* (London, 1957), pp. 130–35.
4. I personally recall a debate over this issue between family friends in Ras Beirut who were among the founders of this club.
5. For a detailed account of the negotiations of Abdullah with the British government and the Jewish Agency behind the scenes, starting from the meeting in London between Bevin and Abul–Huda, see Avi Shlaim, *Collusion across the Jordan*, pp. 132–95.
6. From the reminiscences of Hajj Amin, as recorded in *Haqa'iq 'an Qadiyyat Falastin* (Cairo, 1957), pp. 77–8.
7. King Hussein, in 1961, invited Hajj Amin to return to Jordan, but he declined the invitation. In March 1967, while visiting Jordan to see Jerusalem for the last time, Hajj Amin was accorded a royal welcome in Amman by King Hussein, who urged him to stay in the country; but the mufti preferred to return to Lebanon.
8. Solh was assassinated by a Lebanese member of the PPS. This party, which had attempted a coup in Lebanon in 1949, held Solh personally responsible for the execution of its founder and leader, Antun Saadeh, after the failure of his attempted coup.

8
Learning the Game of Nations

Viewed in retrospect, the assassination of King Abdullah in 1951 was not an isolated event, but one in a series of Arab political murders which followed the Second World War, and more particularly the débâcle in Palestine.[1] The same period also witnessed political upheavals in a number of Arab countries. The first took place in Syria, where an army colonel, Husni al-Zaim, overthrew the constitutional government and seized power by a military coup on 30 March 1949, only to be overthrown and killed on 14 August of the same year when a similar coup was carried out against him. These two coups, following one another in quick succession, set the pattern for Syrian politics for nearly two decades. In Egypt, repeated riots and incidents of violence, which included the assassination of a number of leading public figures, among them two prime ministers, and the burning of Cairo, culminated on 23 July 1952 with the dethronement of King Farouk by the Free Officers of the army. This paved the way for the subsequent transformation of Egypt into a military republic, first under General Muhammad Naguib, then under Colonel Gamal Abdul-Nasser, commonly known in the West as Nasser. In September of that same year, the so-called 'rose water revolution' in Beirut forced the president of the Lebanese Republic, Bishara al-Khoury, to resign from office, to be replaced by Camille Chamoun – a change achieved for once by parliamentary action, without any intervention from the army. In Iraq, the nationalist feeling which had followed the suppression of the anti-British revolt of 1941 continued to simmer underground for eighteen years. On 14 July 1958, it exploded with phenomenal violence when an army coup, led by Brigadiers Abdul-Karim Kassem and Abdul-Salam Aref, resulted not only in the replacement of the Iraqi monarchy by the first of a succession of military republics, but also in the brutal murder of the entire royal family, along with the veteran prime minister Nuri al-Said and others. What was surprising during those highly turbulent times was not that King Abdullah should have been murdered, but that his succession to the Hashemite throne in Amman – first by his son Talal, then by his grandson Hussein – should have been as orderly and constitutional as it was.

The turbulence of this period in the various Arab countries can be explained by popular dissatisfactions and frustrations with the Arab state system dating back to the 1920s. By 1949, the failure of Arab governments to prevent the emergence of Israel by a concerted military effort had transformed these dissatisfactions into a general rage which ideologists and political adventurers could easily exploit. The Arab troubles of those years, however, were also caused by fundamental political changes on the international scene, which played havoc with the Arab order as originally established by Britain and France.

By the end of the Second World War, the United States had emerged as the world's supreme power, challenged only by the Soviet Union. Consequently, the Americans after 1945 were determined to indicate to the British and the French that their days as major world powers were over, and that they had henceforth to follow American directives, in the Middle East as elsewhere. France had already lost her former control over Syria and Lebanon. Britain, however, still retained a strong position not only in Jordan but also in Egypt and Iraq, as well as in South Arabia and the emirates and sheikhdoms of the Gulf. Local British officials, along with many Arabs, perceived the United States as set on destabilizing Britain's position in these countries, and suspected it of encouraging nationalist agitation against the British presence. Meanwhile the Soviet Union, eager to gain political access to the Middle East, launched open attacks on the British position in the region, exploiting the revolutionary situation which existed there, using communist ideology as the principal weapon. Britain, for its part, took a strong stand against the increasing Russian influence – partly in self-defence and partly to prove its regional usefulness to the United States. Accordingly, the British set out to promote a system of regional alliances directed against the Soviet Union. The Americans, however, had enough confidence in their supremacy not to take the communist threat to their interests in the area as seriously as they pretended. While they openly attacked the Soviet Union and denounced communism, they appeared at the same time to be intent on heckling the British in the Middle East. This left many people convinced that the United States secretly condoned the Russian regional infiltration, as one way to get Britain out. Among those who held this view was Lieutenant-General Glubb in Amman:

Many Americans are genuinely imbued with deep suspicions of Britain and her attitude to the people of Asia. . . . The American people are . . . suspicious of British 'colonial methods'. . . . Some people would have us believe that American Big Business is deliberately endeavouring to oust Britain from all Asia and Africa, in order itself to be able to exploit these countries without a competitor. . . . Americans have little or no appreciation of the immense amount of love and benevolence which . . . Englishmen have devoted to many Eastern races. If, in reality, big American financial interests are striving to destroy Britain's position, will their 'exploitation' be in reality more benevolent? It is certainly striking how often the USA seems to lead the attack on Britain's position in some Eastern country – it is even more remarkable how often the USA and Russia speak with one voice in attacking Britain. . . . In the Arab countries, America is believed to be Britain's worst enemy. I remember well a prominent Arab personality saying to me that he could not understand why Britain was always worrying about Russia. 'Believe me, Pasha,' he said, 'Britain has one enemy in the Middle East, and that enemy is the USA. The Americans will never rest until they have destroyed Britain's position.'[2]

Actually, this negative American attitude towards the British in the Middle East was not new, having started with the scramble for the oil of the region which followed the First World War. In 1914, shortly before the outbreak of that war, an enterprising Armenian, Calouste Gulbenkian, had organized a Turkish Petroleum Company (TPC) to exploit the oil resources of Iraq. Almost half the shares were owned by the Anglo-Persian Oil Company, which the British government came to control. The other half were divided between Royal Dutch Shell, which was an Anglo-Dutch concern, and the German *Deutsche Bank*. At the San Remo Conference of 1920, the German share in the company was confiscated and given to the *Compagnie Française des Pétroles*. This turned the TPC into a British, French and Dutch consortium. The Americans, who took no part in the San Remo talks, had been expecting to be accorded a share in this regional consortium of international oil interests without formally asking for it. The United States, since 1918, had been projecting an image of itself as the bulwark of idealism in world politics, and was reluctant for the time being to tarnish this image by open bickering with her European associates over questions such as oil.

Thus, rather than openly demanding a share in the projected arrangements for the exploitation of the oil of Iraq, the United States tried to force the hands of France and Britain over this issue by stepping in to champion Arab national demands in the region against French and British imperial ambitions. The venue for this American political intervention was the King–Crane commission which was sent by President Woodrow Wilson to Syria in 1919, ostensibly to discover how the Arabs envisaged their political future. Of the two heads of this commission, the second, Charles Crane, was a Chicago businessman who had close connections with American oil concerns.[3] Like many Americans of his generation, Crane appears also to have been a genuine idealist, convinced that the United States had a role to play in helping the less fortunate nations of the world determine their own destinies. He certainly succeeded in winning Arab confidence in his country. According to the King–Crane findings, the first preference of the Arab people was for complete national independence. However, they were prepared to accept an American mandate if national independence was not immediately forthcoming. If forced to choose between a British or a French mandate, they would reluctantly opt for the former, considering the latter to be out of the question.

Openly denounced by France as an Anglo-Saxon conspiracy, and accorded cavalier treatment by the British, the King–Crane report was ignored at the San Remo conference which divided the territories of Syria and Iraq into French and British mandates. But this report did serve another purpose: that of convincing the Arabs that the United States was their only true friend among the world powers. Meanwhile, Syrian Arabs who had been associated with the King–Crane investigations were sent on political missions to peninsular Arabia, to establish contacts with the leading potentates of the region and win them over, wherever possible, to the American side.

The British, however, did not take long to get the message. In 1922, they divided their share in the Iraqi oil consortium with the

Americans, who thus became equal partners in the TPC. Before the end of the decade, the company was renamed the IPC, or Iraq Petroleum Company. By then, a newly formed company called the British Eastern Syndicate had secured a concession for the oil of Bahrain, which was later sold to an American company, Standard Oil of California. Another American company, Gulf Oil, had meanwhile secured a concession for the oil of Kuwait. These two American companies were both outsiders to the IPC. Shortly after, in 1928, the so-called Red Line Agreement was concluded between the IPC partners, whereby none of them could seek oil concessions in the former territories of the Ottoman empire (interpreted to include the whole Arab region east of Egypt, barring Kuwait and Bahrain) except through IPC channels. With American concerns owning nearly a quarter of IPC, and others holding concessions outside the area marked out by the Red Line Agreement, the United States could finally feel confident of having guaranteed a substantial American share of the region's oil.

By this time, the assignment of the King–Crane Commission had long been over. However, Charles Crane had remained in personal contact with his Syrian Arab associates, encouraging the nationalist spirit among them. One of these was George Antonius, a Christian of Lebanese origin and an official of the British government in Palestine, who became the author of the standard history of the Arab national movement in its formative years. This remarkable book was published in 1938 under the title *The Arab Awakening*, and was, in fact, dedicated to Charles Crane. Meanwhile, the American University of Beirut, or AUB, originally established in 1866 as the Syrian Protestant College, had become the stronghold of the new, American-inspired brand of Arab nationalism. The American administration of the AUB actually made a point of encouraging pan-Arab activism among its students. More important, however, was the fact that this university, as the most prestigious academic institution in the Arab world, attracted students from all Arab countries – in most cases, the pick of the local crop. As the activists among these students graduated and returned home, they came to form a network for political activism which covered the whole area.

* * * * * * * * * *

In 1919, the year when the King–Crane commission arrived in Syria, a pan-Arab student society called *al-'Urwa al-Wuthqa* (meaning the 'Firm Handhold') was established at the AUB. This society, after 1936, became the leading student platform for a pan-Arab political party called the *'Usba* (*'Usbat al-'Amal al-Qawmi* or League of Nationalist Action), whose set aims were to press for Arab national independence, and to keep aspirations for Arab national unity alive and strong in the face of increasing trends towards regional particularism. Among the founders of the 'Usba, in 1936, were veterans of the Arab Revolt who had served under Abdullah during the early years of the Transjordanian emirate (see Chapter 6), and had since maintained a strong dislike for the Hashemite emir and his regime. This dislike began to colour the political stand of the 'Usba more intensely after 1941, when Abdullah helped the British crush the revolt in Iraq (see Chapter 7), in which leading members of the 'Usba were involved. After that year, in fact, the stance of the party became anti-Hashemite in general.

By this time, the 'Usba, as a party, had started to disintegrate. But a nuclear group of its members, many of them graduates or students of the AUB, had meanwhile organized themselves as a secret fraternity. This clandestine body, called *Harakat al-Qawmiyyin al-'Arab* (Movement of Arab Nationalists), had its principal cell in Beirut, around the AUB; but it also had active cells operating in different Arab countries, among them Jordan. After the Arab defeat in the Palestinian war of 1948, the leadership of this movement passed into the hands of a group of radical young men who called themselves *Shabitat al-Tha'r* (the Youth of Revenge). Under this new leadership, the Movement of Arab Nationalists became more revolutionary, condoning the use of violence when necessary. In other respects, however, the fundamental principles of the movement remained virtually unchanged.

At about the same time that the original 'Usba – which was the direct ancestor of the Movement of Arab Nationalists – was being organized, two Syrians, Zaki al-Arsuzi and Jalal al-Sayyid, were beginning to write about an Arab national 'rebirth', rendering this term into Arabic as *ba'th*, from the Italian *risorgimento*. Their concept of the Arab national *ba'th* was actually inspired, to a great extent, by the writings of the Italian revolutionary patriot Giuseppe Mazzini (1805–72). The ideas popularized by Arsuzi and Sayyid were later picked up by two secondary school teachers in Damascus, Michel Aflaq and Salah al-Bitar, who became the political founders of the Arab Baath Party (*Hizb al-Ba'th al-'Arabi*). The first congress of this party was held in Damascus in 1947, shortly before the United Nations' partition of Palestine. Bitar and Aflaq, like Arsuzi and Sayyid, had been students in France, and the political platform of the party they founded reflected the influence of the French intellectualism of the period. Meanwhile, a Syrian politician from the town of Hama, Akram al-Hawrani, had organized the Arab Socialist Party (*al-Hizb al-'Arabi al-Ishtiraki*); and a merger between this group and the Baath followed, transforming the Arab Baath Party into the Arab Baath Socialist Party (*Hizb al-Ba'th al-'Arabi al-Ishtiraki*).

The pan-Arab aspirations of the Baath party were no different from those of the Movement of Arab Nationalists. Former 'Usba members were among the founders of both groups; and both groups had Christian as well as Muslim leaders and followers. But while the Movement of Arab Nationalists was not doctrinaire, taking the national unity of the Arabs for granted, and slurring over the historical connection between Arabism and Islam, the Baath party took a different stand on this matter. Apart from advocating socialism as a fundamental condition for Arab national 'rebirth', the party was also an ardent advocate of Arab secularism, which made it particularly appealing not only to Arab religious minorities, Muslim as well as Christian, but also to Sunni Muslims whose social and political thinking had developed beyond the point of confusing political and religious allegiance. Of the four men who contributed to the formation of the Baath ideology, Sayyid and Bitar were Sunni Muslim; but Arsuzi was a Muslim of the minority Alawite sect, and Aflaq was a Syrian Orthodox Christian.[4] In Jordan, as in other Arab lands where the Baath ideology spread, the party attracted Christians as well as Muslims to its ranks, and thus contributed to the political activation of the Transjordanian Christians, which had hitherto been limited. The only competitors to the Baath in Jordan, in this respect, were the Syrian Nationalists of the PPS (see chapter 7), and the officially banned communist party, both parties being staunch advocates of secularism. The Jordanian followers of these two parties, however, and more particularly of the latter, were for the most part Christian: a fact which militated against them in Muslim circles.

The pan-Arab parties and the communists, however, were not the only political organizations which set out to compete for popular support in the Arab world in those days. There were also the Muslim religious parties: the Community of Muslim Brethren (*Jama'at al-Ikhwan al-Muslimin*) and the Tahrir, or Liberation Party (*Hizb al-Tahrir*). The first, originally an Egyptian party which later became active in other Arab countries, including Jordan, preached a return to the law of Islam, but was not opposed in principle to the Arab state system as it actually existed. All it demanded was the Islamization of legislation and methods of rule under the established Arab regimes, without necessarily overthrowing these regimes. The Tahriris, for their part, were an indigenous Jordanian party founded by a Palestinian religious preacher, Sheikh Taqi al-Din al-Nabhani. They demanded the re-establishment of the pan-Islamic caliphate as the only Muslim political institution whose legitimacy was religiously acceptable, which implied a rejection of the legitimacy of the existing Arab state system. In 1956, the Tahrir party was banned in Jordan, following an announcement by the Lebanese authorities that its leader, Sheikh Nabhani, had been apprehended in Beirut and discovered to be in possession of party funds which could not be accounted for locally. Nabhani was consequently to spend the remainder of his life in Beirut under careful security watch. The Muslim Brethren, on the other hand, were permitted to continue operating in Jordan, as their political ideology was not regarded as presenting any real danger to the country. In fact, at a time when the Hashemite regime in Amman found itself under attack by pan-Arab nationalist groups from one direction, and the communists from the other, the Muslim Brethren, it was felt, was one party whose existence in Jordan could serve as a useful political counterpoise to the nationalists and communists alike.

* * * * * * * * * *

In their basic political stands, the Movement of Arab Nationalists and the Baath party were no less anti-Western than the communists. The same was also true of the Muslim parties wherever they happened to be active. But while this worried the British in Jordan, as in other Arab countries where Britain still wielded influence, it did not appear to cause as much anxiety to the United

States. The American preference was clearly for Arab nationalist activism, which was then at the height of its popularity among the Arab masses. The role played by the United States in securing the creation of the state of Israel had caused grave damage to Arab–American relations; and it was hoped that some show of American sympathy for pan-Arab aspirations would help repair that damage. Moreover, the United States was extremely eager to get the Arabs to end their political boycott of Israel, and recognize the Israeli state. To reach this end, the Americans needed to regain the lost confidence of the Arabs. They felt they could only achieve this by intensifying their contacts with the nationalist parties representing grass-roots feelings in Arab society, despite the anti-American rhetoric of these parties.

To Arab statesmen of the older generation, the American support of Arab radicalism – whether discreet or overt – was incomprehensible. King Abdullah, in Amman, had never understood why the Americans delayed their recognition of Jordan's independence until June 1948, almost one full month after their recognition of Israel, considering that he had lost no opportunity to express his unconditional support for the West against the Soviet Union. On the same day, in the summer of 1958, when the dead body of Nuri al-Said was being dragged by a frenzied mob through the blood-stained streets of Baghdad, an interview with Nuri in *Life* magazine was in press, in which he was quoted in the headlines as saying: 'As an Arab and a friend of the West, I am fed up!'. The Lebanese president, Camille Chamoun, was equally perplexed by American policy in the area. When he called upon the United States to help him crush an Arab nationalist insurrection against his staunchly pro-American regime that same summer, he found the Americans instead reaching an understanding with his political opponents once their forces had landed in Beirut.

* * * * * * * * *

Clearly, times were changing, and new political accommodations accordingly had to be made in the Arab world. Such accommodations could take different forms; but they had ultimately to take the American imperative into consideration. In Jordan, it fell to King Hussein, the grandson of King Abdullah, to initiate this process.

However, it was only in 1953, two years after his grandfather's assassination, that Hussein was actually to assume his functions as king. Upon King Abdullah's death in July 1951, the Jordanian throne had passed automatically to the crown prince, who was his forty-year-old son, Talal. The new king, by all accounts, was a model of princely sweetness, a patriotic man full of good intentions. But for several years he had been suffering from attacks of schizophrenia, and had been receiving medical treatment in Switzerland when his father was assassinated. Abdullah's younger son Nayef, acting as regent, was on the point of taking over the throne himself when Talal returned to Amman in September to assume his royal functions. Within a few months, however, King Talal's mental illness began to take a turn for the worse, until it became clear that his condition rendered him unfit to reign. Consequently, on 11 August 1952, the Jordanian parliament held a secret session in which the decision was taken to have the king deposed and succeeded by his eldest son, Hussein, who had become crown prince upon his father's succession.

Born in Amman on 14 November 1935, Hussein had received his elementary education in the Jordanian capital, and had started his secondary education in Egypt at Victoria College, a British-run institution in Alexandria modelled on an English public school. When his father became king, he was sent to England, to complete his secondary studies at Harrow. He thus succeeded to the throne when he was still a student, not yet seventeen years old. According to the Jordanian constitution, he could not begin exercising his royal prerogatives until he reached the age of eighteen by the Muslim calendar, where the year is eleven days shorter than the Christian year. In the meantime, his functions were to be performed by a council of regency appointed by the cabinet, while Hussein himself was sent to Sandhurst to take a condensed course in military science, in preparation for assuming his constitutional powers. Once he had come of age, Hussein returned to Amman, to begin his active reign as king on 2 May 1953.

The smoothness of the transition between the reign of Abdullah and that of his grandson Hussein was remarkable, indicating the extent to which King Abdullah had succeeded in putting the Jordanian monarchy in constitutional order. A political establishment had developed around the Jordanian throne which could handle emergencies with loyalty and responsibility. Heading this establishment during the interim period between 1951 and 1953 was the experienced statesman Tewfiq Abul-Huda, who had been prime minister twice during the reign of Abdullah, and who was called upon to form a new government shortly after the king's assassination. While King Talal was still under treatment in Switzerland, Abul-Huda's government had enough confidence in its constitutional standing to call for general elections, which brought a new parliament to power. Shortly after, when King Talal returned to Amman, Abul-Huda duly tendered the resignation of his government; but the king asked him to form the government again, this time with instructions to provide the country with a new, liberalized constitution. This constitution, for the first time, made the government collectively, and the ministers individually, responsible before parliament. The work on it was completed shortly after King Talal was deposed, so that it was formally promulgated on 8 December 1952, during the period of the regency council. King Hussein was to start his active reign under the new constitution, and in keeping with its spirit. The circumstances of the period, however, did not enable him to abide by it as strictly as he intended.

* * * * * * * * * *

During the months that Hussein had spent as an officer cadet at Sandhurst, the Jordanian ambassador in London was Fawzi al-Mulqi, who in the later years of Abdullah's reign had held ministerial posts – including that for foreign affairs. In London, Mulqi became the young king's friend and confidant. Mulqi had been a student at Liverpool University before the outbreak of the Second World War, and was deeply imbued with ideas about democracy and political and social freedoms, as practised in Britain and other Western countries. Three days after his coronation in May 1953, King Hussein, having accepted the resignation of the government of Abul-Huda, called upon Mulqi to form the first government under his reign, with instructions to introduce liberal reforms, including freedom of speech and freedom of the press.

This first experiment in introducing full democracy to Jordan, however, did not work well. While the country already had a mature political establishment to run its day-to-day affairs, this establishment was limited to a circle of professional politicians. Outside this relatively small circle and its political clients, public opinion among the Jordanians, as among the nationals of other Arab countries, was as yet unrestrained by a sense of civic responsibility and respect for the established order. The vast majority of the Palestinians who had become citizens of Jordan in 1950, in both the West Bank and the East Bank, still could not reconcile themselves to the loss of their original identity and accept that they had become Jordanian nationals. Meanwhile, loyalty to the Hashemite monarchy was far from being general among the Transjordanians of the country. This was particularly the case among urban Transjordanians of the younger generation who had come to consider monarchic rule as anachronistic, and many of whom were strongly influenced by the Arab Nationalist, Baathist or communist political platforms. In the Jordanian armed forces, Arab officers in general were becoming increasingly dissatisfied with the British command of the Arab Legion, which they regarded as an insult to their race. Among these officers, there were some who felt that the time was opportune for the Jordanian monarchy to be overthrown in favour of a republic. The examples of the military coups in Syria, and the Free Officer coup which had done away with the monarchy in Egypt, were clearly beginning to whet military appetites in Amman, as in other Arab capitals.

It was in this political atmosphere, so highly charged with radical and revolutionary ideas and ambitions, that the government of Fawzi al-Mulqi set out to introduce liberal reforms. The outcome was that these reforms were pounced upon by various radical groups to wage relentless attacks on the Jordanian regime, in a seemingly concerted effort to undermine it. The reaction from the king, however, did not take long to come. On 2 May 1954, the first anniversary of Hussein's coronation, Mulqi was asked to tender his resignation, and Tewfiq Abul-Huda returned to power as prime minister. His government inaugurated its work by dissolving parliament and calling for new elections to be held after four months. Next, the publication of newspapers speaking for the Movement of Arab Nationalists, the Baath party, the communists, and other groups of the radical opposition was suspended for a period of six months, as a warning of the measures the government was prepared to take to suppress freedoms when necessary.

Such had been the support accorded by the outgoing government for the right of free speech, that the new government could not easily restrict this freedom, particularly at a time when campaigns for the forthcoming elections were in progress. By pouncing on the freedom of the press, however, while taking no measures to limit free speech, Abul-Huda and his government had provided the opposition in the country with good cause for political agitation, and also with ample means for such agitation. The communists, operating under the name of the National Front, were particularly successful at making political capital out of the situation. The agitation in the country reached its climax on 16 October, the day of the elections, when the Arab Legion had to be brought out, for the first time, to crush an organized riot in the streets of Amman, leaving ten civilians killed by the official count. What followed was the expected outcry – in Jordan as elsewhere in the Arab world – denouncing the Hashemite establishment in Amman, not only as a stooge of Western imperialism and an enemy of true nationalism, but also as a brutal oppressor with Arab blood on its hands.

The events of October 1954 in Amman were only the beginning of Jordan's troubles. Provocations of the regime, normally organized by the same combination of hostile parties, and cynically calculated to elicit violent reactions from the government and armed forces, became a pattern in the political life of the country, giving the Jordanian system a bad name in the Arab world and in liberal circles abroad. King Hussein had started his rule with the best of liberal intentions; but his attempts at liberal reform had been thwarted. This left him at the head of what became virtually a police state – a far cry from the 'happy little country' of his grandfather Abdullah.

By his own account, King Hussein, as a boy, had idolized his grandfather and learnt much from him. He had also been the only member of the family who had accompanied the old king to Jerusalem on the day of his assassination. As a student at Victoria College, Hussein had smarted at the manner in which his grandfather used to be spoken of in Egyptian circles as a defeatist and a traitor, 'because someone had to take the blame for the failure of other Arab statesmen':

My grandfather was a full-blooded extrovert. . . . He was a man of desert ways. . . . He felt, to his dying day, that he had been a leading figure in the struggle for Arab independence for a decade, but that total victory had been snatched from him by duplicity. Yet he was much more than a soldier. He was a diplomat – and an extremely able one at that. . . . He was a wonderful old man, fierce and sometimes autocratic, who transformed Trans-Jordan, as it then was, into a happy, smiling country. . . . I also remember the devastating way he would crush people when he was angry. . . . He also had a wonderful sense of humour. . . . This was the man who taught me so much, who loved me so dearly, and to whom I owe more than I can say. . . . Though . . . his influence on me was profound, it was his death that taught me the ultimate lesson. . . . Firstly, I learned the unimportance of death: that when you have to die, you die. . . . I learned one more thing. If life is cheap, man is cheaper yet. Nothing can ever blot from my memory the falseness of man as I saw it on that day. The cowardly behaviour of my grandfather's so-called friends distressed me so deeply that I had no wish then ever to reign as King of Jordan. . . . Within a matter of hours the politicians had started their intrigues. . . . Powerless for the moment, I was forced to watch the way some of my grandfather's former friends changed allegiance without a thought for the country. I saw his great work jeopardised by weakness on the part of those who had been close to him, by the way they permitted opportunists to step in, even if that meant the ruin of little Jordan.[5]

While young Hussein, no doubt, did learn a lot from old Abdullah, the political style of the two men – not to speak of their manner of life – was different in a number of respects. True, there were many clear resemblances between the grandson and the grandfather. Underlying the political character of Hussein, as that of Abdullah, was a natural affability and a basic humaneness which made him incapable of being cruel or vengeful, or of bearing political or social grudges for long. And Hussein, like his grandfather, was by nature a forgiving person, taking adversity in his stride, and generally given to optimism. He was also, again like his grandfather, a firm believer in the special mission of the Hashemites to lead the Arab nation towards a better future; and the tenacious manner in which King Hussein held on to this belief in the worst moments of crisis could only have been generated by such a sincere conviction. While Abdullah, however, had created a kingdom for himself practically from scratch, Hussein had been destined to be king from birth, which in itself made a difference.

Moreover, while Abdullah, born in the Hijaz, had grown as a boy among the tribes of the Arabian desert, Hussein, born in Amman, had been raised mainly in urban surroundings, and only knew the desert and its people from a relative distance. The staunch bedouin support he readily came to enjoy after ascending to the throne was largely a legacy from his grandfather, although he did manage to preserve and to cultivate it by his own initiative.

Hussein was also to prove different from his grandfather in the manner of his rule. King Abdullah, who is reputed to have played chess like a master, was a man who pondered his political moves, calculating each individual one to achieve a specific end. By contrast, King Hussein, whose favourite sports were driving fast cars, water-skiing and flying aeroplanes, was a man of swift political reflexes. More often than not, he could take political decisions on the spur of the moment, and seemingly by instinct. Unlike his grandfather, who was given to dealing mainly with politicians, and therefore lacked the common touch, Hussein possessed an uncanny ability to identify with popular passions, which often saved the day for him in situations of emergency. King Abdullah was normally a trustful man who could rarely keep his inner thoughts to himself, let alone keep a secret, even from his political enemies. In contrast, King Hussein, by his own admission, succeeded to the throne having the poorest opinion of human nature in political operation, as proved by the earlier quotation from his memoirs. While this did not detract from his natural affability, nor prejudice him unnecessarily against people with whom he normally worked or co-operated, it did contribute to making him highly cautious and alert. From the very start of his rule, he tended to play his political cards very close to his chest, accepting advice only when solicited, and rarely admitting anyone to the inner workings of his mind.

* * * * * * * * *

It was by following his sharp political instincts that King Hussein managed to weather the political storms of the first two decades of his reign, starting in 1954. By this time, the continuing presence of Britain in Jordan had come to be regarded as a flagrant anachronism, not only in Arab but also in international circles. The United States appeared to share this view. In Cairo, Colonel

Nasser, the original organizer of the Free Officer movement, had overthrown General Naguib and replaced him in the presidency of the Egyptian republic. The new Egyptian president had a political charisma which his predecessor had lacked. Within two years of coming to power, Nasser started bidding for pan-Arab leadership, encouraged by the overall regional context and the American effort to change the character of Western stewardship over the area. Nasser had unusual personal charm, and a phenomenal ability to inspire popular confidence in his person by a vernacular rhetoric which could reach the hearts of the simplest folk. The portable transistor radio, which was just beginning to hit the Arab markets in those years, and which practically everybody could afford to buy in its cheaper models, provided him with access to the masses of the Arab world on an unprecedented scale. In Jordan, Nasser's pan-Arab propaganda was particularly successful among the Palestinians, especially those of the refugee camps, who began to idolize the Egyptian leader as the expected redeemer of their lost homeland. But Nasserism also had a vocal political following among the many Transjordanians who had no wish to see their country continue to appear as the black sheep of the Arab flock. Practically everybody in Jordan, as in other Arab countries, stayed tuned to the Voice of the Arabs broadcasting from Cairo, to hear the man they considered the new Saladin address them in person on the issues of the day.

The Americans appeared to be happy with Nasser and satisfied to see him develop so rapidly into a pan-Arab idol. The feeling in Washington was that only an Arab leader of his calibre – a man who could speak for all the Arabs at once – could finally make the desired pan-Arab peace with Israel. Nasser's propaganda machine, moreover, was successfully mobilizing public opinion against the British in the Arab countries where they were still politically entrenched, which was a free bonus for American regional policy. Sensing this positive American attitude towards Nasser, and surmising the reasons behind it, Britain began to exert increased efforts to fortify her regional position. The outcome was the so-called Baghdad Pact: a British-designed defensive agreement against possible Soviet aggression first signed between Iraq and Turkey in February 1955, and later subscribed to by Iran and Pakistan, and by Britain herself. The conclusion of the Baghdad Pact appeared for the moment to be a British master-stroke. Because the pact was ostensibly directed against the Russians as the enemies of the West, of which the United States was the leader, the Americans were in no position to object to it openly. Certainly, the British and American governments were in agreement on general lines of global policy; but American percep-tions with respect to particular regional situations and problems often differed from those of Britain.

In April of that same year, however, a conference of Asian and African nations convened in the Indonesian city of Bandung to formulate a concerted policy of 'positive neutrality' between the Western powers and the communist bloc. President Nasser of Egypt was among the leading participants at this conference, along with President Jawaharlal Nehru of India, and Premier Chou En-Lai of communist China. In the Arab world, the idea of 'positive neutrality' – which later came to be called 'non-alignment' – had been in the air for some time, promoted chiefly by the Movement of Arab Nationalists. The leaders of this movement, who began to converge on Cairo after 1954 to place themselves at the political disposal of Nasser, saw the weakness of the Arabs as deriving from the fact that their armies depended exclusively on the West for their military equipment. From their point of view, the Arabs could easily redress this weakness by securing arms from whoever was ready to supply them, not excluding the nations of the communist bloc. The Arabs, they maintained, were under no compulsion to remain politically committed to the West while the West was in fact the friend of Israel; and there was no point in their becoming involved in defence pacts against Russia when the real threat to them came from Israel. There were other nations of the world, they argued, in Asia and Africa, and in Eastern Europe and South America, whose real interests did not lie in continued subservience to the West or to the Soviet Union. It was the friendship of such nations that the Arabs should aim at cultivating, to create a 'third bloc' in the world standing between the two existing blocs. The Baath party, no less than the Movement of Arab Nationalists, subscribed to these new ideas.

About a year before the Bandung conference, the Syrian government had secured a modest consignment of military sup-plies from Czechoslovakia through a Lebanese intermediary. This Syrian deal, concluded in 1954, had gone virtually unnoticed, but now set a precedent. When Nasser, after the meeting at Bandung, announced a major Czech arms deal of his own in September 1955, his announcement was met by an outburst of Arab enthusiasm: among other places, in Jordan, and within the ranks of the Jordanian army. The Arab giant, it was generally believed, was finally breaking loose from his chains, to prepare for the final showdown with his real enemy. How different Nasser's defiant behaviour seemed from that of the rulers of Iraq, who were signing British-led defence pacts against Russia when Arab interest dictated that they should be aligning themselves with Egypt to fight Israel!

Caught in the tug of war between Egypt and Iraq, Jordan was at a loss what to do. The country had special treaty relations with Britain, and to adhere to the Baghdad Pact involved no more than an extension of these relations. Adherence would also make it possible for Jordan to ask for badly needed financial aid from the richer countries of the region who belonged to the pact. Moreover, it would give Britain an added incentive to help strengthen the Jordanian army and increase its subsidies. These questions apart, King Hussein, as a Hashemite, was naturally more inclined to ally himself with his Hashemite cousins in Iraq than with President Nasser of Egypt, who was already proving to be a highly ambitious and possibly dangerous man. On the other hand, Hussein could not afford to alienate Nasser, nor do anything behind his back. Nasser had clearly acquired an unrivalled command of the Arab masses, which alone provided him with strong political leverage in all Arab countries. More important, if he chose to cause trouble to Jordan, Nasser had the traditional enemies of the Jordanian regime – Syria from one direction, and Saudi Arabia from the other – to assist him.

What further added to the Jordanian predicament was the inscrutable attitude of the United States. Apart from perfunctory criticism of Nasser's leading role in the Bandung conference, and of his Czech arms deal, Washington did not appear to be as disturbed as Britain by the Egyptian president's defiance of the West. Nor did the American government seem particularly enthusiastic about the Baghdad Pact. In fact, from the very beginning, the United States gave out clear signals that her attitude towards Nasser was positive, and likely to remain so. Clearly, developments were taking place on the regional scene in which the Americans and the British were not necessarily on the same side. For a small country such as Jordan, the safest thing to do was to remain uninvolved in these developments. However, this was easier said than done.

Of the Arab countries which were direct neighbours of Israel, Jordan had by far the longest frontier, and one which could easily be infiltrated at many points, in both directions. Since 1953, Palestinian fedayeen, or commandos, had been crossing into Israel from Syria, Lebanon or Egypt by way of Jordan. The operations carried out by these fedayeen, with encouragement from Syria and Egypt, and sometimes with financial support from Saudi Arabia, were causing far more harm to Jordan than to Israel, because of the Israeli reprisals they provoked against villages of the West Bank. While Jordan frequently manged to intercept fedayeen infiltrations into Israel from her territory, the authorities in Amman could not openly condemn the fedayeen operations in principle without exposing themselves to general Arab censure.

Even without prompting from Saudi Arabia, Egypt had always aligned herself with the Arab enemies of Jordan, taking special delight in instigating trouble in the country and embarrassing its rulers. The behaviour of Egypt towards Jordan did not change after Nasser came to power. Starting in 1954, the Egyptian government began deliberately to encourage Arab fedayeen infiltrations into Israel from the Egyptian-controlled Gaza strip, which further compromised the position of Jordan on this issue.

In the following year, the Jordanian government sent a delegation to Bandung, no doubt with a view to indicating goodwill towards Nasser. Later in that same year, when King Hussein was seriously considering the idea of adhering to the Baghdad Pact, he made a point of presenting the details of the Jordanian plan to the Egyptian president, indicating to him that Jordan would not go ahead and sign the pact without his full approval. In response, Nasser indicated a sympathetic understanding of the Jordanian position, and a willingness to endorse the Jordanian proposals. He had hardly done so, however, when his Voice of the Arabs radio unleashed a fierce campaign of invective against the Jordanian regime, and also against the king in person, accusing him of selling out to the British and, worse still, to imperialism and the Jews. Faced with this relentless propaganda campaign, the Jordanian government – then headed by an ageing Circassian politician, Said al-Mufti – fell on 13 December of that year. This was immediately followed by anti-Hashemite demonstrations and riots throughout the country, in which a number of public buildings were stormed. The agitation was chiefly the work of the Baath party and the communists. However, the king decided not to yield in the face of pressure from the populace, and quickly formed a new government:

As the mobs roamed the streets, I brought out Hazza Pasha Majali, who had been Minister of the Interior under Said Mufti, a man of courage, not afraid to shoulder responsibility. He announced publicly that he was in favour of the Baghdad Pact. . . . But we were virtually helpless. This was no ordinary rioting. Though some demonstrations were spontaneous, most of them were cold-bloodedly organised by avowed Communists with the authority and discipline of well-trained officers. Still we might have held on, but on 19 December the Minister of the Interior and two others of Majali's government resigned. Majali tried to find replacements in vain. There was nothing I could do but dissolve the Government, letting a caretaker government carry on with the promise of elections in three or four months. There was an immediate calm over the country and I believe this calm would have continued but for a most unfortunate factor. Some deputies . . . claimed that the Government action in dissolving Parliament was illegal. The law proved them right. I had signed it, and so had the Prime Minister, but the signature of the Minister of the Interior was missing, for he had resigned just before the decree was made. The Jordanian High Court ruled that the decree was unconstitutional and the old deputies had to be reinstated. Now all hell had broken loose. Riots such as we had never seen before . . . disrupted the whole country. This time bands of fire-raisers started burning Government buildings, private houses, foreign properties. I had no alternative but to call out the Legion, who . . . met force with force. I imposed a ten-day curfew on the country. . . . That was the end of Jordan and the Baghdad Pact.[6]

* * * * * * * * * *

The riots of December 1955, being far more violent than those of the preceding year, drove home the message that a major change of policy was required from Amman. In the post-war contest between the great powers over the Middle East, the British had already sustained serious losses; and certainly in some cases, as for example in Iran, the ultimate beneficiary had turned out to be the United States rather than the Soviet Union. For Jordan, this was a matter to be taken seriously. The country had special treaty relations with Britain; and the Jordanian army, still commanded by Lieutenant-General Glubb, was practically run as well as subsidized by the British. If the Hashemite monarchy in Amman was to survive the on-going 'game of nations',[7] it had to reconsider its position with respect to this game. To persist in depending exclusively on Britain in the changed circumstances would be tantamount to leaning on a broken reed. To turn and put one's trust in the United States, however, would be courting adventure. Unlike the British, the Americans had no sentimental attachment to the Jordanian monarchy, and did not consider it indispensable. If trust in the United States involved risks, turning to the Soviet Union – an interloper in the Middle East, and therefore ultimately unreliable – was out of the question. The only other alternative was for Jordan to try to stand on her own feet as an Arab country, in the true spirit of 'positive neutrality', keeping all her options open and hoping for the best.

To dissociate herself from Britain, Jordan had first to put an end to the anomaly of having British officers run her army. Since the end of the 1948 war, Arab officers in the Jordanian armed forces had been manifesting increasing discontent with the command of Lieutenant-General Glubb. One of them was Lieutenant-Colonel Abdullah al-Tall, from Irbid, who was generally regarded as the hero of the battle for Jerusalem (see Chapter 6). Tall had subsequently been appointed military governor of Jerusalem, but when he asked for a promotion in military rank, this was refused on the advice of Glubb. Tall thereupon defected from the Arab Legion in 1949 and went to Cairo, where he became the focal figure in the campaign of vilification which the Egyptians were then waging against King Abdullah. After the king was assassinated in 1951, Tall was charged with having been an accessory before the fact and condemned to death *in absentia*. Tall himself insisted on his innocence, accusing Glubb of having fraudulently contrived the charge against him. The court that handled the case, however, was convinced of his guilt.

Glubb, in fact, did have a strong dislike of Tall, as he disliked other Arab officers of the Legion who came from towns such as Irbid. He suspected these men of disloyalty to the Hashemite crown either because he knew them to be ambitious, or because he considered them infected with nationalism. Among them was

Captain Ali Abu Nuwar, from Salt, and six friends of his who were sympathizers or secret members of the Baath party. In 1952, when the question of King Talal's suitability to remain on the throne was being considered, Abu Nuwar had been overheard talking politics in an Amman hotel, saying that Jordan needed neither British help, nor indeed a king. The information was reported to Glubb, who in turn reported it to the government. Abu Nuwar was thereupon removed from the Arab Legion and appointed military attaché in Paris. It was there that King Hussein met him in the summer of 1954, while on holiday in France; and a little over a year later, Abu Nuwar was recalled from Paris to become the king's ADC, against Glubb's advice. What followed were intrigues and counter-intrigues between Abu Nuwar and Glubb, in which Abu Nuwar, as Hussein's constant companion, naturally had the upper hand.

In Abdullah's time, Glubb had the ear of the king all to himself. Between Glubb and Hussein, however, there was a generation gap which paralleled the generation gap between Abdullah's and Hussein's Jordan. The young Hussein appreciated the loyalty of the British commander of his army, and his genuine concern for the security of the Jordanian throne. Before long, however, he began to grow weary of Glubb's negative attitude towards his Arab subordinates, and of his warnings about their secret political affiliations and ambitions. These young Arab officers were not much older than the king, and he could understand the nationalism that motivated them. He thought of them as friends rather than potential conspirators, and could see why they were dissatisfied with Glubb and the other British officers who were their superiors in the Arab Legion. After all, it seemed only natural for the nationals of a country to wish to run their army themselves, rather than leave its command in the hands of outsiders, no matter how loyal or competent.

Moreover, by the end of 1955, the Egyptian propaganda campaign against the Jordanian regime was making great issue of the fact that the armed forces of Jordan were still under the command of a British officer – and of Glubb in particular. This campaign, and the internal troubles it unleashed in Jordan, decided King Hussein to abandon the thought of adhering to the Baghdad Pact, to which his attitude had been somewhat ambivalent from the start. Having come to this decision, Hussein had one more step to take to redeem the Arab credibility of the Jordanian regime: to get rid of his British general. Broad hints to the effect that it was time for the Pasha to 'enjoy a rest' did not suffice.

On 1 March 1956, Glubb was summoned to the office of the prime minister, Samir Rifai, to be told in plain words that the king had decided to dismiss him. The prime minister, who was the general's old friend, made it clear to him that he would have to leave the country as soon as he could get his packing done. The next morning, as Glubb and his family were on their way to the airport, the court chamberlain, who was one of the two government officials accompanying him to bid him farewell, presented him with a portrait of the king in a silver frame. Across the portrait ran the words, in the king's own handwriting: 'With our acknowledgement of the good services and untiring exertions and with our best wishes for His Excellency General Glubb Pasha.' This was followed by the date of the general's dismissal and the royal signature.

* * * * * * * * * *

Within a few weeks of the departure of Glubb Pasha from Amman, King Hussein dismissed the government of Samir Rifai. He also dissolved parliament and called for new elections in October, giving strict instructions that these elections – unlike those of 1954 – should be free. The outcome was a legislative body similar to that of 1951, with the nationalist parties, together with the communists, forming the largest single bloc. In this bloc, the party that had won most seats was a coalition called the National-Socialist Front. The leader of this party, Suleiman al-Nabulsi, had actually failed to secure a parliamentary seat for himself, but no fewer than eleven of his partisans had been elected. The king, accordingly, called upon him to form a government; and the new government, like the new parliament, was dominated by radical groups, with the leading deputy of the Baath party, Abdullah Rimawi, holding the portfolio of foreign affairs.

On 23 July 1956, about three months before the Nabulsi government was formed in Amman, President Nasser, in Cairo, had celebrated the fourth anniversary of the Egyptian Revolution by the nationalization of the Suez Canal Company. This action had precipitated an international crisis which culminated in

October–November of that year with the so-called Suez War. First, Israel waged a surprise attack to occupy the Gaza strip, ostensibly in response to repeated fedayeen raids against Israel from this Egyptian-controlled territory. The aggression began on 29 October, on the same day that the Nabulsi government was formed in Amman. Next, the French and the British proceeded to land forces in Port Said, ostensibly to stop the fighting between Egypt and Israel and protect the Suez Canal. Actually, the aim of this Anglo-French operation, carefully co-ordinated with Israel beforehand, was to bring Nasser down. Hardly had the French and British forces landed in Port Said, however, when the United States intervened to rescue Nasser. Washington demanded the immediate and unconditional cessation of hostilities, and the withdrawal of the three aggressors from all the territories and positions they had occupied. As a result, the Suez War represented a political victory for Nasser which made him stronger than ever before in the Arab world.

In the course of the Arab nationalist fury triggered by the Anglo-French aggression against Egypt, and in response to a demand by Nasser pressed on all the Arab countries, the Nabulsi government in Amman broke off diplomatic relations with France. It also succeeded in securing unanimous votes from parliament to recognize the Soviet Union and Communist China, and to abrogate the Anglo-Jordanian treaty. Accordingly, this controversial treaty was terminated on 14 March 1957, just over a year after the dismissal of Glubb. Meanwhile, on 19 January, Jordan had signed an Arab Solidarity Agreement with Egypt, Syria and Saudi Arabia, whereby these three countries undertook to pay Jordan the subsidy hitherto provided by the British government.

King Hussein was perfectly prepared to end Jordan's special relations with Britain, and co-operate with the Nabulsi government in mending political fences with the Egyptians and the Syrians. In a personal show of goodwill towards his Arab neighbours, he had actually gone ahead and signed a security pact with Egypt and Syria a few days before Nabulsi took power. By the terms of this pact, Major-General Abdul-Hakim Amir of Egypt was to be joint commander of the armies of the three countries. What Hussein was adamant in opposing, on the other hand, was the general drift towards the left initiated by Nabulsi, which was already giving free rein to communist activism in the country. After the dismissal of

Glubb, the king, as commander-in-chief of the Jordanian armed forces, had promoted Major Ali Abu Nuwar (as he then was) to the rank of general and made him his chief of staff. Abu Nuwar, however, had come out in support of the left-wing policies of the Nabulsi government, which added to the king's problems.

The king, at this point, decided to take matters in hand. Two months before the parliamentary decision to abrogate the Anglo-Jordanian treaty was implemented, President Dwight Eisenhower had promulgated the so-called Eisenhower doctrine (January 1957), offering defence and economic aid to Middle Eastern states which felt threatened by communism. From Amman, King Hussein immediately expressed interest in the American aid offered, provided it was not tied to conditions. This set him on a collision course with the Nabulsi government, which was then pressing for the recognition of the Soviet Union and communist China, as already agreed by parliament. Faced with such strong resistance from the king, Nabulsi and his cabinet were forced to resign on 10 April.

Seizing the opportunity offered by the king's preoccupation with forming a new cabinet, General Abu Nuwar attempted a military coup against him on 13 April. For some time, however, the movements of Abu Nuwar had been under close watch, which gave the king prior knowledge of his plans. Consequently, the coup attempt was easily foiled within a matter of hours. Abu Nuwar was permitted to leave Jordan the following day, first to Syria, then to Egypt, where he remained for nearly ten years. His fellow conspirators fled the country after him, as did a number of political activists, among them Abdullah Rimawi and another minister of the Nabulsi cabinet.

In the interval, a Jerusalem notable, Hussein Fakhri Khalidi, had succeeded in forming a new cabinet on 15 April, after Suleiman Nabulsi had agreed to co-operate with him by assuming the portfolio of foreign affairs. One week later, however, the nationalist parties and the communists held a national congress in the West Bank city of Nablus. In response to a call from this congress, a general strike was organized on 24 April, accompanied by massive political demonstrations in the major cities which threatened to turn into riots. In the face of this new wave of trouble, the Khalidi government immediately tendered its resignation. But another government was formed right away, this time by Ibrahim Hashim, a veteran member of the Jordanian establishment. The next day, a curfew was proclaimed throughout the country, and martial law was imposed. All political parties were dissolved, and the leading activists were arrested.

Once again, the Jordanian regime was meeting 'force with force', for lack of any feasible alternative, and, as before, Arab condemnations fell upon it thick and fast from many quarters. However, this time a signal of Arab support came from an unexpected direction. Since the time of the Suez War, King Saud, in Riyadh, had started to have serious misgivings about the pro-Russian policies which Egypt and Syria seemed to be pursuing. These policies, he thought, were opening the way for a communist infiltration of the Arab world that could become difficult to resist. Moreover, Saudi Arabia had hitherto been supporting republics against monarchies, because of an old feud between the house of Saud and the Hashemites which no longer made much sense. From King Saud's point of view, should Nasser succeed in overthrowing Hussein, who could guarantee that he himself would not be next?

As a signatory of the Arab Solidarity Agreement, Saudi Arabia was due to pay the first instalment of her share of the subsidy for Jordan in that April. In a calculated show of goodwill towards Amman, King Saud hastened to pay the amount to the Jordanian government while the crisis in their country was still at its peak. The gesture was much appreciated. Before the end of the month, as the situation in Amman was being brought under control, King Hussein went to Riyadh in person to thank the Saudi ruler for his timely show of friendship; and King Saud returned the visit in June. The old feud between the two Arab royal houses was finally being overcome.

Egypt and Syria were also due to ratify the Arab Solidarity Agreement and pay their respective shares of the promised Jordanian subsidy, which the Jordanian government formally requested of them. Instead, however, Cairo and Damascus intensified the ferocity of their propaganda attacks on the Jordanian regime, and on King Hussein in person. Towards the middle of June, shortly after King Saud had ended his visit to Amman, diplomatic representation between Egypt and Jordan was suspended, and Jordan closed down her embassy in Cairo. Two weeks later, King Hussein went on a state visit to Iraq, to consolidate relations with his Hashemite cousins in Baghdad. By this time, the Arab Solidarity Agreement, still unratified by Egypt and Syria, had died a natural death, and Jordan no longer felt morally bound by its terms.

Egypt and Syria were still continuing their media campaigns against Jordan and King Hussein, when the two countries decided to unite under the presidency of Nasser in what came to be known as the United Arab Republic (UAR). The decision to form this union was taken on 1 February 1958, and implemented on 22 February amidst wild popular rejoicing throughout the Arab world. The formation of the UAR brought Nasser to the peak of his power as a pan-Arab leader. Meanwhile, on 14 February, Jordan and Iraq had formed a union of their own on a federal basis: hence its name, the Arab Federation. The government of this federation was to be headed by the Iraqi prime minister, Nuri al-Said, with the Jordanian Ibrahim Hashim as his deputy. Two other Jordanians were to hold portfolios in the federal cabinet, one of them, Suleiman Toukan, as minister of defence. Also, members of the Jordanian parliament were detailed to serve on the federal legislature.

In Lebanon, the implementation of the union between Egypt and Syria immediately activated the latent tensions between the Muslims and Christians of the country. While the Muslims began to clamour for Lebanon to become the 'third province' of the UAR, the Christians, led by President Camille Chamoun, decided that the time had come for them to make a stand against the threatening Nasserist wave. The political tensions between the two sides finally exploded in a Muslim insurrection against President Chamoun which lasted from May to October 1958, receiving active support from the UAR. Chamoun had been the only Arab ruler who had dared to subscribe to the Eisenhower doctrine. Failing to crush the insurrection against his regime by himself, he invoked this doctrine to call on the United States for military help. Washington, however, advised the Lebanese president to attempt a political settlement to the crisis without external intervention for as long as such a settlement remained possible.

On 14 July, however, a bloody military coup took place in Iraq, whereupon the United States immediately sent forces to Beirut to bring the Lebanese situation under control. Meanwhile, with the overthrow of the Hashemite regime in Baghdad and the massacre of the royal family, the Arab Federation between Jordan and Iraq automatically ceased to exist. Of the Jordanian officials and army officers who happened to be in Baghdad on that fateful day, four were killed in the random violence that followed, among them two of the three Jordanian members of the federal government, Ibrahim Hashim and Suleiman Toukan.

To the masses of the Arab world, the violent end of the monarchic regime in Iraq seemed to have removed one of the major hurdles along the road to full Arab unity under President Nasser, whose leadership was commonly believed to represent the wave of the Arab future. These were the only remaining obstacles to be overcome: Lebanon and Jordan. Once these were removed, whatever remained of Arab resistance to the Nasserist wave would be easily mopped up. In Lebanon, it was true, the Christians were proving a hard nut to crack. On the day the Iraqi monarchy fell, however, few people in the Arab world thought that the Hashemite regime in Amman stood the slightest chance of survival. Its liquidation, it was commonly believed, was bound to follow in a matter of days or, at most, weeks.

NOTES

1. The assassin of Abdullah, a tailor's assistant, was shot dead by the king's guard on the spot. Of the five local conspirators behind him, four were arrested, tried by a special court and executed, one of them being a relative of the *mufti* of Jerusalem, who was then in Cairo. The fact that the conspirators had been in contact with political agents in Egypt made it appear that the *mufti* was their political instigator; but the attorney general who handled the case, and whom I interviewed, rules out this suspicion. It has not yet been established who were the ultimate political instigators of the conspiracy.
2. John Bagot Glubb, *A Soldier with the Arabs* (London, 1957) pp. 326–8.
3. Charles Crane was later (in 1930) to become involved in the negotiations with Abdul-Aziz Al Saud which ultimately resulted in the establishment of the Arabian–American Oil Company (ARAMCO).
4. The Alawites, or Nusayris, are an esoteric Shiah Muslim sect mainly concentrated in the so-called Alawite mountains forming the coastal fringes of northern Syria, in the Latakia region. The Syrian Orthodox (or Jacobite) church was a minority Christian communion in the area following the Syriac rite, unlike the much larger Greek Orthodox church which followed the Greek rite – hence its name.

5. H. M. King Hussein of Jordan, *Uneasy Lies the Head; an autobiography* (London, 1962), pp. 3, 13–20.
6. *Ibid.*, pp. 92–3.
7. This expression was coined by Miles Copeland as the title of his book, *The Game of Nations* (London, 1969), which purports to relate the inside story of international politics in the Middle East during this period.

9

The Difficult Years

King Hussein was not yet twenty-three when the Hashemite monarchy in Iraq was overthrown, but he was already becoming a master in the practice of politics. To begin with, he realized the nature of his assets and his liabilities. The Jordanian ruling establishment was on his side, still composed mainly of old hands – some Transjordanian by origin, others Palestinian – whose interests as well as sentiments dictated unwavering loyalty to the throne. Alongside this civilian establishment he also had the loyalty of the army, largely composed of tribal elements, whose discipline and commitment to the defence of the Hashemite monarchy had been proved by the facility with which the coup attempt of 1957 had been foiled. Politicized elements still existed in the officer ranks, but these could easily be monitored. In the country at large, the king could count on support from a considerable body of public opinion. This support was not as vocal among the Palestinians of either the East Bank or the West Bank as it was among the Transjordanians, and it naturally tended to vacillate in moments of crisis, but nonetheless it existed to a certain degree. Jordan, after all, was the only Arab country where Palestinians had been readily accorded full citizens' rights. Many Palestinians, who were generally well-to-do and economically content, now enjoyed these rights on a par with their Transjordanian compatriots, which made the political stability of Jordan something worth preserving for them.

The internal support on which the Jordanian regime could depend was not only considerable, but also solid at the core. There was certainly no question regarding the readiness of the political establishment and the main body of the army to stand on the side of King Hussein in all circumstances. Among Jordanians of the younger generation, there were educated elements who were potentially an asset to the country: a reserve of fresh talent and skill on which the regime could draw to strengthen itself in due time, a fact of which the young king was appreciative.

However, because these elements in Jordan as in most Arab countries, were often out of touch with the intellectual trends of the modern world at large, they tended not to discriminate between genuine new ideas and the cut-and-dried party ideologies to which they were exposed at home. Also, these elements were generally eager to attain power, which set them on a collision course with the established system. While this applied to the Transjordanians, their Palestinian counterparts took a negative attitude towards the regime for two different reasons. First, they felt politically excluded from the system as established (and had some reason to do so, because the Transjordanians tended to regard them as unwelcome competitors). Second, most of the younger Palestinian intellectuals had inherited the anti-Hashemite sentiments of the older generation. They were also revolted by the idea of having to live under a monarchy, and to be forced to abide by traditions which were not to their republican taste.

It was these Transjordanian and Palestinian elements – many of them privileged young people, with a potentially secure future – who formed the mainstay of the political opposition in the country. On the surface, this opposition appeared to be no less solid and determined in its aims than the regime. Appearances, however, can be deceptive. It was true that the opposition parties were well organized, and could easily have mobilized the Palestinian masses to political action, both in the refugee camps and in the towns. This potentially provided them with more than enough social and political muscle to present a true challenge to the existing system. However, the important activists in these parties were more ambitious than serious, which led them to pursue the tactics of political poachers and trouble-makers rather than the careful strategy of people who believed in what they were doing. Thus, while the regime stuck to its guns with grim seriousness when faced by crisis, its opponents ordinarily behaved as if they were engaged in a game of 'cops and robbers' in which the 'cops' invariably won, and the 'robbers' ended up either in exile or in prison. This lack of a sense of real purpose in the ranks of the opposition partly explains why King Hussein, in time, could so easily pardon his worst enemies once he was convinced that they had tired of their old pranks. By the mid-1960s, practically all the officers and civilian politicians who had risen against the regime at one time or another – including Abdullah al-Tall and Ali Abu Nuwar – were being recalled from exile, or brought out of their prison cells, to be politically rehabilitated.

All things considered, the Jordanian regime was not as precarious as was commonly supposed. In fact, it had a distinct advantage over its Arab opponents because of the economical use it made of its modest political resources. In the Arab world at large, the resources that President Nasser could tap from Cairo were immeasurably larger than those available to King Hussein in Amman. Nasser, too, had everything it took to make a credible pan-Arab leader. As well as having charisma and charm, he was also (to judge from his life career) a true patriot, sincerely committed to the pan-Arab cause, who was personally beyond corruption. His vanity, though enormous, was more than compensated for by his genial sense of humour. His principal problems, however, derived from an inability to control his political behaviour.

Unlike Hussein, Nasser did not have a dynastic heritage behind him, which may explain his inability to temper his instincts to power. Having emerged unscathed from the Suez War, which was rightly counted a political victory for him, he readily became a prisoner of his pan-Arab popularity, which often marred the judiciousness of his political decisions. More than anything else, Nasser became tactless in dealing with Arab heads of state who were legally his equals. The facility with which he proceeded to turn potential friends among them into enemies, merely by treating them as inferiors, was remarkable. Hussein, by contrast, always made a point of operating within his limits, with caution and tact, never crossing swords with his opponents except when absolutely necessary. This unfailing prudence in political behaviour on his part ultimately proved to be to his advantage.

Reviewing the events of the early years of his rule, Hussein complained bitterly of Nasser's 'double-crossing'. The two men, however, appear to have had a secret admiration for one another. Possibly, Nasser would not have persisted in attacking Hussein and his regime as much as he did had it not been for the members of the Movement of Arab Nationalists and the Baath party who surrounded him in Cairo, feeding him daily with talk about the alleged treason of the Hashemites, especially those of Jordan. Also, of course, Nasser ran the risk of alienating his Palestinian activist support if he reversed his anti-Hashemite stand. This support was particularly valuable to him because the Palestinians, by the early 1960s, had come to be politically active throughout the Arab world, and Nasser could depend on them as bulwarks for his pan-Arab policies in a number of Arab countries, all the way from the Arabian Sea to the Atlantic. On this count alone, Nasser must have felt that he stood to lose more than he would gain if he improved his relations with the Jordanian regime.

From Amman, Hussein could appreciate the Arab nationalism of Nasser, with which he readily identified in principle, and, even at a time when he was still in open enmity with the Egyptian leader, he made a point of indicating a respect for his person, while not mincing his words in criticizing his political manner:

My own concept of Arab nationalism . . . is different from what I understand President Nasser's to be. If I interpret his aims properly, he believes that political unity and Arab nationalism are synonymous. Evidently he also believes that Arab nationalism can only be identified by a particular brand of Arab unity. I disagree. This view can only lead, as it has in the past, to more disunity. The seeking of popular support for one point of view or one form of leadership in countries other than one's own has fostered factionalism to a dangerous degree, splitting countries to the point of revolution. It is nothing but a new form of imperialism, the domination of one state by another. . . . This preoccupation with short-sighted objectives, usually attributed – perhaps wrongly – to political ambition, has brought three attendant evils. It has diverted Arab energies from sound, peaceful pursuits into wasteful political intrigue; it has split people into factions . . .; and it has hampered the Arabs in dealing with the greatest political problem confronting us: the Palestine question. . . . The fault lies partly in the situation created by the policy of divide-and-rule, and partly in the lack of sincerity and honesty of some Arab leaders. Every Arab problem suffers from irresponsibility of the responsible Arab class. . . . It is indeed unfortunate that, having been victimised by the disheartening and deceitful policies of the West, we have been able to do nothing but divide ourselves further. . . . Ambitious men have made claims without foundation, and promises they could not keep. They have been aided indirectly by outside forces which seek control over this area, both the Communists and those who attempt to preserve their interests in ways that have failed them before.[1]

One matter which Nasser was careful to keep concealed was the degree of support accorded him by the United States – a support which was more fundamental to American policy than the assistance which Washington began to accord Hussein following the termination of Jordan's special relations with Britain. The Americans, for their part, were careful not to speak of Nasser as an Arab leader whose role in the area was compatible with their interests. They did not need to exercise the same discretion with respect to Jordan. In April 1957, shortly after the coup attempt against King Hussein was foiled, fourteen units of the American Sixth Fleet, including a battleship and an aircraft carrier, left their bases in Italy and proceeded to the eastern Mediterranean, in a show of American concern for what was happening in Amman. Meanwhile, the White House issued a statement declaring the independence and integrity of Jordan to be vital to the United States. Nasser's propaganda machine was quick to exploit these American moves by presenting them as ultimate proof that the Jordanian king was no more than a stooge of the Americans. Hussein, however, did not feel any need to apologize for the American help he received. In fact, he was frankly thankful for this help, and also for the much-needed American financial assistance which followed in its wake. While his pan-Arab standing was far from being equal to that of the Egyptian president, the Jordanian king, as an Arab ruler, was actually the more independent man, because he could openly admit to the policies he pursued, without being unnecessarily deterred by what people might say. An astute man, Nasser no doubt noted this fact.

No matter how hard he tried, President Nasser could never get King Hussein embarrassed to the point of laying down his arms. Immediately following the overthrow of the Hashemite monarchy in Baghdad, Jordan ran out of oil, and the Americans were asked to help. The road for the tankers which had once brought oil to Jordan from Lebanon by way of Syria had already been barred, and now so was the road from Iraq. One possible solution was an American airlift of oil from Saudi Arabia, but King Saud was afraid of doing anything that could be interpreted as a provocation to Nasser, who now seemed all-powerful. Consequently, the oil lift from Saudi Arabia was stopped after the delivery of only one consignment. In the circumstances, Hussein was forced to receive the indispensable oil from the only remaining direction, which was over Israeli airspace. This required the official approval of the Israeli government, which was given. King Hussein agreed to the arrangement, turning a deaf ear to the barrage of insults which followed from the Voice of the Arabs radio. Jordan, after all, could not survive without oil.

At the same time, fearful of the consequences to Jordan of what had just happened in Iraq, King Hussein had appealed to Washington and London for military help. By this time, American marines had just started landing in Lebanon in response to an earlier appeal by President Camille Chamoun, who had also been marked out by the Nasserists for destruction (see Chapter 8). However, Washington was reluctant to undertake the defence of President Chamoun and King Hussein simultaneously. The solution was to detail the defence of Jordan to the British, who still felt morally committed to the Hashemite regime in Amman. The British military airlift to Jordan, like the American oil lift shortly before, could arrive only by flying over Israeli airspace. Again, a great propaganda issue was made of this matter. King Hussein, however, could not afford to refuse the British military help simply because of the political embarrassment involved. From his point of view, it was the ill will of his Arab enemies that had forced him into this otherwise impossible position. Consequently, he maintained that responsibility for the results lay with those other Arab parties rather than with himself.

* * * * * * * * *

Contrary to the general Arab expectation, the Jordanian regime successfully withstood the revolutionary storm of that terrible summer. During the three months in which the British forces remained in Jordan, serving as a deterrent to external Arab intervention, the Jordanian government, now headed by Samir Rifai, took all the security measures needed to prevent any possible disorder in the country. In the army, whose command since 1957 had been entrusted to a fully loyal chief-of-staff, General Habes al-Majali, the intelligence branch was rapidly developed to top form. Since the time of the Abu Nuwar coup, correct constitutional procedure in Jordan had been dropped. The country had come to be ruled by governments appointed by the king and responsible to him, not to parliament, and with the army standing by on alert all the time. Democracy had to be sacrificed for stability until further notice,.and no pretence was made to the contrary.

In the absence of the necessary evidence, one cannot determine the exact extent to which agents of Nasser were directly or indirectly involved in attempts to destablilize Jordan before and after 1958. Certainly, there were Nasserist involvements in a number of cases, but not necessarily in all. There were many people inside Jordan who felt hostile enough towards the regime, for one reason or another, to attempt acts of sabotage or terrorism either on their own initiative or prompted by the political parties to which they adhered. The vigilance of the Jordanian security services was successful in reducing incidents of this kind to a tolerable minimum, but their occurrence could not always be prevented. In the autumn of 1958, for example, shortly after the British troops had completed their withdrawal from Jordan, a bomb exploded inside the USIS (United States Information Service) library building in Amman, causing some damage. The bomb had been planted by two Palestinians – the daughter of a prosperous Christian businessman and her fiancé – who had become actively associated with the Movement of Arab Nationalists during their student years at the AUB (see Chapter 8). The two culprits were arrested, brought to court, and received prison sentences; but they were subsequently allowed to go free before completing their prison terms.

Nasserism, at the time, was still so much in the air that it continued to permeate the officer ranks of the Jordanian army, though to a lesser extent than before. In February 1959, while King Hussein was visiting the United States, accompanied by his deputy chief-of-staff General Sadek al-Sharaa, news arrived that thirteen army officers had been arrested back in Jordan on a charge of plotting to overthrow the monarchy. The coup was planned for 15 March, and there was evidence that General Sharaa, who came from Irbid, was the chief figure in the plot. The worried behaviour of Sharaa, as the reports regarding the arrests began to pour in, convinced Hussein of his guilt; and when Sharaa, on the way back from the United States, asked the king for permission to stay on for a while in Britain, ostensibly to undergo an urgent surgical operation, permission was refused. Once the royal party was back in Amman, General Sharaa was arrested, court-martialled and condemned to death, the king commuting the sentence to life imprisonment. As normally happened, the man was pardoned after spending twelve years in prison, whereupon he was appointed to no less sensitive a post than that of director-general of the passport office.

The attempted coup of General Sharaa was to be the last of its sort in the realm. However, other means were already being tried to put an end to the Jordanian monarchy. Towards the end of October 1958, King Hussein flew a twin-engined De Havilland Dove over Syrian airspace, on his way to take a holiday in Switzerland, and barely managed to get safely back to Amman after a scrape with two Syrian MiGs. The incident appeared to be an assassination attempt, being otherwise inexplicable. Other attempts at the assassination of the king were to follow. The king, from now on, had to be continually on his guard, even in his own household, where repeated attempts to kill him by poison were uncovered. On 29 August 1960, Hussein was on his way to the office of Hazza al-Majali, who had recently been appointed to replace Samir Rifai as prime minister, when he heard two explosions in the distance and was advised to return home. Two bombs had been placed in the building towards which he had been heading. The first to go off had been tucked into the prime minister's desk, and its explosion killed Majali and ten other government officials who were with him. The second went off shortly after in another room of the building. The bombs, it was believed, had been planted by two Syrians who had subsequently managed to escape across the border. A Jordanian official of the prime minister's office was arrested and accused of being an accessory to the crime. However, the full truth regarding the plot could not be legally established.

The death of Majali was a severe blow to King Hussein, and appeared to many to augur ill for the regime. In Amman, however, a point was made of going on with business as usual. The chief of the royal court, Bahjat al-Talhouni, was almost immediately appointed to replace Majali at the head of the government, in which most of the ministers were persuaded to retain their portfolios. By the spring of 1961, King Hussein was confident enough of the solidity of his position at home to initiate a correspondence with President Nasser. Repeated attempts to destabilize Jordan by one means or another had failed, and the economy of the country was beginning to do relatively well.

With the capital provided by British and American financial aid since the mid-1950s, the potash, phosphate and cement industries of Jordan were already undergoing development by the early 1960s, and an oil refinery – the first of its kind in the country – was under construction in the town of Zarqa, east of Amman. A network of modern highways, well constructed and maintained, was taking shape to knit the various parts of the country together. In the absence or near absence of graft, the financial resources of Jordan, though still relatively meagre, could be put to highly efficient use. Substantial remittances from the many Jordanians working in the Gulf countries, most of them Palestinians, were helping to develop the national economy. In Amman and Jerusalem and their suburbs, a boom in the construction industry provided opportunities for employment and work for skilled and unskilled labourers, again mostly Palestinians, many of them from the refugee camps. In addition, the country derived some income from tourism. Christians from all over the world came to visit the holy places in the West Bank, after which they toured the rich archaeological sites of the East Bank, most notably the fabulous ruins of Petra. The resulting prosperity in Jordan was reflected in the rapid growth of a new middle class of entrepreneurs, merchants and professionals. The country already had a well-run elementary and secondary school system. To enhance the development of its human resources, however, which were the principal source of its wealth, Jordan needed a national university; and a project for the establishment of such a university in one of the suburbs of Amman was already under way.

Whenever the general progress of the country threatened to slow down or halt, the king was always prepared to use the royal prerogative and cut across any bureaucratic hitch standing in the way. By 1961, he could declare with justified pride:

As Jordanians, we have learned one lesson that contributes daily to our progress: we have clarity of purpose. Having escaped death as a nation . . . Jordan wishes to play only one role, that of a model state. . . . We propose to devote . . . our full time and energy to the creation of a way of life that we hope in time all Arabs will achieve.[2]

Like the king, Jordanians in general felt they had good reason to boast of the progress their country was achieving in the face of great political hardship. Many among them, however, had fears that the good fortune they had come to enjoy was too precarious to last. The continued success of the Jordanian experiment appeared to depend entirely on the personal safety of the monarch. It took no more than one bullet to reverse the progress of the country beyond the possibility of redemption. To prevent this bullet from being fired, let alone reaching its target, constant security was required. And, as long as this remained necessary, the restoration of proper constitutional democracy to the country had to wait. Jordan was to receive much criticism on this count. However, by this time, the only Arab country where democratic procedures were still followed in principle was Lebanon, and even here the security system and the intelligence department of the army had to be allowed extensive rein, often at the expense of normal democractic rights, to help maintain national stability in the face of internal and external opposition.

* * * * * * * * * *

Meanwhile, in the Arab world at large, the political tide was beginning to turn against President Nasser, despite the fact that Arab popular opinion remained, for the most part, solidly behind him. In Baghdad, Brigadier Abdul-Karim Kassem had scarcely assumed power as president of the Iraqi Republic in 1958, when it became clear that the new Iraqi regime was not going to be any less hostile to Nasser's pan-Arab policies than the monarchy which this regime had overthrown and replaced. In Damascus, the growing disillusionment with Nasserism which followed the merger between Syria and Egypt resulted in a strange coalition between the Baath party and the surviving leaders of the old conservative establishment in the country. This coalition, by September 1961, had gathered enough strength to force the secession of Syria from the UAR. Syria next began to prepare to make common cause with Iraq and Jordan against Egypt. In the flush of his earlier triumphs, Nasser had grossly overplayed his hand, and was now beginning to pay for his faults.

For Nasser, however, the worst was still to come. In September 1962, a military coup by the pro-Egyptian commander of the

Yemeni army, Abdullah al-Sallal, resulted in the flight of Imam al-Badr from Sanaa, and the proclamation of the Yemen as a republic, with Sallal as its president. Imam al-Badr, however, remained in the country for several years, leading his Zeidi followers in guerrilla campaigns against the republican forces, in the hope that he could return to power. From Egypt, Nasser promptly announced his support of Sallal, and began to dispatch forces to the Yemen in increasing numbers to fight on the republican side. As he did so, he came into conflict with the rulers of Saudi Arabia – first King Saud, then his brother, King Feisal, who replaced him on the Saudi throne in 1964. The Saudis, like Jordan (see below), had come out strongly in support of the imam. They were dertermined to keep the Arabian peninsula under their influence, and were therefore opposed to having Nasser gain a foothold in the area.

When Sallal was later overthrown by a coalition of his former republican allies, and forced to flee to Cairo, Nasser's forces remained bogged down in the Yemen, with neither of the two warring Yemeni sides wanting their continued presence. Nasser, however, could not pull out his forces without losing face. Meanwhile, the desultory warfare between the two Yemeni parties dragged on, until Imam al-Badr was finally prevailed upon to retire from the scene, leaving the Saudi government to broker a peace arrangement between his followers and the now firmly established republican regime. As the Egyptian forces in the country were now left in complete isolation, Nasser had to discover some honourable way to have them withdrawn. His Yememi venture had turned out to be a miserable failure; and no matter how hard it tried, his propaganda machine could not present it to the Arab world as a triumph.

King Hussein, like Nasser, had involved himself in the Yemeni war, but only in the early stages. In August 1962, Jordan had formed a joint military command with Saudi Arabia, and when Sallal proclaimed the Yemeni Republic in Sanaa the following month, Hussein, acting against strong advice, decided to dispatch a squadron of his small air force to the Yemen to support Imam al-Badr against Sallal and Nasser. However, the head of the Jordanian air force and two pilots promptly defected to Cairo, whereupon what remained of the squadron was immediately recalled to Amman. The king had committed a disastrous mistake, as he was later to admit.[3] The worst part of this mistake was that it provided a ready excuse for the pro-Nasser opposition in Jordan to resume its open criticism of the regime.

In the early months of the following year, while Nasser's forces were beginning to get bogged down in the Yemen, new political developments in Iraq and Syria provided the Egyptian president with an opportunity to redeem his reputation as a pan-Arab leader in another way. In Baghdad, Abdul-Karim Kassem was over-thrown and killed in February, to be succeeded in power by his former associate, Abdul-Salam Aref. The new president of Iraq subscribed to the platform of the Movement of Arab Nationalists; and no sooner had he taken over power than he proposed a union between Iraq and Egypt. The following month, the Baath party in Syria, having fallen out with its conservative allies of the so-called 'Secessionist Regime' (*'Ahd al-Infisal*), seized the reins of govern-ment in Damascus for itself, and proceeded to press for an expansion of the union project suggested by Aref to include Syria along with Iraq and Egypt.

While the Baath party had long been at loggerheads with Nasser, it could not afford to have Syria left out of the proposed Iraqi-Egyptian union. The Baathists, moreover, stood to lose their pan-Arab credibility if they failed to come out in support of any Arab unity project. What they now pressed for was a union between Syria, Iraq and Egypt under what they termed a 'collec-tive leadership': a tactic aimed at preventing Nasser from domi-nating the union, as had happened in the case of the UAR. Nasser himself was in a hurry to produce some political magic to cover up the embarrassment he was facing in the Yemen, a matter which the Baathists could exploit.

From the tortuous manner in which the unity talks proceeded in Cario, critical observers could see that what was actually involved between the participants – and mainly between Egypt and Syria – was no genuine desire to achieve unity, but a political game in what had clearly become an Arab Cold War.[4] The talks ultimately resulted in a loose agreement, signed on 17 April 1963, providing for a union between Egypt, Syria and Iraq under a 'collective leadership', the union to come into effect after a preparatory period of twenty-five months. Among the Arab masses, however, the conclusion of this improbable union agreement was hailed as a tremendous pan-Arab achievement, and as another personal triumph for Nasser.

In fact, the conclusion of this agreement had hardly been announced when celebrating crowds went out on the streets in nearly every Arab capital shouting 'Nasser! Nasser!' In Amman, as in Jerusalem, the popular celebrations were quick to turn into riots, as the demonstrators proceeded to attack the police, provoking the government to bring out the army in full force to disperse them. Two years earlier, the Jordanian government, feeling confident that it had the country under control, had called for general elections, which returned a new parliament to power. Shortly afterwards, the political parties in the country, which had some vocal representatives in the new parliament, were permitted to resume their activities, on condition that they did not act as agents for outside powers. With a fresh wave of riots on its hands, the regime now became convinced that the earlier relaxation of its policy on the question of political freedom had been premature, and that decisive action was again necessary. Following a major riot in Jerusalem on 20 April in which four people were killed and thirty injured, the king proceeded to dissolve parliament and appoint his uncle, Sharif Hussein bin Nasser, to head an emergency government to handle the situation. The new government was quick to restore order, and the country was brought once more under firm military control.

* * * * * * * * * *

The union agreement between Egypt, Syria and Iraq never took effect; and the political bickering and mutual recriminations that followed between the partners to this agreement made a farce of all subsequent Arab unity proposals. King Hussein was being proved right, and Nasser's pan-Arab line had succeeded only in achieving greater political disunity in the Arab world. In the final analysis, no Arab regime was willing to have its sovereign prerogatives compromised for the sake of a union which only Nasser was in a position to dominate. From Amman, King Hussein could now pursue the Arab nationalist line following his own special interpretation. As he saw it, Arab nationalism could only succeed in promoting unity of purpose and action among the Arabs if it respected the special character of the different Arab countries and regimes, and did not threaten to trespass on their individual national sovereignties. As hitherto practised, Arab nationalist policy, in his view, was actually consecrating Arab disunity:

> Arab nationalism can survive only through complete equality. . . . It is in our power as Arabs to unite on all important issues, to organise in every respect and to dispel friction between us. . . . Given sincerity and sound leadership, the Arab League has great potential. It is the anvil on which Arab nationalism must be forged. . . . The Arab nation has a common tongue, a common cause, a common future, and a common challenge of survival. Combining the best of its past and the best it can absorb from modern civilisation, it should prosper. . . . In Jordan . . . we are Arabs first and Jordanians second. Jordan has borne the brunt of the burden laid on the Arab world by the unsound, emotional policies of the Arab leaders. We are not prepared to do so again. . . . Over the need for Arab unity there is no difference of opinion. So, instead of debating an accepted principle, let us debate a practical plan. . . . Let all of this be undertaken through an active, respected Arab League, in which . . . danger of domination by any member of the family would be eliminated.[5]

By the autumn of 1963, there was no longer any doubt that the union agreement between Egypt, Syria and Iraq had foundered. Meanwhile, in Jordan, King Hussein had already succeeded in getting everything under control again. The political strategy he had followed had hitherto been generally defensive, which did not reflect well on his pan-Arab standing. The situation now seemed ripe for a change of political course. The first signal that a change of policy in Amman was already under way came that same autumn with the opening of diplomatic relations between Jordan and the Soviet Union. The restoration of good relations with Egypt were to be the next item on the new Jordanian agenda.

In Cairo, Nasser was in a difficult position. Still saddled with involvement in the Yemen to no purpose, he had come to be further frustrated by the collapse of the union agreement with Syria and Iraq. In the circumstances, he was anxious to find a way to restore his image as the paramount leader of the Arabs. From Amman, King Hussein was one Arab leader who stood ready to help him. For the Hashemite monarch, the correspondence he had initiated with the Egyptian president in 1961 had been encouraging, and could have resulted at that early date in improved relations between Jordan and Egypt, had it not been for one hitch. At a conference of foreign ministers of the Arab League held at Shtura, in Lebanon, in August 1960,˙ Nasser had committed himself to supporting the formation of a Palestinian army, and also to the creation of a 'Palestinian entity' (*kayan Falastini*) in the West Bank, which was Jordanian territory. To improve his relations with Hussein, Nasser needed somehow to go back on at least the latter part of this commitment, which he was not prepared to do, considering the value he set on the support of the Palestinians for his pan-Arab ambitions. Also, Nasser and Hussein had been involved on opposite sides in the Yemeni war, which had put an end to the first attempt at reconciliation between the two men.

Now, however, the situation was different. Having repeatedly failed in attempts to impose his will on other Arab rulers, President Nasser was starting to present himself as no more than the first among equals. He invited fellow Arab rulers to come to Cairo in January 1964 for a summit conference. King Hussein accepted the invitation with unconcealed enthusiasm; and when he arrived in Cairo, Nasser went out of his way to show him brotherly affection.

The most important item on the agenda of the conference was the question of the Jordan waters, which was of special interest to Hussein. In 1955, a representative of the United States government, Eric Johnston, had proposed a plan for the distribution of the water of the Jordan river and its tributaries, whereby 40 per cent of these waters would go to Israel, and the remaining 60 per cent would be distributed between Lebanon, Jordan and Syria, with Jordan as the principal beneficiary. The plan was never officially accepted, because the Arab states thought that their adherence to it would involve a *de facto* recognition of Israel. Jordan was to bear the brunt of the consequences, because the non-acceptance of the Johnston plan held up irrigation projects which the country badly needed.

The problem for Jordan became particularly urgent in 1963, when the Israelis announced their intention to begin drawing their share of the Jordan waters, in accordance with the Johnston plan, to irrigate the Negev desert. The natural reservoir of these waters was Lake Tiberias, and a pipeline from this lake to the Negev was already nearing completion. The prospect of this was catastrophic for Jordan, especially as there was no way to tell how much more than their allotted share of the waters the Israelis intended to draw. Clearly, Israel was determined to take advantage of the Arab refusal to accept the Johnston plan and to abscond with as much of these waters as she could, threatening to turn the rich lands of the Jordanian Ghor into a saline desert.

At the meetings of the Cairo conference, Nasser and Hussein propounded the same line. While the Syrians pressed for military action to stop the Israeli diversion of the Jordan waters, the Egyptian president and the Jordanian monarch insisted that war with Israel over the issue must be avoided, as its consequences were bound to be disastrous. Even if one ignored the political disunity among the Arabs, which alone sufficed to make them the losers in any confrontation with the enemy, the superiority of the military capacity of Israel remained a basic factor to reckon with. Nasser and Hussein were both determined to resist the Syrian overbidding on this issue. However, the realistic solution to the problem – Arab adherence to the Johnston plan – remained out of the question politically.

In an attempt to solve the problem while ruling out the use of military force, at least for the time being, the Cairo conference finally decided to attempt the reduction of the flow of water into Lake Tiberias, by the diversion of some of the upper tributaries of the Jordan river in Lebanon and Syria. To prepare for defence in the event of Israeli military action to prevent these diversions, a joint Arab force was to be created, composed of Lebanese, Syrian, Jordanian and Egyptian elements, under a United Arab Command headed by Lieutenant-General Ali Ali Amer of Egypt. Having had previous experience of such joint defence arrangements between the Arab states, Hussein was not particularly enthusiastic about the establishment of this new United Arab Command, but he endorsed it nonetheless. Having effected a successful political reconciliation with Nasser, the Jordanian king was not going to take chances with it.

Another decision of the Cairo summit which King Hussein endorsed was the establishment of the Palestine Liberation Organization. The leader of this organization was to be Ahmed Shukairy, a Palestinian lawyer, formerly associated with Hajj Amin al-Husseini (see Chapters 6 and 7). Shukairy had been a member of the Higher Arab Committee for Palestine in 1948, and had later served as Syria's representative at the Arab League, and as the Saudi Arabian representative at the United Nations. The PLO was supposed to preserve the national identity of the Palestinians and to provide them with the political and military mechanism they needed to reclaim their national rights from Israel. King Hussein could recognize the need for an organization of this kind to satisfy and co-ordinate Palestinian aspirations. His only conditions were that the PLO should co-operate with Jordan, and that its military activities should be strictly controlled by the United Arab Command, lest they inadvertently led to a war with Israel for which the Arabs were not prepared.

The conditions set by Hussein for his acceptance of the PLO indicated the extent to which he was wary of the project. Acting in full sincerity, and with the enjoyment of full Arab dedication to its cause, all the PLO could really achieve, once it became operative, was to keep the controversy over Palestine alive on the agenda of world politics. Given the strength of Israel, and the firm commitment of the United States and other world powers to maintain and even further promote Israeli military superiority in the region, the PLO did not stand the least chance of liberating any part of the Palestinian territory which had gone to form the Jewish state. Granted, the organization could play an important ancillary role in the defence of what remained of the former territory of mandatory Palestine: the West Bank, now part of Jordan; and the Gaza strip, still administered by Egypt. The military forces at its disposal could also contribute to the defence of Arab host countries against possible Israeli aggression, by closely co-operating with the armed forces of these countries.

That there were Palestinians who thought in these realistic terms is certain. The dominant Palestinian mood, however, was one of bravado. From past experience, King Hussein and the Jordanian political establishment had good reason to fear that PLO activities would ultimately prove more of a danger to Jordan than to Israel. Fears of the same sort were openly expressed in Christian Lebanese circles – and more discreetly among some Lebanese Muslims – with respect to Lebanon. What compounded these fears, in Jordan as in Lebanon, was the Arab summit decision to divert the headwaters of the Jordan river, with a United Arab Command under Egyptian leadership standing by. Sooner or later, this projected diversion of the Jordan was bound to provoke Israeli military retaliation. Meanwhile, the United Arab Command, ostensibly formed as a precaution against this

expected eventuality, provided Egypt with ready means to inter-
fere with the mechanism which kept Jordan and Lebanon stable.
Considering the special political value of the Palestinians to
Nasser, there was no question as to where Egypt was going to
stand – at least ostensibly – in the event of conflict between the
PLO on the one hand and Jordan or Lebanon on the other.

To many observers, King Hussein, at that turning point in his
career, appeared to have been finally caught in the general Arab
frenzy. Actually, however, his ready endorsement of the decisions
of the Cairo summit had been the outcome of careful premedita-
tion. The king was fully aware of the dangers involved in subscrib-
ing to Nasser's adventurous policies; but he was now set on going
along with the Egyptian leader all the way, hoping for the best
and prepared for the worst. Essentially, he was sacrificing sound
political judgment for stability, because circumstances demanded
that he do so. In the final analysis, he had apparently deemed it
preferable for Jordan to join the Arab states in their frenzy and
accept her share of the expected consequences, rather than to
remain in isolation, continually at the mercy of destabilizing forces
from both without and within her frontiers.

* * * * * * * * * *

It was in keeping with the spirit of the Cairo summit that King
Hussein hosted the first Palestine National Congress, which
opened in Jerusalem on 28 May 1964, with more than 400
delegates present. The Palestinian National Charter adopted by
this congress defined Palestine as an indivisible territorial unit,
with a concession to the effect that Jordanian sovereignty over the
territory of the West Bank would not be contested. By the terms
of the charter, the role of the PLO was to liberate the Palestinian
'occupied territory' (*al-ard al-muhtalla*), meaning Israel. The
existence of the Jewish state on this territory was declared illegal.
The headquarters of the executive committee of the PLO, headed
by Ahmed Shukairy, were to be in Amman. The organization was
to co-operate with all Arab states, without interfering in the
internal affairs of any of them.

To undertake the liberation of the 'occupied territory', the PLO
required regular armed forces, to be called the Palestine Liberation Army, or PLA. Shukairy's job in Amman was to organize

this army; and the beginning of conflict between the PLO leaderi-ship and the Jordanian regime originated with this issue. To get the PLA organized, Shukairy demanded the right to tax and conscript Palestinians who were legally Jordanian nationals. The Jordanian government rejected these demands, on the grounds that they involved unacceptable trespasses on Jordan's sover-eignty. Shukairy also wanted to distribute arms to the inhabitants of the West Bank villages bordering Israel: something which had been tried before, with calamitous results, and which the Jordan-ian government was not prepared to allow again.

Saddled with the PLO in Amman, the Jordanian government soon found itself facing another difficulty. At about the same time as the PLO was established under the umbrella of the Arab League, and the sponsorship of Nasser, King Feisal of Saudi Arabia encouraged a group of young Palestinians working in Kuwait to found a secret organization under his own sponsorship called Fateh (Arabic *Fath*, meaning 'conquest').[6] The founders of this organiz-ation had first become involved in Palestinian activism when they were students together in Cairo; and the leading figure among them was a celibate engineer, Muhammad Abdul-Rauf al-Qudwa al-Husseini, who chose for himself the *nom de guerre* of Yasser Arafat, or Abu Ammar.[7] Arafat and his companions did not toe any particular ideological line, their principal commitment being to organize fedayeen raids into Israel. This they could not do without having a base in one of the countries bordering Israel from which to operate; and in January 1965 the Baath regime in Damascus, after some hesitation, gave them permission to operate from Syria.

Anxious to avoid Israeli retaliation against Syrian territory, the Baath authorities in Damascus forbade Fateh to send its fedayeen into Israel directly from Syria. Instead, these fedayeen were directed to infiltrate into Israel either by way of Lebanon, or preferably by way of Jordan, where the long armistice line could be easily infiltrated at many points, as already explained. For Syria, the repeated Fateh infiltrations through Jordan yielded the added bonus of embarrassing the Jordanian regime, and also of scoring a point over Nasser, who had no wish to provoke Israel into war, and therefore forbade Fateh from operating from the Gaza strip. The Syrians, at the time, were unhappy with the *rapprochement* between King Hussein and President Nasser, and with the latter's success in establishing himself as the sponsor of the PLO. The support they now gave Fateh thus became another ploy in the Arab Cold War in which Syria, for the moment, felt isolated.

King Hussein, for his part, was anxious to maintain the good relations he had recently succeeded in establishing with Egypt. Following the Cairo summit, he had made a point of holding more personal meetings with Nasser, to consolidate the new friendship with him. In a further gesture of goodwill towards the Egyptian president, Hussein withdrew his recognition of the imam of the Yemen, and offered to mediate between Egypt and Saudi Arabia on the Yemeni issue. It was during this period, also, that Hussein invited Abu Nuwar and other Jordanian political and military renegades to return from Cairo to Amman, while releasing from prison those who were still in Jordan. Nasser reciprocated, for the time being, by upholding the position taken by the Jordanian government with respect to the PLO. In September 1965, for example, when the third Arab summit was held in Casablanca, Ahmed Shukairy, eager to twist the arm of Jordan, urged that the PLO be empowered to deal directly with the Arab League, rather than with individual Arab host states. President Nasser, taking the side of Jordan, would not hear of this, and Shukairy's request was turned down. The Jordanian regime was consequently able to reassert its authority on home grounds, by closing down the PLO head office in Amman, along with the branch offices throughout the country, and ordering arrests of PLO and Fateh personnel whose activities were deemed a threat to Jordan's security. With the Jordanian army keeping careful watch over the full length of the Israeli border, only one fedayeen operation against Israel by way of Jordan was registered between December 1965 and June 1966.

Nasser, however, had never really been as strong as he was thought to be; and with his insatiable craving for the sort of pan-Arab popularity which the Palestinians were particularly qualified to give, he was not the sort of man on whose support Jordan could rely indefinitely. By 1966, Egypt's position in the Yemen had become hopeless. Meanwhile, the Syrians had upstaged Nasser on the Palestinian issue by the overt and vociferous support they accorded Fateh. In his anxiety to make up for his political losses, Nasser was forced to make a *volte-face* by the summer of that year, when he openly declared himself in favour of unbridled fedayeen activity against Israel, not only by the official PLO, but also by the clandestine Fateh. Ahmed Shukairy, who had been forced to leave Amman earlier on, was invited to establish the PLO head office in Gaza. Finding himself again in isolation, with a ruthless propaganda attack unleashed once more against him, King Hussein was compelled to relax Jordanian control over the Palestinian organizations. As a result, Fateh was able to carry out fourteen operations from Jordan against Israel between June and October of that year.

* * * * * * * * * *

By the autumn of 1966, Egypt and Syria were competing with reckless abandon for popularity with the Palestinians. Iraq was also beating its drums, albeit from a safe distance. Any disinterested observer could tell that what was going on was no more than a game. But this game was a particularly dangerous one, as none of the participants gave the least thought to the consequences. Jordan was caught in the middle, and there was nothing she could do about it. The Jordanian regime was also falling under attack from Egypt for its stand on the side of Saudi Arabia on the question of the Yemen.

Meanwhile, as the ability of Amman to control fedayeen operations from the Jordanian territory was weakened, Israeli reprisals could easily be provoked, with which the Jordanian armed forces, alone, could not easily deal. The United Arab Command, which had been officially in existence since 1964, had not been operative in the best of times; and by now it had simply ceased to be there to help. In the early morning of 13 November 1966, the Israelis launched a major punitive attack on the West Bank border village of Samua, in the region of al-Khalil (Hebron), where they rounded up the villagers and began to destroy their houses, on the grounds that they had been giving shelter to fedayeen infiltrators. A Jordanian armed column hastened from al-Khalil to Samua to repel the attack; but the Israelis were able to ambush this force and decimate it as it entered the village. By the time the Israeli operation was over, a minimum of eighteen Jordanians had been killed and at least double that number wounded.

Rather than awakening Arab public opinion to the perils which

Jordan was now facing, all that the tragedy of Samua did was provide the enemies of the Jordanian regime with a ready excuse to harden their attacks against it. The regime, it was argued, was principally to blame for what had happened to Samua, and for what was going to happen to other West Bank villages along the Israeli border, because the authorities in Amman persisted in refusing to have the local Palestinians armed so that they could defend hearth and home. As radio broadcasts from Cairo, Damascus and Baghdad recited such arguments, inciting the Jordanian people to rise against their rulers, crowds composed mainly of Palestinians went out on the streets of all the major Jordanian towns and cities, clamouring for the abdication of the king and the establishment of a PLO government to replace him. The rioting continued for twelve days before the Jordanian army decided to take action against it. Even then, it took weeks for order to be restored throughout the country.

The situation for Jordan remained precarious. Much as they hated one another, Nasser and the Baathists of Syria on the one hand, and the Syrians and the Iraqis on the other, had all allied themselves with the Palestinians. Incongruous as this alliance was, it had come to be popularly viewed as representing the Arab nationalist mainstream. For Jordan to emerge from its predicament, it ultimately had no choice but to add to the incongruities of this alleged mainstream by joining it.

Meanwhile, new developments in the regional situation were beginning to indicate a drift towards war. As the Syrians continued to attack Jordan for refusing to allow the Palestinian fedayeen to operate freely from Jordanian territory, they had to open their own borders with Israel to fedayeen operations. Thus Syria, like Jordan, became exposed to Israeli retaliation. Nasser, meanwhile, against his better judgment, found himself compelled to sign a defence pact with the Syrians on 4 November 1966. Nasser's own borders with Israel were secure. Since the end of the Suez War in 1956, a United Nations force had been stationed in the Gaza strip to see that hostilities between Egypt and Israel were not renewed. As long as this force remained in place, Nasser had a ready excuse not to carry out his military commitments to other Arab parties as promised. By the spring of 1967, however, the situation on the Syrian–Israeli border had become extremely tense. In April, six Syrian aircraft were shot down by the Israelis in a dogfight close to the Jordanian border, and at least one of the Syrian warplanes that were hit fell inside Jordan.

For several months, Radio Cairo had been broadcasting insults and taunts against the Jordanian regime. King Hussein and Radio Amman now had the opportunity to retaliate. Did not Nasser have a defence pact with Syria? And how was it that, while the Syrian and Jordanian borders were becoming the scene of repeated Israeli–Arab confrontations, all was quiet on the Egyptian front? Was it not because Nasser was hiding behind the United Nations forces? Given the circumstances, should these forces be allowed to remain in place? Furthermore, Egypt controlled the straits of Tiran, which led into the Gulf of Aqaba, and thus had a stranglehold over the strategic port of Elath, which was Israel's only outlet to the Red Sea. Did not 'logic, wisdom and nationalism'[8] dictate that Egypt close these straits in the face of Israel?

With his concern for his pan-Arab image, Nasser could not ignore the Jordanian taunts. On 16 May, he surprised the world by asking the United Nations to withdraw its forces from Sinai, and his request was complied with two days later. Worse still, on 22 May, the Egyptian president announced the closure of the straits of Tiran. In Amman, King Hussein reportedly received the news with horror. He had not expected Nasser to respond so promptly to his taunting. War with Israel now seemed imminent; and Jordan, as an Arab country which had unwittingly shared in setting the stage for it, would have to share in bearing the consequences.

* * * * * * * * * *

On 28 May, King Hussein took the initiative to re-establish contact with President Nasser, offering the entry of Jordan into a tripartite alliance with Egypt and Syria against Israel. His decision to do so, given the expected outcome, appeared rash, but it had actually been taken after a careful balancing of alternatives. Regardless of the rights and wrongs of the case on the Arab side, was it better for Jordan to join Egypt and Syria in a defensive war against Israel, and share defeat with them? Or was it more prudent for Jordan to keep out of such a war, no doubt to pay a much heavier price – and this time a deserved one – if it did so? Israel was sending repeated signals to Amman to opt for the latter course. But King Hussein, though alert to these signals, was fully set on ignoring them. In a showdown with Israel, Jordan could take only the Arab side, no matter what the cost. As a semi-official statement from the palace was later to explain:

. . . to meet with Nasser may seem strange when one considers the insults and abuse which Radio Cairo had been hurling at the Hashemite throne for the past year; nonetheless, it would have been impossible for us to justify our remaining aloof from so momentous a matter which engaged the entire Arab world.[9]

Hussein's new overtures were immediately accepted by Nasser, whereupon the king proceeded to Cairo to sign the suggested Arab defence pact with the Egyptian president on 30 May 1967. King Hussein agreed that, in the event of war, Jordan's forces would be placed under the command of General Abdul-Moneim Riad, the assistant chief of the resurrected United Arab Command. Before signing the pact, Nasser made it clear to the Jordanian monarch that he expected him to become reconciled with the PLO. Incorrigible gamesman that he was, Nasser had actually summoned Shukairy from Gaza to be present when the Egyptian-Jordanian defence pact was signed. Furthermore, the Egyptian president insisted that King Hussein take the PLO leader back to Amman with him on the same aircraft. The king, as Nasser saw it, had to undergo some penance before being accepted back into the Arab fold.

Syria did not agree to adhere to the Egyptian-Jordanian defence pact, and went to the extent of denouncing this pact as a betrayal of the Arab cause. Saudi Arabia, on the other hand, promised to send a brigade to Jordan as its contribution to the Arab defence arrangements. Iraq, after some hesitation, did agree to sign the pact. King Hussein announced this fact at a press conference in Amman on 3 June, adding that he now expected Israel to launch her offensive within forty-eight hours.

The expected Israeli offensive began on the morning of 5 June with an attack on Egyptian air bases, which put the Egyptian air force out of operation in one blow. In response, General Riad ordered the Jordanian army to go into action against positions inside Israel on the same day. By 7 June, a swift Israeli counterattack on the Jordanian front had resulted in the fall of the whole of the West Bank, including the Arab sector of Jerusalem. As Syria entered the war, to wage an attack from the north, her forces were driven back all the way to the outskirts of Damascus. By 11 June, the so-called Six-Day War – the third Arab–Israeli war – was brought to an end by a cease-fire imposed by the United Nations. The Arab defeat in the war had been total, leaving Israel in occupation not only of the Jordanian West Bank, but also of the Syrian Golan heights overlooking Lake Tiberias, along with the Gaza strip in southern Palestine, and the Egyptian territory of Sinai. The price paid for the catastrophic Arab adventure had turned out to be much higher than expected.

NOTES

1. H.M. King Hussein of Jordan, *Uneasy Lies the Head* (London, 1962), pp. 74–6.
2. *Ibid.*, pp. 79–80.
3. Peter Snow, *Hussein: A Biography* (London, 1972), p. 152.
4. This term was coined by Malcolm Kerr as the title of his insightful book *The Arab Cold War 1958–1964* (Oxford, 1965).
5. *Uneasy Lies the Head*, pp. 75–80.
6. The name by which this organization came to be known is the vocalized acronym, in reverse, of an abbreviation of its full name, *Harakat al-Tahrir al-Watani al-Falastini*, meaning the 'movement of Palestinian national liberation'. It was King Feisal, reportedly, who suggested the reversal of the acronym, which would otherwise have been *hatf*, meaning 'demise'. The initial contacts between the Saudi monarch and the founders of Fateh were undertaken by an officer of the Saudi army called Fahd al-Marek.
7. A number of Arabic personal names have *Abu* (meaning 'father of') sobriquets that automatically go with them, so that anyone called Yasser, after the father of Ammar ibn Yasser, one of the Prophet's companions, would automatically be an Abu Ammar. The use of Abu sobriquets in addressing seniors in age, or social superiors, combines informality with deference, thereby dispensing with the need to use titles; hence their popularity.
8. Quoted by Peter Snow in *Hussein: a biography*, p. 172.
9. Quoted by Clinton Bailey in *Jordan's Palestinian Challenge, 1948–1983: a Political History* (Boulder, Colorado, 1984), p. 27, from the Arabic edition of King Hussein's *My War with Israel*.

10

Two Sovereignties in Conflict

Jordan paid by far the heaviest price for her share of the blame for what befell the Arabs in June 1967. In Cairo, President Nasser could somehow afford to speak of the outcome of the Six-Day War with Israel as a *naksa*, or temporary reverse. The Sinai desert lost by Egypt in the war was important mainly for its strategic value. The same was true of the Golan heights lost by Syria. But this was not the case for the Jordanian West Bank. Effectively, this area comprised about half the inhabited territory of the Jordanian kingdom; and its fall to Israel could in no way be dismissed as a mere *naksa*. Little wonder that among the Arab losers in the war, Jordan came out particularly crestfallen.

Until 1967, the Jordanian regime could justifiably take pride in having managed to preserve as much as it did of the territory of Arab Palestine since 1948. More than anything else, it could boast of having kept the historical and religiously hallowed sector of Jerusalem in Arab hands, at the cost of Jordanian blood. To the rulers of Amman, Arab Jersualem had been the priceless jewel in the Hashemite crown. But the loss of Jerusalem and the rest of the West Bank in 1967 was not limited to matters of symbolic value only. It also robbed Jordan of the most developed part of her territory, dealing a death blow, among other things, to the recent boom in her tourist trade. Having lost Jerusalem, along with other hallowed Palestinian sites, notably Bethlehem and Hebron, the kingdom could no longer advertise itself as being the Holy Land, as it had previously done. Tourists were unlikely to be attracted to Jordan in large numbers simply to visit the ruins of Jerash or Petra, or those of the Umayyad desert palaces.

Moreover, of the Arab lands lost to Israel as a result of the June war, the West Bank stood the least chance of being easily regained. The Israelis considered the area to be part of their biblical heritage; and the hard-liners among them regarded its occupation as a legitimate Jewish re-conquest of what had once been the Israelite territory of Judah and Samaria. Israel was certainly not prepared to compromise on the question of Jerusalem. Having occupied the Arab sector of the city, the Israeli government immediately proceeded to annex it to the Israeli sector. Jerusalem, as 're-unified', was forthwith proclaimed an integral part of the territory of Israel; and the world was called upon to recognize the holy city as the rightful historical capital of the Jewish nation.

The problem which Jordan was to face on this issue began to assume its full proportions after 22 November 1967, when the United Nations Security Council adopted Resolution 242, calling upon Israel to withdraw from the Arab territories it occupied, as a pre-condition for an Arab–Israeli peace. Upon the insistence of the United States, Resolution 242 was carefully worded so as to avoid any ruling on specific points. From the American point of view, which other permanent members of the Security Council came round to appreciating, the important thing was to get the Arabs and the Israelis to the peace table, rather than leaving the United Nations as a constant umpire between the two sides while the conflict between them remained unresolved, as had happened after the Suez war. Thus, the official English text of Resolution 242 established the principle of Israeli withdrawal from 'occupied territories' (rather than from *the* occupied territories), leaving the technicalities of the withdrawal to be worked out by direct negotiations between the regional parties concerned. In effect, the wording of the resolution added a further dimension to the outstanding Arab–Israeli conflict. Arabs perceived the ambiguity in Resolution 242 as an American and Western trick, deliberately designed to compromise the Arab right to territories which Israel seemed bent on keeping in flagrant disregard of international law. Israelis, for their part, interpreted the equivocal wording of the resolution as giving them the option to keep or return whatever parts of the occupied territories they chose. From the very outset, Israel officially made it clear that the return of Jerusalem, at least, was out of the question.

Before tackling the knotty question of how to exchange peace for lost land, the more immediate problem facing Jordan, as a consequence of the fall of the West Bank, was the influx of masses of refugees into the East Bank. These refugees, arriving destitute, had somehow to be accommodated and attended to, at a time when the Jordanian economy stood shattered, seemingly beyond the possibility of effective repair. Worse still, these refugees, as Palestinians, blamed their plight on the Jordanian authorities, accusing them of having virtually surrendered what had remained of Arab Palestine to the Jews. 'They sold it to them furnished,' the slogan ran. A country, the Palestinians argued, can only be properly defended by its own people, but the Jordanian regime had never permitted the people of the West Bank to be adequately armed so that they could share in the defence of their own land. The Jordanians – perceived as being in fact Transjordanians – were accused of having consistently treated West Bank Palestinians as subjects rather than as fellow citizens. The West Bank, it was said, was 'neither their home nor that of their fathers', which was why they had relinquished it so easily. Before 1967, it was claimed, the chief function of the Jordanian army in the area had been to repress and brutalize the local population, particularly in the villages, rather than to attend to the proper defence of the territory. The Syrians, eager to deflect attention from their share of the responsibility for the general Arab tragedy, encouraged Palestinians to persist in thinking along these lines, and in pinning the blame for what had happened to them chiefly on Jordan.

Having courted disaster and paid the price for it, the Jordanian regime, for its part, set itself immediately to work to make the best of what remained of the kingdom's assets. A year before the outbreak of the June war, King Hussein had chosen his youngest brother, Hassan, to be the crown prince. The young man had just completed his studies at Christ Church, Oxford, and was thus the first member of the royal family to have received a complete university education. Setting store by his competence and diligence, the king entrusted him with the task of attending to the problems relating to the reconstruction and development of the country. The seriousness of purpose on the part of both the king and the crown prince attracted a group of highly competent and resourceful Palestinian academics to place themselves at their service. These were serious-minded individuals who were not blinded by the prevailing Palestinian hostility towards the Hashemite monarchy. It was largely with their help that the crown prince founded a Royal Scientific Society in Amman in 1968, to dedicate itself to the development of Jordan's human resources, particularly in the field of technology.

This was a promising beginning. But, for the moment, Jordan's reconstruction and development efforts continued to be over-shadowed by the political situation in the country and the region. King Hussein was fully aware of the Israeli danger, and at the same time convinced that this danger could only be averted if the Arabs could reach some form of understanding with Israel. The Jewish state thrived on the hostility of the Arabs towards it; at the same time, it was strong enough to win in war against any combination of Arab forces, as had been amply demonstrated in 1948, and more dramatically in 1967. An Arab peace with Israel, on the other hand, would remove the acknowledged military superiority of Israel from the political equation, reducing the Jewish polity to the status of an ordinary Middle Eastern state, preoccupied with day-to-day affairs. After the Arab defeat in the Six-Day War, there was a meeting of minds between President Nasser and King Hussein on this matter. At an Arab summit held in Khartoum between 29 August and 1 September 1967, which Syria and Algeria refused to attend, it was tacitly agreed to 'eliminate the effects of the aggression and to ensure the with-drawal of the aggressive Israeli forces from the Arab lands' by peaceful means, provided there was '*no* peace with Israel, *no* recognition of Israel, *no* negotiations with it'. These three 'nos', taken at the time to be an indication of continuing Arab intransi-gence, were actually intended to be no more than a face-saving formula. With the Syrians and the Palestinians, backed by the Algerians, intent on opposing any move in the direction of peace with Israel, the decision adopted by the Khartoum summit stood no hope of being politically marketable in the Arab world without some verbal concessions to the hard-line platform.

It was following the Khartoum summit that the United Nations Security Council finally came round to adopting Resolution 242, calling on Israel and the Arabs to exchange land for peace. Israel accepted the resolution as a basis for negotiation, as did Jordan, Egypt and Lebanon on the Arab side. But Syria rejected the proposal outright, providing the Palestinians with the political backing they needed to oppose it from their own direction. King Feisal of Saudi Arabia put at least some of his considerable political weight on the side of the Syrian and Palestinian position – on more than one occasion, by solemnly announcing that he intended to pray at the Aqsa mosque in Jersualem before he died. Having been instrumental in the founding of the Fateh movement in 1964 (see Chapter 9), the Saudi monarch now made no secret of his continuing support for this Palestinian fedayeen organization, and for the Palestinian resistance movement in general. By following this strong pro-Palestinian line, King Feisal threatened to undermine the move towards Arab moderation which President Nasser was beginning to pursue. It is possible that the embarrassment of the Egyptian leader over this matter was actually intended as a settlement of earlier political scores. Following the reverse suffered by Egypt in the Six-Day War, Nasser had endured the further humiliation of pulling his troops out of the Yemen, unconditionally and without fanfare. The Saudi ruler continued to nurse strong grudges against Nasser over the Yemeni issue, even after it had become a thing of the past.

With Syria overbidding on the Palestinian question from one direction, and Saudi Arabia and her peninsular satellites – notably Kuwait – rejecting peace moves from the other, the hand of the Egyptian president was forced. Still setting high value on Palestinian popular support, Nasser was compelled to take a more indulgent attitude not only towards the PLO, which was still under Shukairy's leadership, but also towards Fateh, which he knew to be Saudi-backed. To secure the leverage he needed to deal with Fateh, however, the Egyptian president sponsored the establishment of two Palestinian fedayeen groups of his own, which he could direct as he pleased. The same was also done by Syria and Iraq, and, later, by Libya, where Colonel Muammar al-Qaddafi had overthrown the Idrisi monarchy in 1969 and seized power, proclaiming his recognition of the pan-Arab leadership of Nasser. Like Saudi Arabia and the Arabian Gulf states, Libya derived a large revenue from oil, and was thus in a position to provide financial support for Palestinian fedayeen organizations willing to toe her line.

Of the numerous fedayeen groups that proliferated after 1967, the only one which was independent of Arab state sponsorship from the very beginning was the Popular Front for the Liberation of Palestine, or PFLP. The founder of this group, Georges Habash, was a Christian Palestinian from Lydda, and a medical graduate of the AUB, who had formerly been the leading figure of the clandestine *Shabibat al-Tha'r* – the nuclear group which came to head the Movement of Arab Nationalists after 1948 (see Chapter 8). As the leader of the PFLP, Habash proclaimed his ideological adherence to Marxist socialism, and proceeded to seek support for his organization from the Soviet Union and communist China. Of all the fedayeen leaders, Habash was the most uncompromisingly hostile to the Hashemite regime in Amman, his PFLP having inherited its strong anti-Hashemite stance from its political ancestor, the Movement of Arab Nationalists. The splinter groups of the PFLP, notably the Popular Democratic Front for the Liberation of Palestine, or PDFLP, led by the Christian Transjordanian Nayef Hawatmeh, from Salt, were no less vocal in their opposition to the Jordanian monarchy than the mother organization.

* * * * * * * * *

In the course of 1968, Fateh and most other Palestinian fedayeen organizations joined the PLO. The Arab states having hitherto failed to live up to their promise of redeeming Palestine, the fedayeen organizations made it clear that they intended to assume the responsibility of liberating their lost homeland by their own efforts. By now, they had come to consider themselves as representing a sovereign Palestinian resistance (*muqawama*), or Palestinian revolution (*thawra*), independent of any non-Palestinian Arab control. Naturally, the Palestinians could not easily take such an openly defiant stand with respect to Arab states which were their political or financial sponsors, and to which a number of their fedayeen groups were in fact politically answerable. On the other hand, they could easily pit the sovereignty of their revolution against that of Arab states with seemingly precarious regimes, notably Lebanon and Jordan. The pretext, in the case of both these countries, was that their territories provided ideal bases for fedayeen operations against Israel. In Lebanon, the Palestinians had been insinuating themselves into the endemic rift between the Muslims and Christians of the country since 1965, with encouragement from Muslim Lebanese parties. In Jordan, where more than half the population in the East Bank was already Palestinian, the fedayeen could act with even more temerity. Their leaders seemed to take for granted their ability to override the sovereignty of the Hashemite regime in Amman.

Immediately following the Arab defeat in the June war, the whole Arab world seemed to be supporting the Palestinian revolution. Jordan, for the time being, was not strong enough to prevent the different Palestinian fedayeen groups from freely operating on her national territory. The Jordanian government, however, took the necessary precautions to keep constant track of all fedayeen movements in the country through the Mukhabarat, the intelligence branch of the Jordanian army. By this time, there was hardly an Arab or non-Arab intelligence service operating in the region which had not infiltrated the Palestinian fedayeen ranks, normally at more than one echelon; and Jordan's sophisticated Mukhabarat was certainly no exception. From the very beginning, the Jordanian army felt confident that it would be able to handle the fedayeen problem when the right moment came. The plain fact was that the fedayeen organizations had an exaggerated estimate of their own power. Moreover, their conditioned political reflexes, compounded by the latent or open rivalries among their leaders and the indiscipline prevailing in their ranks, made them easy to manipulate by any agency interested in their destruction.

Initially, Jordan made a point of lending military backing to Fateh and other fedayeen groups operating against Israel from her territory. Most Palestinians, however, doubted the motives behind this support. The Jordanian army, they suspected, was simply going through the motions of backing them, being in no position to do otherwise. Regardless of whether they were right or wrong in their suspicions, the Palestinian fedayeen in Jordan clearly wanted the military show in the country to be exclusively their own, which was enough to drive a wedge between them and the many Jordanians who were loyal to the monarchy. To such Jordanians, the fedayeen appeared more set on discrediting the Jordanian regime and effecting a Palestinian takeover of the country than on fighting Israel. How else to explain the fact that they misconstrued the behaviour of Jordan towards them at every turn?

On 21 March 1968, the Israelis carried out a major raid, with tanks, on a Fateh stronghold at Karameh, in the Jordan valley, where they began to destroy the village houses with dynamite.

The raid was repelled after a fierce battle in which the Jordanian army fought alongside the fedayeen of Fateh, using its artillery to destroy a number of the Israeli tanks. In Amman, King Hussein praised the role of both the army and Fateh in achieving this victory, declaring that 'we have reached the point where we are all fedayeen'.[1] But the masses of Palestinians who went out on the streets of the capital, first to celebrate the event, then to honour the Palestinian dead, claimed the victory entirely for Fateh. To their mind, the Israelis had been beaten for the first time in an open encounter, and it was the Palestinian resistance that had achieved this feat. The Jordanian army, for its part, maintained that the fedayeen could not have won the battle alone, and that the brunt of the fighting had been done by its own men, but this claim was ignored by the celebrating Palestinian crowds. No matter what the Jordanian forces did, the fedayeen were obviously not prepared to accept them as true brothers in arms.

Until that time, the main concentrations of the fedayeen had been in the Jordan valley, and their pressure was felt little in Amman. In the flush of Palestinian enthusiasm that followed the battle of Karameh, however, their ranks everywhere were suddenly swelled with new recruits. By a tacit understanding between the Jordanian government and the PLO, Palestinians of Jordanian nationality could escape compulsory service in the Jordanian army if they joined the fedayeen organizations. These organizations, being for the most part more than adequately funded by their Arab sponsors, were in a position to pay them salaries. Meanwhile, in Amman as in other urban centres, popular militias were organized, ostensibly to serve as auxiliaries to the Palestinian resistance. At the same time, repeated Israeli shelling of the fedayeen hideouts in the Jordan valley was causing increasing numbers of Palestinian fighters to move their bases away from that border area, to entrench themselves in and around the Jordanian capital and the principal towns. The resulting breakdown in law and order provided the banned political parties of the Jordanian opposition with a long-awaited opportunity to come out into the open again. In April 1968, they formed a left-wing coalition under the chairmanship of Suleiman Nabulsi (see Chapter 8),[2] declaring themselves openly in favour of the fedayeen, whose forceful presence they sought to exploit in pressing for the restoration of the political freedoms suspended in the country first in 1957, and then again in 1963. During the months that followed, Palestinian fedayeen, mainly from Lebanon and Syria, began to converge on Jordan, virtually taking over the Jordanian capital and making it their principal stronghold. On the immediate outskirts of Amman, the Wahadat and Husseini refugee camps came to be popularly referred to as independent republics. Here, as elsewhere, the Jordanian army and security forces offered the fedayeen no open resistance for the moment, and practically ceased to be visible. The Palestinian leaders, however, were aware that Jordanian preparations were under way for an ultimate showdown.

In October 1968, the Fateh radio station, operating from Cairo, began to speak of a plot to destroy the Palestinian revolution inside Jordan. Shortly afterwards, in early November, members of a small fedayeen organization called *al-Nasr* ('the victory') had an armed clash with the Jordanian police in Amman. The head of this organization was Taher Dablan: a Palestinian who had recently retired from service as an officer in the Syrian army, and whom the Palestinians alleged was actually a secret agent of the Jordanian Mukhabarat. In response to the armed attack by Dablan's men on the police, the Jordanian government ordered the army to strike back at his organization; Dablan himself was seized and put in prison, after being condemned to death by a military court. By striking at al-Nasr, no matter what the Palestinians thought of this group, the Jordanian regime was issuing a warning to other fedayeen organizations of the fate that awaited them if they persisted in ignoring the legitimate authority in the country.

Plainly, a sovereign revolution and a sovereign state could not continue living under the same roof. Sooner or later, one of them had to destroy the other. For the time being, however, pretences at co-operation were kept up by both sides. Following the action taken by the Jordanian army against al-Nasr, the Palestinian organizations agreed to respect the full authority of the Jordanian regime, and to restrain the indiscipline of their unruly elements. But their promises, even when sincerely meant, could not be kept; and, as a result, the situation in the country continued to drift further towards total anarchy. In February 1969, the Fateh leader, Yasser Arafat, took over the leadership of the PLO from Ahmed Shukairy, whereupon he immediately proceeded to hold friendly talks with King Hussein. Attempts to heal the rift between the Jordanian regime and the Palestinian revolution by contacts of this kind were repeated time and time again. However, every time an agreement was reached, something happened to make it break down. As far as the Palestinians were concerned, the Jordanian authorities could not be trusted; and as far as the Jordanian regime was concerned, the Palestinian fedayeen had no business being in Jordan in the first place.

By now, the regime, in its determination to crush the fedayeen, could count on a large body of Jordanian opinion – mainly, but not exclusively, Transjordanian – to provide it with moral backing. By pressing its luck too far, the Palestinian revolution had awakened, for the first time, a strong and vocal patriotism among the many Jordanians who remained loyal to the Hashemite throne. The more the fedayeen flexed their military muscle in the country and its capital, the stronger this Jordanian patriotism grew. At the American University of Beirut, where the PLO had one of its principal student strongholds, Jordanian students – about half of them of Palestinian or Syrian origin – set up what they called the Jordanian Organization (*al-Tanzim al-Urduni*) to confront the Palestinian taunts directed against their king, or against their government and army. The Palestinians tried to discredit this Tanzim by branding it an agency of the Jordanian Mukhabarat, which was not in fact true.[3] The Palestinians, confident at the time of the grip they had over Arab popular opinion, simply failed to appreciate the extent to which other Arabs, such as the Jordanians or Lebanese, could be sincerely committed to their own national causes. This lack of empathy with the patriotism of other Arabs was to prove, in time, one of the principal weaknesses of the Palestinian revolution.

* * * * * * * * *

After holding his first talks with Yasser Arafat, King Hussein went to Washington in March 1969 for talks with the new American president, Richard Nixon. The Jordanian monarch proposed that the Arab peace initiative with Israel be renewed on the basis of a six-point plan which did not differ greatly from Resolution 242. To the Palestinians, this meant that King Hussein was going back on his policy of resistance to Israel by force. Palestinian suspicions were further fed by statements issuing from Washington that Hussein was confident of being able to curb the fedayeen movement in Jordan once a sastisfactory settlement with Israel had been reached. A few months later, in August, King Hussein tried to ease the violent PLO attacks on his peace move by assuring the Palestinian people that they would have the right to determine their future as they pleased once an end had been put to the Israeli occupation of the West Bank territory. He even insinuated that the Arabs might have to go to war against Israel to achieve this end. The Palestinians, however, construed the assurances made to them by the king as emanating from weakness. By the end of 1969, there was no sign of Israel being prepared to withdraw from any of the occupied territories, least of all the West Bank. Meanwhile, the behaviour of the Palestinian fedayeen in Jordan had reached the point where it had become intolerable. To all intents and purposes, the PLO within the country, now dominated by Fateh, had become a state within the state. It showed no signs of being able to control the indiscipline of the various fedayeen groups in the slightest, with each of them continuing to answer to a different Arab political sponsor.

As the major Palestinian organization which depended on Arab governments for its funding, Fateh was committed to non-interference in the internal affairs of Arab states. Its leadership, therefore, was disinclined to take an open stand against the Jordanian regime, for as long as that could be avoided. The same, however, did not apply to organizations such as the PFLP of Georges Habash, or the PDFLP of Nayef Hawatmeh. By the start of 1970, Habash and Hawatmeh were already calling for the overthrow of the Jordanian monarchy and its replacement by a militant left-wing regime. The liberation of Palestine, they maintained, could not be achieved unless Jordan was liberated first.

With the notable exception of Syria, most of the Arab states, including Egypt, seemed to be in sympathy with Jordan over the fedayeen question. However, there was not much they could do to help, beyond offering their services as mediators between the Jordanian regime and the PLO. Throughout the Arab world, the fedayeen movement had fired the enthusiasm of the masses; and every Arab regime had to reckon with this fact. By creating the PLO in 1964, the Arab League had let the genie out of the bottle; and not even Nasser, with all the pan-Arab popularity he still enjoyed, could get it back in again. Hussein was led to understand this from Nasser personally, when he flew to Cairo in February 1970 for talks with the Egyptian president. Nasser was prepared to use his good offices to reduce the Palestinian pressure on the Jordanian regime, provided Hussein restrained his army from openly clashing with the Palestinian fighters. King Hussein's position was further compromised over the fedayeen issue by the fact that the Arab countries on which Jordan depended for financial subsidy – notably Saudi Arabia, Kuwait and Libya – were openly committed to supporting the fedayeen cause.

* * * * * * * * * *

Following the return of King Hussein from his meeting with Nasser, the situation in Jordan rapidly deteriorated. The government, from its side, began to exert pressures to limit the freedom of activity of the Palestinian resistance. The fedayeen organizations, from their side, began to vie with one another in defying the efforts of the Jordanian regime to curb their power. Agreements between the two sides were no sooner concluded than they collapsed. On 9 June 1970, some fedayeen opened fire on the Mukhabarat headquarters in Amman. As the king made his way there to see what was happening, his motorcade came under heavy machine-gun fire, and one of the soldiers accompanying him was killed. The news of the attack on the king was hardly out when the Bedouin crack forces of the Jordanian army took matters into their own hands. The two major refugee camps on the immediate outskirts of the capital – al-Wahadat and al-Husseini – were shelled; and clashes between the Jordanian troops and the fedayeen continued for three days. Meanwhile, the PFLP seized fifty-eight foreigners from the two leading hotels in Amman, declaring that these people would continue to be held as hostages until the shelling of the refugee camps was stopped. When a cease-fire was finally arranged, Fateh stepped in to outbid the PFLP by demanding changes in the army command and the dismissal of the king's leading advisers before the cease-fire could be accepted and the hostages released. The king was advised by his chief ministers, including the prime minister Bahjat Talhouni, to agree to these terms. The army was left enraged.

In a last attempt to agree terms with the Palestinian resistance,

King Hussein invited officials from Algeria, Tunisia, Sudan, Egypt and Libya to act as a committee of reconciliation. The efforts of this committee resulted in yet another agreement between the Jordanian and Palestinian sides, which was concluded on 10 July. By the terms of this new agreement, which was signed by Yasser Arafat on behalf of the PLO, the Jordanian government undertook to recognize a Palestinian 'central committee' and permit the fedayeen free movement in the country, provided they disbanded their bases and arms depots in the cities, and stopped carrying their weapons in the streets. Neither side really expected this arrangement to last for long, but both of them, momentarily exhausted, needed a pause for breath.

The regional issue at stake at that particular moment was the so-called Rogers Plan. On 25 June, the American secretary of state, William Rogers, had announced a new diplomatic initiative to bring about peace between the Arabs and Israel. It called for a cease-fire between Egypt and Israel along the Suez Canal, and a renewal of efforts on the part of the United Nations to reach an overall peace settlement based on Resolution 242 of the Security Council. King Hussein was in favour of the Rogers Plan, but was not willing to endorse it unless Nasser did so first. On 24 July, the Egyptian president accepted the new American initiative; Jordan's acceptance followed on 26 July. 'What you accept, we accept, and what you reject, we reject', ran the cable which King Hussein sent to President Nasser on this occasion.[4]

The fedayeen in general were opposed to the Rogers Plan, and went to the unprecedented length of taking Nasser to task for having endorsed it. From their point of view, any negotiated peace with Israel meant the end of Palestinian armed resistance, which in turn meant that their organizations would have to disband. In response to the open Palestinian criticism of his policy, Nasser had the PLO and Fateh radio stations which broadcast from Cairo closed down. The Fateh leadership, however, preferred not to quarrel with Nasser over the issue. While Yasser Arafat continued to attack the Rogers Plan, he stopped making open reference to Egypt or even Jordan in his attacks. In fact, at times he even hinted that Egypt, and the Arabs in general, possibly stood to benefit by accepting the American initiative. The PFLP and the PDFLP, on the other hand, held firm to the extremist stand, as did a new splinter of the PFLP: the PFLP-General Command, headed by Ahmed Jibril. From their point of view, any negotiated Arab settlement with Israel would involve the sacrifice of the fundamental principles of the Palestinian revolution, which called for the liberation not only of the West Bank and the Gaza strip, but of the whole of the original Palestine. These organizations, of course, could not do much about the acceptance of the Rogers Plan by Egypt; so they turned their full wrath against the Hashemite regime in Jordan.

As the responsible leader of the PLO, Yasser Arafat urged the Palestinian organizations to stay out of Jordanian politics, warning that the fedayeen movement stood to lose if the Jordanian regime was provoked to unleash its considerable military force fully against it. Georges Habash and Nayef Hawatmeh, however, having opted out of the PLO, paid no attention to Arafat's warnings. In the summer of that year, they resumed their earlier attacks on the Hashemite monarchy in Amman with increased ferocity. As far as they were concerned, the existing regime had to be overthrown: replaced perhaps by a combat state run by popular militias; perhaps by a Palestinian government sharing power with the Jordanian government; or perhaps by some other constitutional arrangement, whereby the Jordanian parliament would be dissolved and reconstituted with pro-fedayeen representatives. Habash and Hawatmeh formally advanced such proposals at an emergency session of the Palestinian National Congress held in the Wahadat refugee camp towards the end of August.[5] If the Jordanian regime needed any pretext to proceed with the destruction of the Palestinian revolution in its territory, this pretext was being freely provided.

Yasser Arafat, from his side, continued to press for Palestinian moderation, and to warn of the consequences of extremism, but without success. While the PFLP and the PDFLP campaign against the Jordanian regime went on, the fedayeen reverted to lawlessness on an unprecedented scale, ambushing army vehicles, and, on one occasion, waging an armed attack on the central post office in the capital. On 1 September, an armed ambush opened fire on the king while he was on his way to the airport.

The Palestinians maintained that the Jordanian Mukhabarat were behind much of what happened, to prepare Jordanian public opinion for the final showdown. Nevertheless, the fact remained that the PFLP and PDFLP, as well as other fedayeen groups, were making no secret of their intent to destroy the established system in Jordan.

On 6 September, fedayeen of the PFLP hijacked three international airline flights, bringing a Swissair and a TWA aircraft to a desert airstrip called Dawson Field, north-east of Amman, and a Pan-Am aircraft to Cairo. The Pan-Am plane, with its passengers and crew set free, was blown up in Cairo airport a few minutes after landing. At Dawson Field, however, the 310 passengers and crew were kept on board the two aircraft, which the PFLP threatened to blow up if several fedayeen imprisoned in Western Europe and in Israel were not released within seven days. On 9 September, yet another hijacked plane – a BOAC airliner, with 115 passengers and crew on board – was brought to Dawson Field. On 12 September, all three of the hijacked airliners there were blown up, shortly after their total of 425 passengers and crew had been allowed to disembark. Of these, 371 were freed immediately, while 54 were kept as hostages by the PFLP for about two weeks.

Ostensibly, these spectacular hijackings were intended to demonstrate to the world the lengths to which the Palestinian revolution was prepared to go to achieve its rightful ends. At that particular moment, however, the PFLP was more directly concerned with forcing the Palestinian revolution in Jordan to pursue its own radical course. To this extent, the PFLP was successful in its aim. The Arab governments were by no means happy with the hijackings, nor actually was Yasser Arafat, who reportedly thought that acts of this kind did far more harm than good to the Palestinian national cause. Such was Arab popular enthusiasm for the hijackings, however, that Arafat stood to lose his prestige as a Palestinian leader if he failed to endorse the revolutionary legitimacy of these remarkable feats of Palestinian daring. In the game of revolution, moderation rarely carries the day; and at a meeting of the PLO central committee on 10 September, the Fateh leadership finally joined in approving the demands of the PFLP hijackers two days before the three aircraft at Dawson Field were blown up. Certainly in Jordan, Fateh and the PFLP, not to mention other radical fedayeen groups, now stood on the same side, to fight together what they called the 'final battle'.

Skirmishes had already been happening between the Jordanian army and the fedayeen, in towns such as Irbid, Zarqa and Maan, since the last attempt on the king's life on 1 September; and the two sides began to take up positions for the expected final confrontation in Amman. The real showdown, however, was not to start until 16 September. On the preceding day, the fedayeen had taken over the city of Irbid, where they proclaimed a 'people's government' (*hukuma sha'biyya*). That same night, King Hussein decreed military rule throughout the country, and set up a military cabinet for the purpose headed by a Palestinian officer, Brigadier Muhammad Daoud, but otherwise composed mainly of Transjordanians. At the same time, General Habes al-Majali was placed in charge of the army as chief of staff. The next day, the Jordanian artillery, from positions inside and around Amman, opened fire on the Wahadat and Husseini refugee camps, where the fedayeen had their headquarters, reducing large parts of them to rubble. The army had originally calculated that it would take no more than two days to break the back of the Palestinian resistance, but this was not to be the case. Once the initial attack on the camps was over, the mopping-up operations continued in Amman for ten days. The fedayeen, who had taken up trench and roof-top positions in the densely populated quarters of the city, were hunted down wherever they were suspected of being found. In other parts of town, buildings which were believed to harbour fedayeen were shelled at minimum notice. The army was taking no chances; and according to the PLO figures, the death toll in the first eleven days of fighting was as high as 3,400.

While all the Arab states expressed concern about what was happening in the Jordanian capital, Syria alone came out openly in support of the Palestinians; and on 20 September, 200 Syrian tanks crossed the border into Jordan to help the PLO. The Jordanian air force, however, went swiftly into action, destroying seventy-five of the invading Syrian tanks and forcing the rest to withdraw to home positions within three days. Meanwhile, at the request of the United States, Israel sent reinforcements to its army on the Syrian border, as a warning to the Syrian government to refrain from further intervention. King Hussein, who had sent urgent messages to Washington and London asking for help, accepted the Israeli move on the suggestion of the United States, after being informed that there was not enough time for either American or British aid. Following this, Libya and Kuwait immediately suspended their subsidies to Jordan. Meanwhile, the rumour had spread like wildfire that Israel's action was part of a concerted plan against the Palestinian resistance which King Hussein and the Israeli prime minister, Golda Meir, had recently worked out at a secret meeting held in one of the rocky enclaves of Wadi Araba.

From Cairo, President Nasser suggested that an Arab summit meeting be held in Cairo to settle the issue between the Jordanian government and the fedayeen, but Hussein declined the invitation, sending his prime minister, Brigadier Daoud, to Cairo instead. Shortly after his arrival in the Egyptian capital, Daoud seized the opportunity to announce his resignation. Earlier on, Palestinian threats had forced Daoud to send his family away from Jordan to secure their safety. Daoud himself was a very sick man, unable to shoulder the grave responsibilities thrust upon him by the king. In Amman, a Palestinian notable from Nablus, Ahmed Toukan, was appointed to replace him at the head of a stop-gap civilian government. The resignation of Daoud was certainly a blow to King Hussein, but it did not deter him from holding to his policy of confrontation. Meanwhile, President Nasser continued to pressure the Jordanian monarch to put an end to the showdown with the Palestinians. However, Hussein persisted in ignoring these pressures, convinced that they were mainly intended for Palestinian and Arab popular consumption. Having subscribed to the Rogers Plan two days before Hussein, the Egyptian president was effectively in the same boat as the Jordanian monarch; hence, he could not easily afford to let the king down.

On 24 September, however, an Arab League team composed of the Tunisian and Sudanese prime ministers, the Egyptian chief of staff, and the defence minister of Kuwait arrived in Amman to hold talks with the king and the PLO leader. By this time, the Jordanian army had clearly gained the upper hand in the fighting, although the fedayeen were far from being completely overwhelmed. Large numbers of them were still entrenched in various parts of the country, retaining a number of positions even inside the capital. It was therefore in the interest of King Hussein, for the moment, to accept the Arab League initiative, and to go to Cairo to meet with Yasser Arafat in the presence of Nasser. On 27 September, a cease-fire agreement was announced between the two parties, by the terms of which all prisoners were to be released, and both the Jordanian troops and the Palestinian fedayeen were to withdraw from the cities. Habash and Hawatmeh had meanwhile taken flight to Damascus, which meant that the cease-fire agreement was essentially one between the Jordanian regime and the PLO, as represented by Fateh. President Nasser, however, did not live to see the outcome of the agreement he had played the major role in brokering. Having long suffered from diabetes, cardiac problems and other ailments, he died suddenly of a heart attack the day after the agreement was signed.

* * * * * * * * * *

Following the death of Nasser, King Hussein, in Amman, dismissed the stop-gap government of Ahmed Toukan, appointing in its place a cabinet of staunch Jordanian loyalists, headed by Wasfi al-Tall: a Transjordanian from Irbid who had been prime minister twice before. Tall had been an officer in the British Army for a time during the Second World War, and also a volunteer officer in the Arab Army of Deliverance (see Chapter 7) in the Arab–Israeli war of 1948. He was thus a man of considerable military experience.[6] Originally, he had been a strong sympathizer with the Palestinian cause; but after 1968, he had come to regard the behaviour of the fedayeen organizations in Jordan as an unwarranted Palestinian violation of Jordanian hospitality. Earlier political experience had taught Tall other lessons. At one time, for example, he was a strong advocate of political liberalism; and during his first term as prime minister, it was he, in 1961, who had lifted the ban on political party activity, which resulted in the tragic riots of 1963. Since then, Tall had come to believe that political liberties, in a country where national loyalties were divided, should always be kept under close watch; and that it was sometimes necessary to resort to repression if the national interest so dictated. In October 1970, the very survival of Jordan as a state appeared to be at stake. As Tall saw it, this was no time for the Jordanian government to have its hands tied, either by brotherly considerations for the fedayeen, or by scruples with respect to constitutional freedoms.

In effect, Tall headed a war cabinet, intent from the very start on completing the liquidation of the fedayeen movement in Jordan. The surge of Jordanian patriotic feeling, which was growing stronger by the day, provided the king and his new prime minister with firm backing for this policy. Yasser Arafat, who no longer had Nasser to back him, was quick to grasp the message. The winds in Jordan were no longer blowing in favour of the PLO, and the Jordanian political opposition, on which the Palestinians had formerly relied heavily, was being made to eat humble pie. On 13 October, the PLO leader was prevailed upon to sign a new accord – the so-called Amman Agreement – confirming the king's control over his country, and imposing the restrictions on Palestinian activity within Jordan which the Cairo Agreement of 27 September had failed to impose. The fedayeen were called upon to disband all their bases, both in the villages and in the towns and cities, and were forbidden to bear arms in public or appear in uniform. In Amman, their leaders and officers could retain their armed guards. Other than this, they were to obey the civil laws of the realm, conforming, among other things, with traffic regulations. In return, all that was required of the Jordanian regime was an amnesty for all fedayeen prisoners and permission for Georges Habash and Nayef Hawatmeh to return to Jordan, provided they operated within the context of the central committee of the PLO, and not independently as before.

The regime in Jordan was set on finally ridding the country of the fedayeen by a strategy of attrition. This was clear to Yasser Arafat. However, the Jordanian regime could not easily pounce on the Palestinian resistance unless clearly provoked; and Arafat tried his best to prevent such provocation from taking place. At the same time, the PLO leader tried to mend his fences with Egypt by a further softening of his position on the question of the Rogers Plan. In response, Nasser's successor, President Anwar al-Sadat, permitted Fateh to renew its radio broadcasts from Cairo, and even agreed to deliver the opening speech at the eighth Palestinian National Congress held in the Egyptian capital in February 1971.

Saddled with Habash and Hawatmeh, however, Arafat could not proceed far in his efforts to save the Palestinian revolution in Jordan. At the same Palestinian National Congress which was opened by President Sadat, the PFLP and PDFLP leaders resumed their attacks on the Jordanian regime, pressing for a resolution to designate Transjordan as part of Palestine. From the point of view of these two men, it was incumbent on the Palestinian revolution to liberate both areas: one from Hashemite rule, the other from Israeli domination. Had such a resolution been passed, it would have been tantamount to a PLO declaration of war against Jordan. The proposal by itself was enough of a provocation. By now, the point had been reached when the Jordanian authorities no longer bothered to distinguish between what was said or done by Arafat, and what was said or done by Habash and Hawatmeh. The moment had come to strike with an iron fist, and destroy the problem once and for all.

The Jordanian army resumed its offensive against the Palestinian fedayeen on its territory in March 1971, by driving them out of the town of Irbid, their principal stronghold in the north. Next, in April, King Hussein ordered the PLO to remove all the fedayeen from Amman and relocate them in the wooded hills between Jerash and Ajlun, at a safe distance from the capital. The request was complied with by the PLO leadership without much fuss. But the fedayeen were deeply resentful of the humiliation they had suffered by being removed from the capital; and from their new positions in the Ajlun forests, they proceeded to launch guerrilla attacks on Jordanian army patrols as well as on military installations in the neighbourhood. As before, there were Palestinian charges that the Jordanian Mukhabarat was the agency that engineered many, if not most, of these attacks. Certainly, though, the fedayeen remained bent on having their 'final battle' in Jordan, in the full knowledge that they stood no chance of winning.

On 13 July, the Jordanian army launched its final assault on the fedayeen in the Ajlun hills and the adjacent parts of the Jordan valley. By 18 July, the offensive was over. Large numbers had been killed; others had fled; and about 2,000 surrendered and were subsequently allowed to leave the country in the direction of Syria. Of those in the Jordan valley, about 200 crossed the river to surrender to the Israelis rather than to the Jordanian army. No Palestinian voice was raised to denounce their behaviour as being in any way treasonable. The Jordanians, however, did not bother to make an issue of this. The following day, 19 July 1971, the PLO in Jordan ceased to exist. On the territory of the Hashemite kingdom, the established sovereignty of the state had won the day, and the attempted sovereignty of the revolution was over.

NOTES

1. Quoted by Peter Snow in *Hussein: A Biography*, p. 205.
2. Suleiman Nabulsi was not a Palestinian, but a Transjordanian notable

from the town of Salt, where his family, though originally from Palestine, had long been established. Since his political rehabilitation in 1963, Nabulsi had been a member of the Jordanian senate.

3. The Tanzim was actually founded at the AUB in 1969 with the encouragement of the Lebanese Student League, and the two groups continued to work in conjunction. One Jordanian student who was believed to represent the Jordanian Mukhabarat was denied membership in the Tanzim, and socially ostracized by its members. Campus clashes between the Tanzim and the Lebanese Student League on the one hand, and the Palestinians and their left-wing Lebanese sympathizers on the other, made the newspaper headlines on several occasions. In July 1971, the president of the Tanzim was abducted and held hostage for eleven days by the PFLP, at about the same time as the last pockets of the Palestinian resistance were being mopped up in Jordan. His release was secured by the personal intervention of the Lebanese president, Suleiman Frangieh.

4. Quoted by Clinton Bailey, *Jordan's Palestinian Challenge*, p. 54.

5. *Ibid.*, p. 56.

6. Wasfi al-Tall was the son of Mustafa Wehbeh al-Tall; see Chapter 5.

11

'A Stone for the Corner'

The expulsion of the Palestinian revolution from Jordan left the Hashemite regime in Amman in a position of unchallenged authority. Since the first armed clashes with the PLO, Transjordanian support for the monarchy had been overwhelming; and with the fedayeen organizations finally gone, hostility to the established order among Palestinians, as among the few Transjordanians who still sympathized with the PLO, was no longer publicly voiced. The Jordanian government was thus determined to prevent any return of fedayeen to the country. The military establishment could now be fully counted upon to attend to this matter. Of the Palestinians once serving under the Jordanian flag, a large body had deserted since September 1970 – along with a number of Transjordanians – to join the fedayeen organizations, and ultimately to leave Jordan with them. Others had been dismissed, or had quietly retired. The Palestinians who remained in service, mainly in the officer ranks, were no less loyal to the crown than their Transjordanian comrades, which left the armed forces of the realm solidly Jordanian in commitment and character.

To Jordanian loyalists, the success of the regime in ridding itself of the fedayeen organizations seemed too good to be true. The haughty and tactless behaviour exhibited by Palestinian leaders and their followers had been mortifying to such Jordanians, as had the many excesses committed by fedayeen individuals or groups who appeared set on disregarding the sovereign prerogatives of the kingdom and the right of its people to their individual opinions and way of life. The PLO invariably attributed such excesses to 'undisciplined elements' (*'anasir ghayr mundabita*), but this did not exonerate them from ultimate responsibility for the harm incurred, considering that an organization of its standing was expected to exercise adequate control over its ranks. This view was held not only by Transjordanians, but also by the many Palestinians who had long been critical of the fedayeen movement, or who had come to be so. For nearly three years, the street power wielded by the PLO, as by the Palestinian organizations operating outside its control, had greatly detracted from the authority and prestige of the Jordanian state. In the resulting anarchy, the fragile Jordanian economy had suffered serious damage, as development projects were halted and ordinary enterprise – Palestinian as well as Transjordanian – came to a virtual standstill in almost every field.

Now that order had been restored, the Jordanian government was not prepared to risk any return to anarchy. Jordan had been under martial law since the June War of 1967, and it was now decided to maintain this emergency measure to prevent attempted fedayeen infiltration back into the country and the smuggling of arms into the refugee camps. For these reasons, and also to reduce the chances of terrorism or sabotage from any direction, additional precautions were also taken at all border points, along the major highways and at strategic road junctions. In the Jordanian capital, as in other cities and towns, the presence of the Mukhabarat was felt everywhere, while desert patrols kept watch over the country-side. The refugee camps were placed under special guard, to prevent them from turning once again into hotbeds of trouble. One fedayeen attempt to hijack a Royal Jordanian flight, foiled in mid-air, was enough to get the strictest security imposed at Amman airport and on every Royal Jordanian flight.

The military control of the country was remarkable for its thoroughness and efficiency, leaving hardly any room for internal dissent. Outside Jordan, however, the Palestinians made no secret of the fact that they remained bent on revenge. In November 1971, the Jordanian prime minister, Wasfi al-Tall, was assassinated in Cairo outside the Sheraton Hotel, as he was returning from a session of routine Arab defence talks. The assassins were Palestinians belonging to a newly formed commando group within Fateh, called Black September. About a month later, the Jordanian ambassador in London, Zeid Rifai, barely escaped death when his car came under heavy automatic gunfire at a street corner close to the embassy. (The fedayeen, allegedly, had nothing to do with this particular incident.) Rifai had been chief aide at the royal palace, and one of the king's closest advisers in September 1970, before he was posted to Britain. In the circumstances, the regime had to remain on full alert to secure its survival and the personal safety of the monarch. For as long as such a high degree of state vigilance remained necessary, Jordanians who identified with the regime refrained from criticizing the elaborate security system to which the country was subjected, regardless of the daily inconveniences incurred.

People visiting Jordan during this period were exposed to two different anthologies of atrocity tales, one Transjordanian, the other Palestinian: myths and counter-myths of the sort encountered in any society emerging from civil war. The Transjordanian anthology was replete with accounts of alleged Palestinian perfidy, ingratitude and malice. It dwelt at length on the outrageous behaviour of the fedayeen, as highwaymen and rapists of whom the country was well rid, thanks to the patriotism and valour of the army. The Palestinian anthology, for its part, was equally replete with allegations about the random savagery and rape committed by the Jordanian troops – particularly those of the dreaded bedouin regiment – as they set out to eradicate fedayeen resistance in the towns and refugee camps. Accounts of indiscriminate brutality meted out by the army to captured fedayeen became more gruesome every time they were retold. There were also reports about continuing night raids on the refugee camps, in which countless innocent Palestinians were allegedly taken from home and family to be humiliated or tortured in the dungeons of the Mukhabarat.

There was some truth behind the exaggerations in the Palestinian allegations, which were the ones given the widest publicity. Raids on the refugee camps, normally in search of hidden arms, did take place; and caches of arms were often found and confiscated. Occasionally, such raids were carried out with unwarranted harshness. But few Palestinians who got into trouble with the authorities on such occasions were as innocent as was claimed. Their treatment under arrest rarely went beyond the ordinary rigours of cross-examination. On the other hand, Palestinians could be victimized in roundabout ways on mere suspicion, by administrative or military officials who happened to harbour strong anti-Palestinian feelings. A word from such an official to the head of a factory or a company manager could get a Palestinian dismissed from his job, or denied employment. Palestinians could also be barred from travel by having their passports confiscated for prolonged periods, often without explanation. Appeal against such injustices was possible, provided one knew which strings to pull; consequently, only individuals with strong government connections could appeal successfully.

As a rule, however, and contrary to the publicized Palestinian allegations, the vigilance of the Jordanian regime after 1971, though extremely strict, followed due process of law and was, if anything, clement rather than vengeful. Shortly after the assassination of Wasfi al-Tall, for example, the government of his successor, Ahmed al-Lawzi, decreed a general amnesty to all Palestinians held in custody since September 1970, regardless of the nature of the charges against them. The beneficiaries of this amnesty were given the free choice of staying in the country and reporting periodically to the police, or leaving to rejoin the fedayeen organizations in Lebanon or Syria. By the terms of the same amnesty, fedayeen carrying Jordanian citizenship who had fled the country since 1970 could return to Jordan as ordinary civilians if they wanted, provided they reported to the Mukhabarat upon arrival to get their political records cleared.

Under the martial law in force, anybody suspected of political activism could be interned and subjected to questioning by the Jordanian security authorities. This procedure, though legal, was sometimes applied with undue severity by the official in charge. Certainly, however, no person suspected of anti-Jordanian activities was ever detained by the Mukhabarat indefinitely; and few, if any, were interned for extended periods without good reason. Also, no political detainee in Jordan ever remained unaccounted for, as frequently happened to political detainees in other Arab countries. Even the most bitter critics of Jordan at the time were prepared to admit this much.

In principle, the quarrel of the Jordanian regime was with the fedayeen as an armed movement, and not with the Palestinians as a people. From the official view, the fedayeen in Jordan had tried to take over the country and failed. The Jordanian regime had been forced to take military action against them in self-defence; and having succeeded in expelling them from the country, it was not going to allow them back as a fighting force under any pretext or condition. With the Palestinians of Jordan, it was a different matter. They were Jordanian citizens entitled to the enjoyment of their full legal rights, on a par with their Transjordanian compatriots, provided they conformed with the law of the realm. In principle, they could not be discriminated against on any basis. The fact that such discrimination did exist derived from the peculiar structure of Jordanian society rather than from state policy. As far as the Hashemite monarchy was concerned, all Jordanians were equal, regardless of origin. To most Transjordanians, however, as to most Palestinians, the question of origin remained politically important. With the Transjordanians dominating the army and holding the key posts in the administration, the status of the Palestinians as Jordanian citizens of full rank and standing was compromised in various ways, especially in cases where their political loyalty was suspect.

* * * * * * * * *

After 1971, the internal policy of the Jordanian regime was chiefly aimed at promoting national unity between the rival sectors of the Jordanian population. From the point of view of the monarchy, such national unity was the ultimate guarantee for the survival and security of the country and its established order. Once achieved, it could transform Jordan into a model Arab state, by opening the way for a full return to democracy. In thinking along these advanced lines, the monarchy was ahead of Jordanian society, where neither Palestinians nor Transjordanians could easily be persuaded of the advantages and virtues of a common citizenship transcending questions of origin. To Palestinian particularists, national unity implied official recognition of their right to behave as Palestinians first, without prejudice to their standing as Jordanian citizens. On this basis, they were willing to settle for the sort of democracy which conceded the right of the citizen to divided loyalty. Transjordanian particularists, for their part, regarded themselves and their fellow Transjordanians as being the true nationals of the country. This made them balk at the idea of sharing Jordanian citizens' rights with the Palestinians on an equal basis. They consequently pressed for a democracy which accorded Transjordanians a special political status, relegating the concept of national unity to little more than a polite formula.

In the circumstances, it remained for the monarchy to take the first steps towards the achievement of the Jordanian national ideal it had in mind, in the hope that others would follow. For the moment, however, the prevailing conditions did not favour much progress in this direction. Having rid itself of the fedayeen movement, the Hashemite regime in Amman could not readily convince all Palestinians of its goodwill towards them, no matter how hard it tried; and as the government was forced by necessity to rely increasingly on Transjordanian support, Palestinian particularist opinion in the country was further alienated. Meanwhile, the Jordanian regime after 1971 found itself once again in relative Arab isolation. This was not because other Arab regimes genuinely disapproved of the manner in which the fedayeen problem in Jordan had been handled. Rather, it was because no Arab state at that time felt it could afford to make an enemy of the Palestinian revolution by taking Jordan's side on the fedayeen issue.

In other respects, the political situation in Jordan, starting from this period, was remarkably stable by comparison with the situation in other Arab countries. The surge in Jordanian patriotism which had grown in the course of the confrontation with the fedayeen, mainly but not exclusively among the Transjordanians, provided the Jordanian monarchy with a substantial popular legitimacy. The Hashemite regime in Amman had never ceased to subscribe to its particular concept of pan-Arabism, defined as a natural bond dictating brotherly co-operation among all Arabs on terms of equality and mutual respect. The Jordanian authorities, however, were not going to make any concessions to the PLO and place the sovereignty of their country once more in jeopardy, simply to provide proof of an Arab sincerity which they considered self-evident.

The established regimes in other Arab countries were in a different position. Uncertain of the degree of internal support they commanded, these regimes apparently felt an urgent need to justify their legitimacy in Arab nationalist terms, virtually on a day-to-day basis. The touchstone for Arab nationalist legitimacy at this time was the degree of support a given regime was willing to accord the Palestinian revolution. Ousted from Amman, the Palestinians had established their new headquarters in Beirut, to become a state within the state in Lebanon, in some ways more effectively than they had ever become in Jordan. The total defeat they had suffered at the hands of the Jordanian army had failed to affect their political fortunes. In fact, the changed Arab circumstances at that particular moment were distinctly in their favour.

President Nasser was dead, and no Arab ruler had succeeded in inheriting his mantle. In Egypt, President Sadat was too deeply engrossed in internal problems to have much real concern for pan-Arab affairs. Syria and Iraq, under their respective Baath regimes, continued to pursue pan-Arab lines, but neither of these two countries stood much chance of replacing a giant Arab state such as Egypt in pan-Arab leadership. Nor could they exercise such leadership jointly, since the Baath parties of Damascus and Baghdad had split into rival branches locked in perpetual conflict, never seeing eye to eye. Two Arab rulers who did try to take over the mantle of pan-Arab leader in the early 1970s were King Feisal of Saudi Arabia and Colonel Muammar Qaddafi of Libya (the latter regarding himself as Nasser's leading disciple, and hence as his rightful successor). But neither had much success in his ambitions, beyond gaining a temporary influence over Arab states in dire need of Saudi or Libyan financial support. In this dearth of inspirational Arab leadership, the Palestinian revolution, despite its recognized shortcomings, stood out as the last repository of the Arab national conscience. The rugged Palestinian fighter, as idealized in the prolific literature and graphic art of the PLO, became the unrivalled symbol of the nationalist dream which still held the Arab masses in thrall; and Beirut, as the new base of the Palestinian resistance, rapidly replaced Nasser's Cairo as the acknowledged nationalist capital of the Arab world.

Operating from Beirut, the PLO was quick to acquire a unique Arab legitimacy, derived from the wide popular support it commanded. A word from Yasser Arafat in favour of an Arab regime, no matter what its actual standing, was enough to guarantee its Arab acceptability. Little wonder that Arab rulers, great and small, vied with one another in courting Arafat's friendship. The PLO also appeared endowed with the authority to excommunicate Arab regimes and place them under interdict if they failed to support its policies or caused the organization displeasure in any way. The one Arab regime which the PLO seemed determined to keep permanently under interdict was the Hashemite monarchy in Jordan.

* * * * * * * * * *

For the moment, there was no question of a reconciliation between Amman and the PLO. The Palestinians were willing to accept such a reconciliation only on condition that their fighters return to Jordan. The Jordanians would not permit this return of Palestinian fighters to the country: certainly not unless they agreed to abide strictly by Jordanian army directives. Under pressure from Egypt and Saudi Arabia, the Jordanian government made one symbolic concession to the Palestinians, by allowing a token force of about 500 PLA officers and troops to be re-established and quartered at Khaw, near Zarqa, under firm Jordanian control. Such was the docility of this force, however, that no Palestinian set much store by its existence.

Apart from the question of the return of the fedayeen to Jordan, the prime bone of contention between the Jordanian government and the PLO after 1971 was the question of the West Bank. Legally, this Israeli-occupied territory was part of Jordan, and it remained for Jordan to reclaim it. The West Bankers, under Israeli occupation, remained Jordanian citizens, carrying Jordanian passports when they travelled. The Jordanian government, though perennially short of money, had never ceased to carry out its administrative and financial responsibilities with respect to the territory and its inhabitants, paying the salaries or pensions of thousands of active and retired civil servants, and subsidizing public institutions and charities. The West Bank, moreover, was economically dependent on the East Bank as the market for its agricultural products. West Bankers kept their savings in Jordanian currency, 'sleeping with the king's head under their pillows', as it was called. The substantial remittances sent to them by relatives working in the Gulf countries had to pass through Amman, where they were changed into Jordanian dinars before reaching them. Little wonder that King Hussein had a political following in the West Bank – and also in the Gaza strip – strong enough to score an overwhelming victory in the municipal elections of 1972. The king's following in these areas, however, was a silent one which did not voice its support for the Hashemite monarchy in the open. The political noise in the occupied territories was the preserve of the PLO, whose political supporters lost no opportunity to go out on the streets, denouncing the Hashemites and their alleged betrayal of the Palestinian cause far more loudly than they denounced the Israeli occupation under which they actually lived.

Certainly, the PLO had neither the desire nor the ability to take over administrative and financial responsibility for the West Bank from the Jordanian government while the area remained under Israeli occupation. But the PLO did not concede the right of Jordan to this territory any more than it conceded the right of Israel to other parts of what was once Palestine. As far as the PLO was concerned, the whole territory of Palestine had to be liberated from Israeli control by what was termed Palestinian *kifah musallah*, or 'armed struggle'. The fact that the Palestinian revolution did not have the military capacity to achieve this end in the foreseeable future made no difference to the principle. Unlike Jordan and Egypt, the PLO had not accepted Resolution 242 of the United Nations Security Council, and was not prepared to agree to a peace settlement with Israel in exchange for occupied land, because peace with Israel meant the recognition of her right to exist. The alternative was to leave the issue of the West Bank and Gaza strip to drift, which was exactly what Israel wanted. As far as the Israelis were concerned, the longer they stayed in these territories, the slimmer the chances that they would be prevailed upon to relinquish them.

King Hussein, for his part, persisted in behaving correctly. He had lost the West Bank to Israel, so it fell to him to secure its restoration to Jordan, which he felt could be achieved only through negotiation, in accordance with the terms of Resolution 242. The West Bankers, however, had been smarting at the loss of their former Palestinian identity since their union with Jordan in 1950. It was necessary, in the circumstances, to make some concession to their regional particularism. Accordingly, on 15 March 1972, the king put forward a plan which envisaged a radical reorganization of the Jordanian kingdom along federal lines, in the event of a peace settlement with Israel being reached. The Hashemite Kingdom of Jordan, in accordance with this federation plan, was to be renamed the United Arab Kingdom. This was to be organized in two autonomous provinces – the East Bank and the West Bank – each with its own parliament and administration. Matters relating to foreign affairs, along with those relating to defence and the unity of the kingdom, were to be the responsibility of a central government and parliament in which the two provinces were to be equally represented. The federal kingdom, moreover, was to have one united army, and its capital was to be Amman. There was talk at the time of the Gaza strip being connected to the West Bank by a corridor, once it was evacuated by the Israelis. In that case, it was argued, this isolated Palestinian area might be integrated into the West Bank province of the proposed United Arab Kingdom, unless other Arab arrangements were made for its administration.

King Hussein's federation plan met with a mixed reception among the Palestinians of both the West Bank and the Gaza strip. The PLO, however, with the backing of most Arab states, denounced the proposal as a devious plot aimed at robbing the Palestinian people of their right to self-determination and independence. From the point of view of the PLO, it was the right of all Palestinians, and not West Bankers alone, to accept or reject proposed solutions to the Palestine problem. The Palestinians scattered over the world far exceeded in number those of the occupied territories; and any solution that denied the right of all Palestinians to return to their land and establish their full sovereignty over it was treason to the Palestinian cause. King Hussein, the PLO claimed, having liquidated the Palestinian resistance in the East Bank, now proposed to kill the Palestinian issue as a whole by reducing it to the procedures for restoring Hashemite sovereignty to the West Bank, possibly with the addition of the Gaza strip. His proposal, according to the PLO, was unacceptable to Palestinians in principle, regardless of any support it might have among the inhabitants of the occupied areas. If the king were truly concerned about the liberation of Palestinian territory, all he had to do was entrust the fedayeen with the job, by permitting their return to Jordan and opening up the full length of the borders with occupied Palestine for their operations.

Beyond continuing to press for the return of the fedayeen to Jordan, and stressing the fundamental importance of armed struggle, the PLO failed to put forward any concrete and workable proposals on the basis of which the Palestinian problem could be settled. To be acceptable to the world community, such proposals had to take the letter and spirit of Resolution 242 into account. However, Yasser Arafat, who personally appeared to appreciate this fact, could not prevail on the PLO to take it into due consideration. Within the PLO, opinion continued to be divided between Fateh on the one side and the PFLP and its splinter groups on the other, the latter side now being supported by the Iraqi-backed Arab Liberation Front. Even within Fateh, there were sharp divisions of opinion between right- and left-wing groups, between moderates and extremists. The only compromise that the various Palestinian parties seemed willing to accept was one which envisaged the establishment of a 'democratic secular state' for the whole of Palestine, in which the Israelis would be transformed into Palestinian Jews sharing the country with Palestinian Arabs. The Israelis, naturally, scoffed at this proposal.

As the paramount Palestinian leader, Yasser Arafat's chief concern was to maintain the internal unity of Fateh on the one hand, and the PLO on the other. This meant that he often had to go against his own judgment, which was normally sound, in the interest of political compromise with parties which refused to consider the Palestinian problem in practical terms. In the expressed opinion of most Arabs, it was for the PLO to rule on all matters relating to Palestine; Jordan, though admittedly a concerned party, had no business intervening. The PLO wielded enough influence in the Arab world to make the majority of its rulers adopt this stand.

King Hussein's federation plan was interpreted by his Arab adversaries as a flagrant intervention in Palestinian affairs. No sooner had it been announced than Egypt proceeded to sever diplomatic relations with Jordan. President Sadat at the time was anxious to silence Palestinian criticism of his own efforts to reach a settlement with Israel over Sinai, and this made it necessary for him to demonstrate support for the PLO for as long as the Sinai question remained under negotiation. On 29 February, a little over two weeks before Hussein put forward his United Arab Kingdom proposal, Sadat had released the assassins of Wasfi al-Tall from prison, arranging for them to leave Egypt and seek safety under the protection of the PLO in Lebanon. To Hussein, this had been an unfriendly act by the Egyptian president, and the severing of diplomatic relations, following so soon after, added to the king's resentment of the hypocritical policy which Cairo now seemed to be set on pursuing. Syria, Iraq, Algeria and Libya had already broken off relations with Jordan in September 1970. With Egypt now added to this list, the truly influential Arab states still maintaining relations with Amman were reduced to Saudi Arabia, Tunisia and Morocco.

However, King Hussein continued to stand on firm ground in his own country, and he could therefore afford not to be too bothered by what other Arab parties said or did. The West Bank was an area inhabited by Arabs living under Israeli occupation and carrying Jordanian citizenship; it was up to these people, and no one else, to decide their political future. The inhabitants of the Gaza strip, though not Jordanian citizens, were entitled to the same right. As for the PLO, it was behaving, in Hussein's judgment, much as irresponsible Arab leaderships had always behaved, pursuing unrealistic policies and making promises which it was powerless to bring into effect. As the king saw it, the only party that stood to profit from the behaviour of the PLO was Israel. Like the PLO, Israel had rejected Hussein's federation plan, on the grounds that the king was putting the cart before the horse. The Israelis argued that Hussein was presuming to regulate the future of an Israeli-occupied territory before negotiating its return. If he wanted to have this territory returned, he had first to talk to them and find out what their conditions were.

* * * * * * * * * *

The king's arguments on the question of the occupied territories were forceful, but hardly anyone in the Arab world was willing to accord them a fair hearing. Jordan, however, remained a country whose standing in the region could not be ignored when important Arab decisions needed to be taken. By the late summer of 1973, President Sadat in Cairo and President Hafez al-Asad in Syria were preparing for a new war against Israel. The defeat suffered by the Arabs in the 1967 war had been so overwhelming that Israel was left feeling no urgent need to accept a settlement involving the required exchange of land for peace. Consequently, the situation in the area had reached an impasse which required another war to break it – one in which the Arab side put up a better military performance. Before embarking on such a project, however, Sadat and Asad thought it necessary to effect a reconciliation with King Hussein. In response to their invitation, Hussein went to meet them in Cairo on 10 September. The details of the war preparations were not divulged to the Jordanian monarch in the course of the meeting, but the Egyptian and Syrian presidents clearly wanted to assure themselves of Hussein's friendship before proceeding with their war plans. Shortly after the Cairo talks, diplomatic relations with Amman were resumed, first by Egypt, then by Syria.

What immediately followed, on 5 October, was the successful Egyptian offensive in Sinai which started the fourth Arab–Israeli war. Jordan did not participate in this war, beyond sending one armoured brigade to Syria in token support. After the initial Egyptian success, the Israelis launched a counter-offensive in which they managed to penetrate deep into the Egyptian mainland, while their forces in the north advanced once again to the outskirts of Damascus. The outcome of the war, however, was counted a stalemate. On 22 October, the Security Council of the United Nations adopted Resolution 338 which imposed a ceasefire, to be followed 'immediately and concurrently' by negotiations between the parties concerned aimed at establishing a 'just and durable peace in the Middle East'. This peace was to be secured in accordance with the principles already stipulated in Resolution 242, which called upon Israel to withdraw from 'occupied territories' in return for Arab recognition of her right to exist.

By specifically calling for the implementation of this earlier Security Council decision, Resolution 338 opened the way once more for Jordan to restore her sovereignty over the West Bank. A peace conference was in the offing, to be held in Geneva; and Jordan was fully prepared to participate. The Jordanian prime minister, who was then the resourceful Zeid Rifai, summed up the essence of the two United Nations resolutions proposed as a basis for the Geneva conference under the slogan 'land for peace'. Arab states other than Jordan made their participation in the conference conditional on PLO attendance, which Israel refused to accept. The PLO itself, still hampered by divided opinion within its ranks, could not easily decide whether it wanted to attend. Certainly, it was not in the interest of the organization to be left out of the Geneva peace talks. Agreeing to take part in these talks, on the other hand, was tantamount to a recognition of Israel.

The one point on which all parties within the PLO were agreed was that Jordan should not be allowed any role in Geneva relating to the Palestinian question, including the issue of the West Bank.

The organization immediately set to work to secure a clear Arab League ruling on this matter, with Syria and Egypt as its principal allies. When the sixth Arab summit conference convened in Algiers, in November 1973, to co-ordinate the Arab position with respect to the proposed peace conference, the Arab heads of state at this meeting took a secret decision, recommending that the PLO be recognized as the 'sole legitimate representative of the Palestinian people'. This recommendation, so obviously directed against Jordan, was first publicly adopted by an Islamic summit conference held in Karachi, in Pakistan, in February 1974. Its official endorsement by the Arab League followed in October of the same year, when the seventh Arab summit conference, held in Rabat, in Morocco, adopted a resolution to the same effect, and with identical wording. Next, in November, Yasser Arafat went to New York to address the General Assembly of the United Nations. The invitation for him to do so had been arranged by the Soviet Union, following an earlier visit by the PLO leader to Moscow. After listening to Arafat's speech, the General Assembly of the United Nations passed its own resolution to recognize the PLO as the 'sole legitimate representative of the Palestinian people'. The General Assembly further recommended the participation of the PLO in all official conferences dealing with the Middle Eastern problem. Subsequently, the PLO was allowed to have an observer delegation in the Security Council whenever issues relating to Palestine were under discussion.

The Rabat resolution, as endorsed by the General Assembly of the United Nations, effectively made the PLO, rather than Jordan, responsible for recovering the West Bank from Israel. With the PLO still refusing to talk to Israel, this meant that the issue of the West Bank, along with that of the Gaza strip, could remain non-negotiable for an indefinite period. King Hussein realized this to be the case, and had given the Arab League prior warning of what to expect. At Rabat, however, Hussein pledged full Jordanian support for the PLO in its new task. Going back on earlier threats to the contrary, the king further undertook to maintain administrative services and financial responsibilities with respect to the West Bank, until the PLO was in a position to take over. Less than a month after the Rabat conference, the Jordanian parliament, in which the West Bankers had equal representation with the East Bankers, was suspended; and the prime minister, who was then Zeid Rifai, was called upon to form a new cabinet in which only East Bank Palestinians were assigned portfolios. The king wanted to make it clear that he intended to abide by the Rabat resolution to the letter.

* * * * * * * * *

With Israel refusing to recognize the credentials of the PLO, the Geneva peace conference never really took off. Meanwhile, the PLO got itself bogged down in the armed conflict that erupted in Lebanon in the spring of 1975, between the Muslim and left-wing parties supporting the Palestinian revolution in the country on the one side, and the Christian parties opposing the Palestinians on the other. In the initial stages of this war, which ended in the summer of 1976, the Palestinians lost all their strongholds in East Beirut and its suburbs to the Christian forces, who had managed to secure military help from the Syrians. In West Beirut, however, the Palestinian organizations, backed by their Muslim and left-wing Lebanese supporters, retained their military predominance, albeit under a measure of Syrian control. In the subsequent phases of the Lebanese war, these organizations, under pressure from Yasser Arafat, tried to stay in the background of the fighting, but they were not always successful in doing so because Fateh and the PFLP, in particular, felt morally committed to their Lebanese allies who were ostensibly fighting to vindicate the Arabism of Lebanon. When Israel invaded Lebanon in the summer of 1982 and besieged West Beirut, it was the Palestinians who led the resistance to the siege. The Israeli invasion had been aimed at destroying the Palestinian revolution in Lebanon, and it succeeded in this aim. As the siege of Beirut was tightened, the PLO was prevailed upon to leave the city, with all the forces under its command, under an international guarantee. Its new headquarters were fixed in Tunisia.

Meanwhile, the Middle Eastern scene had been witnessing new developments. In January 1974, Egypt, without prior consultation with the Arab League, had signed an agreement for a disengagement of forces with Israel in Sinai. A similar agreement was signed by Syria with Israel in May with respect to the Golan area. But while Syria was reluctant to pursue the matter further, President Sadat, who was facing mounting social and economic problems inside Egypt, was extremely eager to reach a final settlement with Israel, with or without general Arab consent.

By 1977, the Arab arguments and counter-arguments regarding the Geneva conference were clearly turning into an exercise in futility. On 19 November of that year, however, President Sadat surprised the world by flying to Israel to address the Knesset (Israel's parliament) and initiate direct talks with the Israeli government. Before doing so, he had taken the precaution of going to Damascus to persuade President Asad of the wisdom of the move he intended to undertake, but his effort in this direction was not successful. In December, Syria, along with Libya, Algeria and South Yemen, severed diplomatic relations with Cairo; and these four countries, joined by the PLO and later by Iraq, formed a Rejection Front which branded the behaviour of Sadat as treason. The Egyptian president nevertheless persisted in his initiative, encouraged by the positive Israeli response, and more so by the enthusiasm of the United States for his peace move. In September 1978, the American president, Jimmy Carter, invited Sadat and the Israeli premier, Menachem Begin, for two weeks of talks at the presidential retreat at Camp David, in Maryland. A peace treaty between Egypt and Israel was finally concluded on 26 March 1979.

At the Camp David talks, Sadat had succeeded in getting Begin to make a substantial concession on the question of the occupied territories. All that Begin was willing to concede in the beginning was a measure of autonomy for these areas, under Israeli sovereignty. Sadat's counter-proposal was to have this autonomy placed under the joint authority of Egypt, Israel and Jordan, and to limit this to a transitional period of five years, after which the political status of the areas involved would be reconsidered. Begin finally agreed to this arrangement, which had the blessing of the American president. The PLO, however, rejected the Camp David package outright, as did the other members of the Arab Rejection Front. Jordan, which stood to benefit from becoming a co-sponsor of the proposed Palestinian autonomy, had not been consulted in advance on the matter, which left the authorities in Amman feeling ambivalent about the project. After careful consideration, the Jordanian government decided not to break the Arab consensus on the issue. Noting the strong Arab reaction to the Camp

David accords, Jordan refused to adhere to them, and even joined in condemning them as a violatioh of Palestinian rights.

At the ninth Arab summit conference, held in Baghdad on 2 November 1978, which Egypt alone did not attend, the Arab rulers, among them King Hussein, were unanimous in blaming Sadat for having infringed the Rabat consensus by presuming to negotiate the question of the occupied territories with the Israeli premier without prior permission from the rightful Palestinian authority. In its final resolution, the Baghdad summit confirmed Arab support for the PLO as the 'sole legitimate representative of the Palestinian people'. Later, when the Egyptian president proceeded to conclude a separate peace with Israel, heedless of all Arab objections, Jordan broke off diplomatic relations with Cairo, as did all the other Arab countries. Amman also agreed to the expulsion of Egypt from the Arab League, whose offices were removed from Cairo to Tunis.

While Sadat, who had been one of the originators of the Rabat resolution, had proceeded since 1974 to pursue independent policies, Jordan did exactly the opposite. Having accepted the Rabat resolution despite expressed reservations, mainly to stay in line with the general Arab trend, the Jordanian government immediately set out to improve the country's relations with her Arab neighbours, beginning with Syria. To make up for his non-involvement in the 1973 war, King Hussein declared, in May 1975, that Jordan would participate in the event of another Arab confrontation with Israel. His message was directed to Damascus; and the response was quick to come. In June, President Asad of Syria arrived on a state visit to Jordan, and negotiations for a political amalgamation of the two countries followed. What was actually arrived at were accords involving co-operation and co-ordination in the realms of defence, foreign affairs, economic policy, information, education and cultural activity. These measures sufficed to secure a considerable improvement in relations between Amman and Damascus. Subsequent disagreements between the Jordanian and Syrian regimes over bilateral or regional issues often reached the brink of crisis. However, the Jordanian government invariably took the initiative to have such disagreements resolved in a manner to satisfy both parties.

The ice was not broken between Jordan and Iraq until November 1978, when King Hussein, who had visited Baghdad only once since the overthrow and massacre of the Iraqi branch of the Hashemite dynasty, arrived in the city to participate in the ninth Arab summit. This conciliatory move on the part of the Jordanian monarch elicited an appreciative response from the Iraqi president, Saddam Hussein; and strong bonds of friendship did not take long to develop between the two men. The resulting *rapprochement* between Jordan and Iraq was one of the major factors which strained the relations between Jordan and Syria during the years that followed. In 1980, when the Iraqi regime went to war against the newly established Islamic Republic in Iran, for reasons that did not bear on Jordan in any way,[1] King Hussein was the one Arab ruler who openly came out in support of Iraq against Iran on Arab nationalist principle, with strong backing from his people, Palestinians and Transjordanians alike. For the duration of the hostilities, which ended in 1988 with the Iranian acceptance of a United Nations cease-fire, the modest resources of Jordan – most significantly, the supply line to Iraq from the Red Sea port of Aqaba – were placed at the disposal of the Iraqi war effort without reserve or calculation as to ultimate loss or gain, even when the Iraqi war fortunes were at their lowest ebb.

* * * * * * * * * *

The nationalist stand taken by Jordan with respect to the Iraq–Iran war consecrated the status of the Hashemite monarchy in Amman as an Arab regime of the front rank. For the Arab standing of the country to be placed beyond challenge, however, a settlement of the outstanding conflict with the PLO was required. Since the Rabat summit of 1974, Jordan had continued to adhere to the Arab League resolution recognizing the PLO as the 'sole legitimate representative of the Palestinian people', on the understanding that the matter ultimately related to the future of the Israeli-occupied Palestinian territories, including the Jordanian West Bank. From the point of view of the PLO, however, the Rabat resolution had accorded the organization the authority to act as the 'sole legitimate representative' of all people of Palestinian origin, including those of the Jordanian East Bank. When pressed on the issue, the PLO disclaimed any territorial ambitions with respect to the East Bank. Nonetheless, the claim put forward by the organization to be the rightful representative of the local Palestinian population challenged Jordanian sovereignty on what was incontestably Jordanian territory. Among the East Bank Palestinians, those who already thought of themselves as Jordanians perhaps constituted the majority; but they were not as vocal in their support as the followers of the PLO, who lost no opportunity to indicate where their true allegiance lay.

By bidding for the political allegiance of the East Bank Palestinians, the PLO reinforced the stand of Transjordanian hard-liners who had never accepted the Palestinians of the country as true compatriots. Similarly, the PLO position, and the local support it commanded, played into the hands of Israeli extremists of the Likud and other right-wing groups, who pressed for the transformation of the Jordanian East Bank into a Palestinian *watan badil*, or 'alternative homeland', so that the West Bank and the Gaza strip could be readily annexed to Israel. This *watan badil* theory – summed up by the slogan 'Jordan is Palestine' – had first been advanced in Israel in 1975; its leading exponent was Ariel Sharon, who was minister of agriculture, and then minister of defence, in two successive Likud cabinets. In the opinion of Sharon and his followers, the Hashemite order in Jordan was the chief obstacle to the annexation of Palestinian occupied territories by Israel. Since 1967, the Palestinians had actually come to form a substantial majority in the Jordanian East Bank. Thus, Sharon argued, Jordan would automatically become a Palestinian republic once the monarchy in Amman was overthrown. If necessary, the Israeli government could hasten the process by massive expulsions of West Bank Palestinians to the East Bank.

Rather than whetting Palestinian political appetites in Jordan, Sharon's *watan badil* proposal actually had the opposite effect: it dampened – and in some cases completely silenced – Palestinian voices which had been calling for the overthrow of the Jordanian monarchy since 1970. Meanwhile, in 1978 Jordan and the PLO found themselves on the same side in the controversy over the Camp David accords. King Hussein, having already settled outstanding differences with Syria, and being on the point of reaching a similar settlement with Iraq, considered the moment opportune to effect a reconciliation with the Palestinian organization. The king accordingly invited Yasser Arafat to Jordan for talks, in company with the Libyan ruler, Muammar Qaddafi. The meeting between the three men took place on 23 September 1978 somewhere in northern Jordan. Almost immediately afterwards, the PLO was allowed to re-open its office in the Jordanian capital. What followed, in early November, was the Baghdad summit, and the burying of the hatchet between the Jordanian monarchy and the Iraqi republic. Later in that same month, two PLO delegations arrived in Amman to discuss with the Jordanian authorities how best to oppose the Camp David autonomy plan proposed for the occupied territories.

On a routine agenda of this sort, the Jordanian regime and the PLO had little reason to disagree. On the fundamental issue dividing the two sides, however, the discord continued. Jordan remained unwilling to lift the ban on fedayeen operations against Israel from Jordanian territory, which the PLO kept demanding. Nor were the Jordanian authorities prepared to concede to the organization the right to act as the 'sole legitimate representative' of East Bank Jordanians of Palestinian origin.

The PLO could afford to be intransigent in dialogue with Jordan for as long as the organization continued to operate from a strong base in Lebanon. Until 1982, the pan-Arab influence wielded by the PLO had more than made up, in political terms, for the ineffectiveness of its armed struggle against Israel. Once the organization had been expelled from Beirut, however, its leadership began to feel an urgent need to deliver on its long-standing commitment to retrieve at least some part of Palestine. Without the help of King Hussein, the organization would be unable to make any advance in this direction.

As the PLO was preparing to leave Beirut, President Reagan of the United States launched the so-called Reagan Plan on 1 September 1982, calling for a self-governing Palestinian authority in the West Bank and Gaza strip in association with Jordan, and the freezing of Jewish settlements in Arab areas under Israeli occupation. The American president did not recognize the PLO, and refused to talk with its leaders. He therefore tried to persuade King Hussein to undertake the necessary negotiations with Israel. The Reagan Plan, in essence, was similar to the United Arab Kingdom project advanced by King Hussein in 1972. Accordingly, the king proceeded to reactivate the project on 20 September, in preparation for the expected peace talks. Eager to participate, Yasser Arafat and other leading PLO figures began to converge on Amman for intensive discussions with the Jordanian authorities:

first, on the procedures for setting up a joint Palestinian–Jordanian delegation to negotiate with Israel; second, on the type of relationship to be established between the Jordanian kingdom and the self-governing Palestinian entity which now appeared to be at hand.

Between October 1982 and April 1983, Arafat visited Amman no fewer than four times to consider the technicalities of implementing the Reagan Plan with King Hussein and leading figures in the Jordanian government. Because the idea of a federal Jordanian–Palestinian kingdom was unpalatable to Palestinian nationalists, Arafat suggested a confederation between Jordan and a future Palestinian state which would otherwise be independent. The Palestinian National Council, to which the PLO executive committee was ultimately responsible, was willing to endorse the idea of confederation. However, the same council, to the embarrassment of Arafat, rejected the Reagan Plan, as it had rejected earlier proposals which involved tacit recognition of Israel. Losing patience with the PLO, Washington urged King Hussein to proceed with the peace negotiations by himself, which he was reluctant to do. The Jordanian monarch was naturally anxious to get the problem of the occupied territories settled, but he hesitated to take any action which could be interpreted by Palestinians as a usurpation of their rights.

Meanwhile, a quarrel had broken out between Yasser Arafat and the Baath regime in Damascus, which proceeded to sponsor a rebellion against the PLO leader within the ranks of Fateh. On 24 June 1983, Arafat was declared *persona non grata* in Syria. This left Jordan as the only Arab country bordering Palestine to which the PLO and the legitimate branch of Fateh could turn. In Amman, King Hussein, who openly condemned the Syrian action against Arafat, was prepared to continue the dialogue with the Palestinian leaderships. In his view, the security and prosperity of the whole Middle Eastern region depended on the peaceful settlement of the Palestine question. Such a settlement, he maintained, could be reached only with Palestinian consent. The PLO, however, never ceased to suspect the king of ulterior motives. These Palestinian suspicions, having hardened rather than weakened with time, proved extremely difficult to eradicate.

* * * * * * * * *

While the dialogue between Jordan and the PLO dragged on, King Hussein found himself under mounting domestic pressure to restore constitutional life to the country. Jordan had been effectively without a parliament since 1974. Elections for a new parliament could not be held in the East Bank alone while the future of the West Bank remained undecided. In the summer of 1978, a National Consultative Council of sixty members – including West Bank Palestinians resident in the East Bank – was appointed by the king to serve in lieu of a legislature. Although this council had no constitutional standing, the king and government were careful not to promulgate any new law without its approval. To many Jordanians, however, the proper return to democracy did not have to await the resolution of the Palestine question, which had hitherto been stalled at every turn. Consequently, in January 1984, the king convened a special meeting of the parliament he had suspended ten years earlier, to amend the article of the constitution which forbade parliamentary elections being held without West Bank participation. The article in question was accordingly amended to permit the appointment of West Bank Palestinians to the Jordanian parliament, for as long as the future of that part of the West Bank remained undecided.

In Palestinian nationalist circles, the initiative taken by King Hussein in the direction of restoring constitutional rule to Jordan, with West Bank representation, was interpreted as an attempt on his part to circumvent the Rabat resolution, which made the PLO rather than the Jordanian government responsible for the future of the West Bank and of the Palestinian people in general. It was also believed that the king had made this move in preparation for entering into negotiations for a Middle East settlement, with or without Palestinian participation. A new *rapprochement* between Jordan and Egypt seemed to confirm this belief. This *rapprochement*, which began in February of that year with a meeting between King Hussein and the Egyptian president, Husni Mubarak, in Washington, in the presence of President Reagan, culminated in September in the resumption of diplomatic ties between Amman and Cairo.

Whatever the interpretation given to the king's new moves, their immediate effect was to get the interrupted dialogue between Jordan and the PLO resumed. The king had hardly returned from his meeting with Reagan and Mubarak in Washington, when

Yasser Arafat arrived in Amman to re-open the file of the regional peace process with the Jordanian authorities. About a year later, on 11 February 1985, the PLO leader initialled an agreement with King Hussein, the text of which was officially released by the Jordanian government twelve days later. This Amman accord, as it came to be called, was ambiguously worded. In a roundabout way, however, it did commit the PLO to the acceptance of United Nations resolutions calling for the settlement of the Arab–Israeli conflict on the basis of Israeli withdrawal from occupied Arab territories, and Arab recognition of Israel's right to exist. The agreement also committed the organization to participation in negotiations with Israel within a joint Jordanian–Palestinian delegation, on the understanding that the negotiations would take place at an international conference attended by the five permanent members of the United Nations Security Council and all the regional parties concerned. With respect to the future of the West Bank and the Gaza strip, the agreement confirmed the principle of confederation between Jordan and an otherwise independent Palestinian state to be set up in these territories.

All the Amman accord achieved, however, was to reactivate Palestinian suspicions with respect to King Hussein's political motives. A rapid deterioration of relations between the PLO and Jordan followed. Palestinian parties opposing the agreement, backed by Syria and Libya, were quick to announce the formation of a Palestinian National Salvation Front, to fight Israel rather than surrender to Israeli and American terms. Arafat himself continued to stand by his acceptance of the accord for some time; but within the ranks of the PLO and Fateh, majority – if not unanimous – opinion was against him. King Hussein, it was maintained, facing pressures from the United States, had acted in bad faith, tricking Arafat into initialling the agreement, then hastening to publish it unilaterally, to commit the PLO leadership to its terms. A last round of discussions between Hussein and Arafat in Amman ended on 8 February 1986 in a parting of the ways. The Jordanian side considered that the PLO leader had reneged on the agreement. The outcome was a new break in relations between Jordan and the PLO, which resulted, in turn, in a heightening of anti-Jordanian feeling among Palestinian supporters of the PLO inside Jordan. As a precaution against any possible outbreak of trouble, the government, in July of that year, ordered the closure of all PLO and Fateh offices which had been re-opened in Jordan since 1978, and instructed their personnel – including leading PLO representatives – to leave the country.

Relations between Jordan and the PLO were at their worst when the popular uprising known as the intifada broke out in the occupied territories towards the end of 1987. The Jordanian government, which still considered itself responsible for the West Bank and its people, came out in support of this uprising, giving it prime coverage in the Jordanian media. Certainly in the initial stages, however, the spokesmen of the intifada lost no opportunity to make public denouncements – both at home and abroad – of alleged continuing interventions by King Hussein in Palestinian affairs that were not his concern. Left-wing Israelis voicing support for the intifada were satisfied to see it take this anti-Jordanian stance. Meanwhile, new scholarly work on the career of King Abdullah, using what had previously been classified material in the Israeli and British archives, although in itself of great value, was put to political use by interested parties to widen further the rift between the Palestinian nationalists and the Hashemite rule in Jordan.[2]

* * * * * * * * * *

Within the Jordanian ruling establishment, opinion had long been divided over the question of what position the regime should take with respect to the Palestinian nationalist claim to the West Bank. Some, like the king, maintained that Jordan should not relinquish her moral and material obligations towards the West Bank Palestinians for as long as the status of the occupied territories remained unresolved. Others opposed this view, urging that Jordanians should settle for the East Bank and abandon all responsibility for the West Bank and its population. The latter view represented the position of Transjordanian hard-liners. As far as they were concerned, East Bank Palestinians who were not happy with being Jordanian citizens were free to forgo their citizens' rights and remain as mere residents of the country, pending the establishment of a Palestinian state to which they could go. The king, who remained firmly convinced that the national unity of the Jordanian people was bound to be realized in due time, frowned on such talk, on the grounds that it did no one any good. Meanwhile,

Palestinian nationalists, taking the Transjordanian hard-line plat-form to represent the actual stand of the regime, retorted that they had not become Jordanians by their own free choice: it had been imposed upon them as a result of the Hashemite appropria-tion of part of their original homeland. Their dearest wish, they insisted, was to return to their country and establish their own independent state on its territory, as soon as its liberation was achieved.

How many East Bank Palestinians were genuinely prepared to drop their Jordanian citizenship and actually leave Jordan, in the event of a settlement being reached on the occupied territories, was a moot point. As Jordan regained political stability in the early 1970s, the return of prosperity to the country quickly reached unprecedented levels, thanks largely to good government plan-ning. By the early 1980s, Jordan was already in the front line of Arab development. In the course of barely ten years, Amman had grown from a relatively small and nondescript provincial town into one of the finest and best-organized cities in the Arab world. The Jordanian capital bustled with enterprise in every field. As much of this enterprise was in Palestinian hands, vested interests alone sufficed to transform the most outspoken Palestinian nation-alists in the East Bank into *de facto* Jordanians. Because of the continuing civil war in Lebanon, the standing of Beirut as the business centre of the Arab world had gone into eclipse after 1975. This opened possibilities for Amman to replace the Lebanese capital as the centre of services for the area, in some cases with considerable success. With the Transjordanians tra-ditionally geared towards employment in the administration and the armed forces, the needed infrastructure for the developing services sector of the Jordanian economy naturally came to be dominated by Palestinians, many of them men and women of high qualification. At the same time, Palestinians working in the Gulf countries invested their savings in Jordanian real estate, which further enhanced the Palestinian attachment to the country, despite protests and pretences to the contrary.

King Hussein was anxious to give East Bank Palestinians a greater political stake in the Jordanian system, in addition to the economic and social stake they had already acquired. However, with the PLO still disputing the Jordanian claim to the political allegiance of these Palestinians, the policies pursued by the monarchy in this direction met with hurdles which often appeared insurmountable. Every step taken by the king to promote Palestinian confidence in the regime was construed by the PLO and its partisans in Jordan as another Hashemite scheme to cheat the Palestinian people and rob them of the right to their own national identity and land. There was only one measure to which the king could resort to circumvent this predicament: providing the Palestinians with the option of individually choosing the national allegiance they preferred, by completely dissociating Jordan from the Palestinian question. This meant terminating the union between the West Bank and the East Bank.

While the slightest hope still remained for a proper settlement of differences between Jordan and the PLO, King Hussein hesitated to take this step. Pending a decision on this matter, the parliamentary elections promised since 1984 could not be held, as West Bank representation in the new parliament depended on whether or not this territory remained part of Jordan. By 1988, however, the last efforts on the part of the Jordanian government to reach a workable understanding with the PLO had ended in failure. Meanwhile, Palestinian activism in the East Bank was once more coming into the open, albeit on a limited scale. In January 1988, at least twenty-three Palestinian nationalists – including members of the PFLP – were arrested by the Jordanian authorities, on the grounds that they had instructions from their Syrian headquarters to create a 'revolutionary atmosphere' in the country. At about the same time, a Palestinian nationalist demonstration in the Jordanian capital was broken up by the police. Such incidents, it was feared, would be repeated, unless the Jordanian and Palestinian national issues were separated once and for all.

The decision on this matter was taken in three steps, which followed one another in swift succession. On 28 July 1988, the Jordanian government announced its intention to scrap a five-year development plan for the West Bank, explaining that this measure was aimed at allowing the PLO more responsibility for the area. Two days later, King Hussein formally dissolved parliament, thereby putting an end to West Bank representation in the Jordanian legislature. Finally, on 31 July, the Jordanian monarch addressed the nation in a televised speech, in which he formally renounced Jordan's claim to the West Bank. Jordan was not

Palestine, he declared; and responsibility for the West Bank was henceforth to rest with the PLO as the sole legitimate representative of the Palestinian people. Jordanians of Palestinian origin could remain Jordanians if they wished, or keep their Jordanian citizenship until there was a formal Palestinian nationality for which they could opt. In the latter case, they were welcome to stay in the country as fellow Arabs of resident status. As an Arab state, Jordan remained committed to its obligations towards the Palestinian cause, as towards all Arab national causes. Jordanians had always been Arabs first, and would continue to be so.

As important as the text of the royal address was the setting. As the king spoke, the television camera turned at regular intervals to the background, to focus on a portrait of his great-grandfather, Sharif Hussein of Mecca: the leader of the Great Arab Revolt, hailed in 1916 as King of the Arab Countries by volunteers arriving from different parts of the Arab world to fight under his banner. To those who understood the language of signs, the message was clear. The Jordanian monarch considered himself the heir to a legitimate Hashemite leadership which was not restricted to Jordan, and which Arabs had originally followed by choice rather than by compulsion. This was to remain the case. As rulers of Jordan, enjoying the confidence of the Jordanian people, the Hashemites were renouncing their claim to Palestine by their own decision, because the followers of the Palestinian revolution wanted it so. But they remained as committed to the championship of the Arab national cause as their forebears had been, in Palestine as elsewhere.

* * * * * * * * * *

The formal renunciation of Jordan's claim to the West Bank opened the way for the resumption of constitutional life in the country. There were some technicalities to attend to first. New laws had to be drawn up which took account of the fact that the West Bank was no longer entitled to representation in the Jordanian legislature. Another matter to be settled – a particularly thorny one – pertained to the distribution of the seats in the parliament to be elected, in a manner that satisfied both Jordanians of Palestinian origin and Transjordanians. While the latter conceded the fact that they were numerically in the minority, they pressed for an electoral law which would preserve their traditional majority status in parliamentary representation, on the grounds that they were the original Jordanians who had always provided the country with its backbone. To resolve this problem, electoral constituencies were re-arranged to guarantee majority Transjordanian representation.

The Jordanians finally went to the polls on 8 November 1989, with women voting – and also entitled to seek office – for the first time. The fairness of the parliamentary elections was acknowledged by winners and losers alike; and the regime was given due credit for the initiative it had taken to secure the return of democracy to the country. A National Charter, worked out by a special commission appointed by the king, established the principle of national unity and full equality of citizenship for all Jordanians. The stipulations of this charter, as passed by parliament in the late spring of 1991, became an integral part of the organic law of the kingdom. What remained for the Jordanian state to do was attend to internal problems of long standing: not least among them, those relating to the endemic penury of the state and its mounting foreign debts.

Meanwhile, as already indicated, the consistent Jordanian support of Iraq against Iran between 1980 and 1988 had earned the Hashemite monarchy in Amman a special nationalist prestige, recognized by Jordanians as well as by Arabs of other countries. At the Arab summit held in Amman in November 1987, King Hussein, having already effected a reconciliation with Libya, played a leading role in trying to secure a similar reconciliation between Syria and Iraq, with the aim of promoting a common stand against Iran. The Saudis were particularly appreciative and supportive of Hussein's gesture, at a time when the Iranians were starting to exploit the right of all Muslims to pilgrimage by having Iranian pilgrims instigate political riots in Mecca. At the same Amman summit, the Jordanian monarch led the drive to re-admit Egypt to the Arab League, so that the organization could function once more as a body representing the whole Arab community of states without exception.

The pan-Arab standing of Jordan was to receive a further boost in connection with the regional developments that followed the Iran–Iraq war. Economically, this war had been extremely costly to Iraq, leaving the country in no position to repay the loans extended to her by the Gulf states since the start of the hostilities. President Saddam Hussein and his government were eager to have these loans cancelled; but Kuwait, as one of the principal loaners, insisted that her war loans to Iraq be kept on the books. The quarrel which developed over this issue was complicated by an old border dispute between the two countries and by the fact that Kuwait was intent on exploiting the rich oilfields of this disputed area. As a major oil producer which was practically land-bound, Iraq, moreover, had long been demanding an adjustment of the coastal frontier with Kuwait so as to secure ready access to the Gulf waters: a demand to which Kuwait would not agree. Furthermore, depressed oil prices, which were then compounding the economic problems of Iraq, were attributed by the Iraqi government to the fact that Kuwait, along with the United Arab Emirates, was producing oil in excess of the quota permitted by the Organization of Petroleum Exporting Countries (OPEC).

Considering the vital importance of Arab oil to the international community, Jordan pressed for a settlement of the outstanding differences between Iraq and Kuwait by Arab mediation, before they led to an international crisis. At first, other Arab countries also urged that an Arab settlement of the Iraq–Kuwait dispute be arranged. Events spiralled out of control, however, when Iraq staged a surprise invasion and occupation of Kuwait on 2 August 1991, forcing the ruling Al Sabah family to take flight. After a failed attempt to set up a pro-Iraqi regime in the country to replace the rule of the Al Sabah dynasty, President Saddam Hussein proclaimed the 're-annexation' of Kuwait to Iraq. The Iraqis had always argued that Kuwait legitimately belonged to Iraq, on the grounds that it had been part of the vilayet of Basra in Ottoman times.

Militarily and politically, the Iraqi action against Kuwait was a breach of international law which could not be allowed to pass. On this matter, the Jordanian government was in full agreement with other Arab states, as with the international community. From the Jordanian viewpoint, however, Arab interests dictated that the issue be treated on a regional basis. The United States, with strong support from Britain, was threatening international intervention, and American forces were beginning to arrive in Saudi Arabia to indicate that Washington meant what it said. At the same time, the United Nations Security Council was beginning to move towards action. Last-minute attempts by Jordan to get the problem resolved through the good offices of the Arab League were unsuccessful. The majority of the Arab states, led by Saudi Arabia, Egypt and Syria, maintained that international intervention, as advocated by the United States, was in order, unless Iraq withdrew immediately and unconditionally from Kuwait. As a number of Arab states decided to send forces to Saudi Arabia, to join the American and international military build-up against Iraq, King Hussein tried his best to persuade President Saddam Hussein to yield to the demands of the Arab and international community and to withdraw from Kuwait, in the interests of Iraq and the region as a whole. The Iraqi president, however, would not be convinced to go back on what he had already done.

In Arab and international circles, the stand of Jordan with respect to the Iraqi–Kuwaiti conflict was interpreted as outright support for Iraq, and strong American and international pressures were brought to bear on Amman to alter its stand, or else prepare to face the consequences of backing a loser. Arab popular opinion outside the peninsula, however, was strongly supportive of Iraq; and this was almost unanimously the case in Jordan. Washington and her allies, it was generally maintained, were pursuing double standards, taking one position with respect to the Iraqi aggression against Kuwait, and another with respect to the policies pursued by Israel in the occupied Arab territories. This was exacerbated by the popular perception of the Gulf states, in Jordan as elsewhere, as greedy countries, unwilling to share the enormous wealth which had come to them as a windfall with poor and needy brethren whom they haughtily dismissed as 'Arabs of the North'. In the common view, it was these oil-rich Arabs whom the Western powers were supporting against the poor Arabs by their proclaimed determination to remove Iraq from Kuwait, if necessary by force. Furthermore, the West was doing so for purposes that had no more than a tangential bearing on the regional issue. The same Western powers which pretended to be so concerned with what had happened to Kuwait had hardly raised a voice of effective protest against what had been happening in Arab Palestine for more than two decades.

These common Arab perceptions did not alter the fact that Iraq's aggression against Kuwait was both regionally and internationally unacceptable. The Jordanian government was fully appreciative of this fact. On the other hand, it could not remain insensitive to Jordanian and Arab national feeling. In the official Jordanian view, the Iraqi action against Kuwait had done tremendous regional damage, and the manner in which the West was reacting to the regional crisis threatened to add greatly to its proportions. In the circumstances, top priority had to be given to limiting the damage caused; but such limitation, as pressed for by Amman, was extremely difficult to achieve in the heat of the moment.

As the United Nations proceeded to impose sanctions on Iraq, Jordan agreed to support these sanctions, pleading for an exception to be made in matters of vital necessity to her own economy. Iraq, for example, was the principal market for Jordanian agricultural and industrial products. More important, Jordan depended on Iraq for free oil supplies, received in repayment for outstanding debts incurred during the period of the Iran–Iraq war. Meanwhile, the escalation of the international crisis triggered by the Iraqi invasion and occupation of Kuwait continued, culminating in the brief but abrupt ground war which broke out in late February 1991.

In Jordan, as in other Arab countries excepting Saudi Arabia and the Gulf states, the war waged by the Western powers against Iraq – no matter the degree to which its ferocity was justified – was generally perceived as a crusade. Under the pretext of liberating Kuwait, the West, it was commonly believed, was set on subjugating and humiliating the Arab people, by destroying whatever remained of their dignity and standing in the world. Among the Arab regimes of consequence, the Jordanian monarchy was the only one which had the courage to articulate what was happening in the mind of the ordinary Arab at that turning point in the history of the region. More important was the fact that it did so with dignity and composure, emphasizing the importance of heeding the dictates of Arab community feeling while remaining equally heedful of the dictates of the international order. Little wonder that the Jordanian state emerged from the frenzy that seized the region and the whole world at the time with its Arab and international credibility enhanced rather than diminished.

* * * * * * * * * *

As matters stand today, Jordan is an Arab country which still has a long way to go to solve all her problems. However, on balance, the success of the Jordanian political experiment so far has been remarkable. Starting virtually from scratch, and working against an amazing array of local and regional odds, the Hashemite monarchy in Amman has managed to create a civil society and political community seen by many as models of their kind in the Arab world. At the same time, a country which began as one of the poorest in the Arab world has come to stand in the front line of Arab development, mainly through the efforts of its human resources, under the guidance of a patient and enlightened leadership.

In the world today, most Arab countries remain at a loss over how to reconcile their individuality as nation-states with the reality and dictates of their common Arabism. Jordan is one Arab country which has managed to resolve this problem, after much trial and error, and without dissimulation in one direction or another. Once regarded as the most precarious of the Arab states, the Hashemite Kingdom of Jordan also managed to devise a formula for its existence whereby it could have stability and stride towards democracy at the same time. This alone has been no mean achievement, in a part of the world where democracy has so frequently been compromised or destroyed by an excess of zeal, or arrogant and irresponsible adventurism. In the present regional situation, it might be too much to predict a better Arab future. Should the Arab world be destined for such a future, however, the success of the Jordanian experiment, as observable today, might well serve as one of its cornerstones.

NOTES

1. The Islamic Revolution in Iran, led by the Ayatollah Ruhollah Khomeini, was a movement of Shiite Muslim political activism whose success in transforming the country into an Islamic Republic threatened to destabilize Iraq, as Khomeini proceeded to condemn the Baath regime in Baghdad, encouraging the Shiite majority in the country to challenge the political dominance traditionally wielded by the Sunnites. Border disputes of long standing further complicated the issue between the two countries. Of the Arab states, only Syria and Libya took the side of Iran against Iraq in the war that followed, on the grounds that Iraq had been the aggressor. Historically, the Iranians

had always claimed rights of dominance over the Gulf region, parts of which had been under Iranjan rule in past centuries; and the existence of Shiite communities in Gulf countries such as Bahrain, Kuwait and Saudi Arabia provided the Khomeini regime in Teheran with ready means to destabilize the Gulf region as a whole. Hence the financial support which the Gulf countries gave in loans to the Iraqi war effort against Iran. The issue of these war loans was ultimately to lead to the regional and international crisis culminating in the Gulf War of February–March 1991.

2. Prime examples are the excellent works, referred to in earlier chapters, of Mary C. Wilson, *King Abdullah, Britain and the Making of Jordan,* and of Avi Shlaim, *Collusion across the Jordan: King Abdullah, the Zionist Movement, and the Partition of Palestine.*

Select Bibliography

Books in English on Jordan and the Hashemites

Abidi, Hyder Hasan, *Jordan; a Political Study 1948–1957* (London, 1965).

Bailey, Clinton, *Jordan's Palestinian Challenge, 1948–1983: a Political History* (Boulder, Colorado, 1984).

Baker, Randall, *King Husain and the Kingdom of Hejaz* (Cambridge, 1979).

Daan, Uriel, *Studies in the History of Transjordan, 1920–1949; The Making of a State* (Boulder, Colorado, 1984).

Dearden, Ann, *Jordan* (London, 1958).

El-Edroos, Syed Ali, *The Hashemite Arab Army. 1908–1979* (Amman, 1980).

Faddah, Mohammad Ibrahim, *The Middle East in Transition; a Study of Jordan's Foreign Policy* (London, 1974).

de Gaury, Gerald, *Rulers of Mecca* (New York, 1951).

Glubb, Sir John Bagot, *A Soldier with the Arabs* (London, 1957).

—*Britain and the Arabs, a study of fifty years* (London, 1959).

—*The Changing Scenes of Life: An Autobiography* (London, 1983).

—*The Story of the Arab Legion* (London, 1946).

Gubser, Peter, *Politics and Change in al-Karak, Jordan* (London 1973).

Haidar, Musbah Ali, *Arabesque* (London, 1944).

H.M. King Abdullah of Jordan, *Memoirs of King Abdullah of Transjordan* (London, 1950).

—*My Memoirs Completed* (London, 1978).

H.M. King Hussein of Jordan, *Uneasy Lies the Head: an autobiography* (London, 1962).

—*My War with Israel* (London, 1968).

Kirkbride, Alec Seath, *A Crackle of Thorns* (London, 1956).

—*From the Wings: Amman Memoirs 1947–1951* (London, 1976).

Lewis, Norman, N., *Nomads and Settlers in Syria and Jordan, 1800–1980* (Cambridge, 1987).

Lunt, James, *Glubb Pasha: A Biography* (London, 1984).

—*Hussein of Jordan; a political biography* (London, 1989).

Morris, James, *The Hashemite Kings* (London, 1959).

Mountfort, Guy, *Portrait of a Desert: The Story of an Expedition to Jordan* (London, 1965).

Nyrop, Richard F., *Jordan; a country study* (Washington, D.C., 1980).

Patai, Raphael, *The Kingdom of Jordan* (Princeton, 1958).

Peake, F.G., *A History of Jordan and its Tribes* (Coral Gables, Florida, 1958).

Shlaim, Avi, *Collusion across the Jordan; King Abdullah, the Zionist Movement, and the Partition of Palestine* (Oxford, 1988).

Snow, Peter, *Hussein: A Biography* (London, 1972).

Sparrow, Gerald, *Modern Jordan* (London, 1961).

Vatikiotis, P.J., *Politics and the Military in Jordan: A Study of the Arab Legion, 1921–1957* (London, 1967).

Wilson, Mary C., *King Abdullah, Britain and the Making of Jordan* (Cambridge, 1987).

Index

violent confrontation and defeat in
Jordan 233–41
from 1971 to 1992
and Jordan 243–9, 260–3, 266
and West Bank 250–5, 262–9
and Egyptian peace moves 257–62
and Egypt 250, 256
and Jordan 243–7, 260–3, 266
and Lebanon 248, 249, 262
and Libya 261, 265
and Saudi Arabia 250
and Syria 256, 263, 265, 268
PLO *see* Palestine Liberation
Organization
pan-Arab nationalism 248
from 1900 to 1919 33–5, 38–42,
45–6, 66–7, 71–2
from 1919 to 1939: consolidation of
Transjordan 92–119 *passim*
from 1939 to 1951 153–4
from 1951 to 1957 172–6, 179,
182–95
from 1957 to 1967: Egypt and Jordan
and opposition to Israel
197–221
see also Hussein, king of Jordan;
Israel; Nasser
Parti Populaire Syrien 154, 167, 174
pashas 60
Passfield White Paper 132–3
pastoralists 8, 9, 11
see also bedouin
Paul, St 12
PDFLP *see* Popular Democratic Front
for the Liberation of Palestine
peace, exchanging land for (UN
proposal) 223, 225, 234, 251,
252, 255, 265
Peake, Captain Frederick 104, 110,
113, 115–16, 118
Peel, Lord: Peel Royal Commission
(1937) 138, 139–41, 144, 159
Perea 11; *see also* Bilad al-Sharat
Perowne, Stewart 28
Persia 15, 16, 17; *see also* Iran
Petra 10, 11, 205
PFLP *see* Popular Front for the
Liberation of Palestine
Philadelphia (Amman) 13; *see also*
Amman
Philby, H. St John Bridger 96–7, 111,
113, 128–9
pilgrimage

road 7, 21, 26, 52–3, 54, 59–60
sites *see* Mecca; Medina
PLA *see* Palestine Liberation Army
PLO see Palestine Liberation
Organization
political parties
rise of 173–5
from 1919 to 1939 85, 93, 101, 114,
115
from 1957 to 1967 198, 239
from 1967 to 1971 229
from 1971 to 1992 247–8, 270
see also Baath; constitution
Popular Democratic Front for the
Liberation of Palestine 227,
232, 234, 235, 240–1
Popular Front for the Liberation of
Palestine
from 1967 to 1971: fedayeen
problems and Palestine 226–7,
232, 233, 234, 235–6, 240–1
from 1971 to 1992 253, 257, 268
population 3, 14
ports 11–12, 25, 219; Jordan's only *see*
Aqaba
Portuguese 56–7
PPS *see* Parti Populaire Syrien
propaganda *see* media
Ptolemaic empire of Egypt 10, 12
Ptolemy II ('Philadelphos') 13

al-Qaddafi, Colonel Muammar 226,
249, 261
Qaramita sect 21, 52–3
al-Qassam, Sheikh Izzuddin 137
Qatrana 83, 86, 97
Qitada ibn Idris of Yanbu, emir of
Mecca 24, 55
Qureish 50, 67; *see also* Hashemites;
Umayyads
Quwwat al-Badiyah 115–16

Rabad 23
Rabat Arab summit (1974) 256–7, 259,
260
radio *see* media
al-Rafiq, Sharif Aoun, emir of Mecca
(1882–1905) 63, 67, 68, 69
railways 7, 69, 71, 82
Ramallah 161
Ramla 18, 21–2, 54, 163
Ramtha 44
Ras al-Khayma 64